LOST HORIZONS

A darkly comic memoir about those Hollywood players
whose dreams never quite matched their horizons.

David Del Valle

WITH PHOTOGRAPHS FROM THE PERSONAL
COLLECTION OF DAVID DEL VALLE
AND THE DEL VALLE ARCHIVES

Published in the USA by:
BearManor Media
P O Box 71426
Albany, Georgia 31708
www.bearmanormedia.com

All program titles and program descriptions are used in editorial fashion with no intention of infringement of intellectual property rights.

All photos are from the personal collection of David del Valle and the Del Valle Archives.

Some chapters are reprinted with permission from Films in Review.

Printed in the United States of America
ISBN 978-1-59393-607-5

Book and cover design by Darlene Swanson • www.van-garde.com
Cover Art: Alan White
Copy Editor: David W. Menefee

Dedication

This book is dedicated to the memory of
Christopher Sven Dietrich
(1954-2004)

"WHOSE HEART WAS AS BIG AS THE SKY"

—BARBARA STEELE

I also need to acknowledge these men who helped make this book possible: Roy Frumkes, my editor at Films in Review, Richard Lamparski, my role model and friend, A. Ashley Hoff, whose friendship and guidance came at just the right moment for this book to happen.

Contents:

Foreword

It's been 101 years since The National Board of Review (NBR) was formed in 1909 as a wedge that was driven between the filmmakers and the self-proclaimed film censors in cities all around the United States. Cinema was in its infancy then. Features weren't even being made yet. But already, theater projection booths were being stormed by politicos, religious leaders, and parent-based organizations, all of them eviscerating 35mm prints before the bewildered eyes of startled projectionists. And it wasn't the same scenes being cut from state to state. No, it seems that different sensibilities were wielding the scissors in different areas of the country. It was a bad time for the fledgling art form.

The NBR fought to defend freedom of expression as much as it could, and it was effective, For several decades, you could see "Passed by The National Board of Review" in the title sequences of films shown around the country.

Initially, the NBR's literary wing was called The National Board of Review Magazine, a stuffy, print-heavy affair bereft of photos. In 1950, it was reduced to digest size and re-titled *Films in Review*. In this new incarnation, it favored career articles, and copious amounts of photographs adorned it's high-gloss pages. The publication continued until 1997, when printing costs were forcing niche magazines like *Films in Review* out of existence. I had started writing for the magazine in 1966, and by 1995, I was its Editor-in-Chief. In 1996, I bought it from the NBR, kept it afloat for a year, and then took it up into cyberspace as filmsinreview.com, where it resides today.

As editor, one of the writers I brought in was David Del Valle, with his invaluable historical knowledge, as well as his infinite arsenal of personal encounters with the denizens of the film capitol. I met David through Barbara Steele, the stunning 'scream queen' of the 1960s, whose work in Mario Bava's *Black Sunday* and many other Italian horror flicks immortalized her within a decade. I was in Los Angeles partially to interview her and her friend, actress Mary Woronov, for another magazine I was editing, *The Perfect Vision*. She introduced me to David while I was out there, and encouraged him to try his hand at a column. Her intuition was correct. In the Jan/Feb 1996 issue, his interview with Curtis Harrington, discussing Harrington's friendship with James Whale and the restoration of Whale's *The Old Dark House*, was a watermark article.

Then, when the magazine went up on the Internet, David proposed, and I heartily welcomed, his column, "Camp David." It became one of our most popular visitation destinations for wanderers through the on-line webzine, and month after month, his encounters with Hollywood luminaries great and elusive appeared, illustrated with rare stills from his private collection, stills which often featured David himself with the personalities being discussed ordissected.

I'd often thought of putting out a book comprised of articles from *Films in Review*'s fifty-year history, but this is the first book of *Films in Review* writings, and I wish David great success with it. Meanwhile, his never-ending deluge of columns keeps coming, which means, I'm sure, that there will be more fascinating tomes to follow this one.

Roy Frumkes
Editor, FIR

Introduction

In 1937, the great Frank Capra adapted James Hilton's novel of a Utopian paradise known as *Lost Horizon* into an unforgettable film. In that film, Ronald Colman plays the world-weary Richard Conway, whose destiny awaits him in a region behind the Valley of the Blue Moon known only as Shangri-La.

In the course of writing these memoirs of my time in a decidedly earthier version of that mythical place—known as Hollywood—I could not help but appreciate the parallels between the Shangri-La of the movies and the real life city of mirrors where "the sun always shines and the air is blue," to quote James Hilton. Hollywood, like Shangri-La, can represent just a lie to hold those who dream of stardom to a false ideal. The serenity one is granted in Shangri-La can also be attained in Hollywood; it is just a matter of how many martinis and how much marijuana one needs to ingest to recapture that *déjà vu* you felt as a starstruck kid watching those "golden lads and lassies" dazzling your imagination on the silver screen and beckoning you to join in the dance.

The same dream was not lost on the rich and powerful, as well. It is a matter of record that in 1940 Howard Hughes bought 138 acres of prime real estate in Hollywood, dubbing it at once "Shangri-La." It was to have been a love nest for him and Ginger Rogers, yet like all things in Hollywood (as well as Shangri- La), shit happens.

I think our own Ross Hunter got it right. In his legendary remake of Capra's masterpiece, Hunter envisioned his Shangri-La on sets leftover from *Camelot*, his plaster wet-dream centered in beautiful, downtown Burbank. That first and only Liv Ullmann musical never achieved the lofty heights of Capra's film, yet it certainly rang true of the Hollywood it came to represent, where fantasy and reality played at odds with the real world, time, and death. It is not surprising that one film critic would describe the High Lama's palace in Hunter's version as "Pickfair if it was remodeled as a hotel." In fact, a trendy hotel in Santa Monica that was known simply as "The Shangri-La Hotel" had fifty-two Art Deco rooms set in a garden-like atmosphere. The myth of Hollywood, like its filmic role model, forever remains a place where destinies will be discovered and the meaning of paradise revealed.

This collection of memoirs from my life in Hollywood is undoubtedly the result of two basic things, the first one being that I have reached an age in life where my mortality is looming closer than these past encounters. Secondly, as each memory presents itself, it unfolds with a definite perspective on one's own life. The tragic death in 2004 of my longtime companion of nearly twenty-five years led me to grow up in ways I had carefully avoided my entire life until the reality of that moment forever robbed me of the luxury of assuming that those things only happen to other people.

So many of the subjects in this collection have also passed away, so in writing about them I feel it is my responsibility to remember them exactly as I found them since no one else in all probability will. I was fortunate that my tastes always ran into the somewhat *outré* when it came to films and the people who made them.

My arrival in Hollywood was, if nothing else, providential, as so many of the objects of my fan-like obsession were alive, well, and very approachable—all the better for my purposes, as things turned out.

The very act of committing a memory to paper is in itself an act of liberation. I have discovered both the good and the bad in myself and especially in the lives of the men and women I revered so much in the world of motion pictures. Gore Vidal once observed that "a memoir is how one remembers one's own life." When I began to edit these together, I couldn't help but notice that the tone and subject matter was rather scandalous in nature.

It reminded me of what one of my old professors observed about the French: "They adore celebrating the vulgar details and gossip in life and virtually created and then made popular what we have come to know as the "scandalous memoir." Therefore, please think of these chapters you are about to encounter as being, for lack of a better word, "French."

As my journey takes shape, you will also discover that it is being presented from a gay man's perspective, as I have no other choice in the matter, since most of life's defining moments were in the presence of actors and directors enjoying the same lifestyles as myself. Coming out when I did in the full flood of the counter-culture of the 1960s, I was spared so much guilt and self-doubt by coming of age in a city like San Francisco, where anything was possible. In those days, sexuality equaled joy, and the city was a beacon for those who expressed that feeling without being judgmental. It was the personification of the Stephen Stills lyric, "Love the one you're with."

This collection had a life of its own, as each chapter was originally put together as a monthly column for the online version of *Films in*

Review. I had been writing the "Camp David" column for years without ever dreaming of including personal reminiscences in the mix. However, when I finally started to reveal one every month, it suddenly became automatic-writing and this is the result. Now, allow me to give you a bit of autobiography to explain the circumstances that allowed all this to begin.

Vincent Price once told me, "If you limit your interests you limit your life." I have tried to keep faith with that concept to be interested in as many aspects of life as fate would decree. I did allow one passion to overwhelm the majority of my other interests as I have always been in love with the movies. The ritual of buying the ticket at the box-office, then going through those gilded doors into a lobby filled with posters of coming attractions. The aroma of fresh popcorn and hot dogs instantly separating me from reality until the time I had to step back through those same doors into the "real world." I really was one of those people that Gloria Swanson, in her career defining moment as Norma Desmond, referred to as being "out there in the dark."

In dreams as in fairy tales, if you wish for something very hard, they say it must come true. In my life, I always longed to work and live around the talented people I admired in the entertainment world, and to a certain extent, this has all come to pass. My journey began from my earliest days at Encina High School in Sacramento, where I talked our principal into allowing me to create a film series out of the drama department so I could show my fellow students' films like Polanski's *Dance of the Vampires* and Roger Corman's *House of Usher*.

That ultimately led to my appearing on the local *Creature Features* television show with host Bob Wilkins, who became a good friend, taking his show later on to the Bay Area, where I would continue to appear as a "film expert" through college at San Francisco State. While studying there, the great Vampire scholar himself, Leonard Wolf, personally introduced me to Anne Rice, as well as taught what would become a landmark Comparative Literature class on *Dracula*. Then finally, full circle to Beverly Hills and at last Hollywood, where after a brief stunt in the mailroom at William Morris in 1978, I became a theatrical agent with the mandatory gold lettering, "Del Valle, Franklyn and Levine," positioned on the front door of my very own agency that was located on the "lucky" thirteenth floor in the twin towers of Century Park East. From 1979 through the 1980s, I would represent and sometimes befriend the very actors I was drawn to from all those late night creature features of my misspent youth.

Always a serious collector of memorabilia, by then I had accumulated a sizable collection of still photographs, which would form the foundation for the current Del Valle Archives. That morphed into a business unto itself for the past two decades, providing visual material for such organizations as the BBC, The Sci-Fi Channel, 20TH Century Fox, MGM/UA, and Taschen Press.

After losing the agency business to an actors' strike in 1980, I became a protégé of the late archivist, John Kobal, traveling with him back and forth from Los Angeles to New York and London, as The Kobal Collection became a world-class archive, which it remains to this very day. John introduced me to another John who would make a difference in my professional life: John Russell Taylor was the Arts Editor for the *London Times*, as well as being a first-rate author and film historian. He took over the editorship of the popular *Films and*

Filming magazine and brought me along as a columnist with my own byline, "Dateline Hollywood." I became an active member of the Hollywood Foreign Press in the bargain and a new career began in earnest. By 1987, the magazine was beginning to stumble, and soon I looked for other things to do. I found myself working as a unit publicist for low-budget films like *The Offspring*, which became one of the last films in which my friend, Vincent Price, appeared in after nearly six decades in the business.

Throughout the 1990s, I continued to write articles and conduct interviews for a wide range of publication both here and abroad. I began interviewing actors and directors on videotape for my own public access program, *The Sinister Image*, in the late 1980s, which produced a now-classic VHS tape now long out of print entitled *Cult People*, and which had excerpts from the shows condensed into ninety minutes.

The advent of video, complete with its ever-changing formats from laser discs to DVDs and then high-definition, brought more projects my way: creating audio commentaries and liner notes for those formats. In 2002, I produced as well as hosted the award-winning *Vincent Price: The Sinister Image* DVD, which contains the definitive interview with Vincent Price as a Horror Icon.

In 1998, I met a young up-and-coming screenwriter and film buff named Roy Frumkes, who was then writing for the longest-running film magazine in America, *Films in Review*. We became fast friends, and soon, I was also writing for that magazine.

When the future began to look bleak for *Films and Review* and the unthinkable was inevitable with the last issue looming on the horizon, Roy bought the right to *Films in Review* and placed the legendary magazine online, where it has remained to this very day. Roy invited me early on to develop my own column, which became "Camp David," now in its tenth year of publication.

It was in fact my essays in "Camp David" that have led to editing the material from the past ten years with *Films in Review* into the chapters for this book. I began the column as a news and gossip piece, and it was only in the last three years that the essays have taken on a decidedly autobiographical slant, giving way to committing to print all the most interesting recollections of living twenty-five years in this façade of paradise known as Hollywood.

Within these pages, you will come to know actors and directors, straight and gay, as well as all sorts of deranged personalities that perhaps you never knew existed until now. It will be my pleasure to share with you these personal and sometimes shocking encounters with that netherworld sometimes referred to as "the other side of midnight." Just relax and follow your collective imaginations beyond the mountains of the Blue Moon to the fabled city of Shangri-La, just this side of the San Fernando Valley. —David Del Valle

Chapter 1
The Lady Ligeia

Elizabeth Shepherd

In 1964, Roger Corman directed his final motion picture based on the works of Edgar Allan Poe, *Tomb of Ligeia*. That film contains a *tour de force* performance by the most talented of all the actresses to appear in Corman's "Poe series," the sublime Elizabeth Shepherd.

Elizabeth embodied the beauty and essence of the "English Rose" with a mystique ideally suited to play the Lady Ligeia and essential to balance her other role of the Lady Rowena.

The production was blessed with superb production values and locations including a ruined eleventh century abbey. The darkly romantic script by Robert Towne channeled the spirit of Poe with vengeful black cats, cursed Egyptian artifacts, necrophilia, and the ubiquitous Vincent Price in wraparound black shades!

Elizabeth dominated the production with her own unique presence, creating an unforgettable impression with her dual role. Later, I was surprised to learn she had tested for and won the role of Emma Peel in *The Avengers*, only to be replaced after one episode due to creative differences regarding her interpretation of the character.

By 1976, I found myself in London working with the late, great John Kobal on one of his first exhibits of Hollywood Glamour Photography for the Victoria Albert Museum. John maintained a large flat that contained The Kobal Collection as well, in an area known as Drayton Court/Drayton Gardens, and directly across the street lived a then young, up-and-coming director named Waris Hussein. Waris had just finished working on a BBC series entitled *Romance*. His segment was written by the woman who created the "It" girl of the roaring twenties, Clara Bow—the playwright, Elinor Glyn, her masterpiece of purple prose *Three Weeks*. The star of the piece was Elizabeth Shepherd!

Over dinner at William F's (a favorite haunt on the Fulham Road) Waris told us about directing this amazing actress, who worked so hard on the show that at one point she broke down in tears because there was not enough time to dress her character as she should have been dressed if they were making a proper film instead of television. Afterwards, he brought us round to his flat, where he gave me a large photo of Elizabeth from *Three Weeks* that showed her posed while lying seductively on a tiger's skin. Waris explained she was currently living in Los Angeles and he knew she would be most pleased to meet such an admirer as myself.

Once back in Hollywood and armed with her home phone number, I wasted no time in ringing the Lady Ligeia to set up a time to call and pay my respects. Well . . . the end result was to be a lasting friendship with a remarkable lady, loyal in her friendships and devoted to her craft. From that first meeting, I found Elizabeth to be a thoughtful, caring woman, who loved the theater with a passion that one does not see often enough in this business. She signed the photo Waris had given me with the following inscription:

"Would you like to sin on a tiger's skin with Elinor Glyn?

Or would you prefer to err with her on some other fur?"

I have many wonderful memories of Elizabeth from that period of time. I recall with pleasure taking her to see Jeremy Brett perform the title role in the west coast premiere of Edward Gorey's *Dracula*. As the curtain went up, wolves howled over the loudspeakers. All at once, she leaned over to me and said, "Takes you back, doesn't it?"

She did a number of personal appearances for KCET, our public broadcasting station in Los Angeles, as they were running her episode of *The Duchess of Duke Street*. I gave her a pin made of shooting stars and she wore it on camera. I remember her happiness at becoming a US citizen, so we threw a "Yank" party celebration complete with a charming cake in the shape of the flag. We toasted with champagne as the United States acquired yet another national treasure for the arts!

Lots of parties followed with colleagues and mutual friends like Ferdy Mayne, Martine Beswicke, and Barbara Steele. In fact, she and Barbara did a one-act play in West Hollywood with the late Fox Harris (*Repo Man*). At the performance I attended, Fox was so over the top that I decided not to speak to him since I had nothing positive to say! Fox was counting on me to represent him, so the next day he turned up at Barbara's apartment already bombed, complaining about me for hours before her then-boyfriend Anthony Herrera came home and kicked him out. Elizabeth gave a funny, understated performance in that show, and Barbara smoked cigarettes and glared at the audience as Fox Harris played out his psychodrama for the entire short run of the play. Fox is gone now, and I wish I had signed him on as a client because, overlooking his "Wildman" antics during that show, he was a talented actor whose work in film was cut short.

During that time, Elizabeth appeared in her first horror film since *Ligeia*. *The Omen* had made box-office history, not to mention millions, for 20th Century Fox, so no one was surprised when they got around to a sequel, *Damien: Omen II*. The filming began in Chicago with a young avant-garde director, who felt the film did not have to follow the formula of set-piece killings but could explore a different avenue. He began to experiment with color and symbolism. Elizabeth loved what he was doing with the film and her role of investigative reporter Joan Hart. However, the powers at Fox looked at the rushes and wanted more blood and gore, so out went the young director and in came old-timer and ex-actor Don Taylor. Taylor arrived in Chicago, matching star Bill Holden drink for drink. They looked at the rushes together and mocked what had gone before. Soon, the film began to look like what it would become—an expensive body-count film with big names going to their rewards in the goriest manner possible. Elizabeth would have her eyes pecked out by a demonic crow, and then blindly wander back onto the road, only to be run over by a ten-ton truck! What made that even more ironic was that director Don Taylor was married to yet another Poe heroine from the Corman films, the beautiful British actress Hazel Court.

Waris Hussein arrived in Hollywood around that time, directing TV movies-of-the-week. Waris loved to tell people he was cursed by a voodoo priest while making a film about the Santeria religion (a blending of Catholicism and voodoo) with Shirley MacLaine called *The Possession of Joe Delaney.* Everyone on that film met with some kind of mishap . . . Shirley didn't make a film for nearly two years, and Waris was banished forever into television!

It is amusing to remember now that Marisa Berenson was seeing quite a bit of Waris in hopes that he would cast her in one of his upcoming projects. He threw little soirées, and he always screened *Three Weeks.* I remember Marisa saying, after watching Elizabeth in it, "Oh Waris, that is exactly the kind of part I want to play." As far as I know, Marisa has never had the opportunity to display such a range! Life for Marisa in Hollywood was defiantly not a "Cabaret."

Eventually, Elizabeth would meet my friend and fellow film buff, director Curtis Harrington, who appreciated her qualities as well, and thus began inviting her to his parties. It was during one of those shindigs that I believe Elizabeth began to think more about theater and how frustrating living in Hollywood could be for theater-trained actors used to working at their craft instead of waiting for an agents call. Hurd Hatfield (*The Picture of Dorian Grey,* 1944) was there, and he too felt the theater was an afterthought in Los Angeles. I had a small cocktail party for Curtis and Hurd a few days later and I noticed Hurd and Elizabeth talking more on the subject of not depending on Hollywood for a career. He certainly did not, and he soon returned to his home in Ireland and semi-retirement.

Life often leads us on to different paths, and so it was with Elizabeth who, after a few years in Hollywood, bravely chose to cast her fortunes toward Canada and the theater, where she would always be appreciated for her range and ability. She came to see me the last day she was in Hollywood, and after wishing her well, I knew an era in my life was about close.

For the last few years, Elizabeth and I had lost touch with each other as she got on with her life. Canada proved to be the right choice, not to mention a perfect working environment for her talents. It was thrilling for me to read about Elizabeth's many projects, which kept her busy and in demand, not only in theater, but films and television. In fact, she had her own mystery series, *The Adventures of Shirley Holmes*, as well. Her unique voice has been utilized in animated shows like *The Avenger* and the *Silver Surfer*. However, it was her work on a very special project that brought us full circle and back together again.

On January 15, 2001, Elizabeth Shepherd brought to life another remarkable lady to enhance her already formidable resume. That time, the Lady is based on fact, proving once again that truth is stranger than fiction. The fabulous *Marchesa* Luisa Casati lived a life of unimaginable debauchery and glamour for decades, a true original until her death in 1957. The *Marchesa* desired nothing less than to become a living work of art. She got her wish as most of the great artists of her day worshipped at her altar of personality, immortalizing her image in almost every form of artistic expression.

That one-woman show entitled *Infinite Variety—Portrait of a Muse* was an instant success for its star. A sold-out performance at the Italian Cultural Institute in New York and London both hailed her uncanny impersonation of the *Marchesa* as superb! In the audience for the London performance was the only living relative of the *Marchesa*, her grandchild, The Lady Moorea Black. Lady Black praised Elizabeth as nothing short of perfection in her interpretation of her grandmother. The authors who created all that magic, Scot D. Ryersson and Michael O. Yaccaarino, have worked a miracle in Cultural scholarship. They have created a labor of love in sharing that outrageous woman's life with a new generation of admirers. Cults are already in place for the *Marchesa,* and their books are responsible for the renaissance.

As for Elizabeth Shepherd . . . her image in my mind's eye will always remain the Lady Rowena sitting by a fire mesmerized and by her husband Verden, as she quotes these lines as Ligeia: "Who knoweth the mysteries of the will? The will herein lieth that dieth not. Man need not kneel before the angels nor lie in death forever, but for the weakness of his feeble will. *I will always be your wife. . . .*"

Chapter 2
Art is Revolution
Steven Arnold

In rediscovering the Marchesa Casati, I was reminded of a more contemporary eccentric genius, whom I first came to know from the glorious days of "The Cockettes" at the Palace and the eternal party that was San Francisco in the late 1970s, the gifted artist, Steven Arnold. Steven was always surrounded by magic, and he attracted a Phantasmagoria wherever he lived or worked. Steven was a master of light and fantasy, an accomplished filmmaker, photographer, and dreamer.

Steven Arnold arrived with his own special entourage to introduce his film, *Luminous Procuress*. It was the talk of the San Francisco Film Festival. The night it played in the magical Palace of Fine Arts, Steven Arnold had arrived. He was a gentle, soft-spoken man and as fragile as an angel who fell from Heaven. You wanted to protect him. After the film, he was asked if he acknowledged the influence of Jean Cocteau in his film. Steven replied, "I am Cocteau . . . with a little LSD in the mix!"

Steven was a guiding force during the Golden Days of The Palace Theatre in North Beach, and the international success of "The Cockettes," his direction, and his concepts, gave way for directors like John Waters to experiment with surrealist theater. I remember that the first time I saw Divine in the flesh was at The Palace. From those humble beginnings, Steven was soon transformed by Salvador Dali, who had met Steven in New York. The two became instant soul mates. Dali saw Steven's film and declared it a masterpiece! Dali asked Steven to work in his private museum in Spain, and the two remained close from that time until Dali's death.

Years later, Steven had established yet another alternative universe off Beverly Boulevard towards downtown Los Angeles. His "Salons" were legendary, as every type of personality was given a chance to mingle with models, artists, film makers, and drag queens . . . all were accepted as long as one kept it non-judgmental. Steven quietly presided over those festivities with grace and humor, films were screened, performance artists showcased their work, and no one wanted to leave! The house itself was non-descript, but once inside, we were in a magical realm of gods and goddesses, sex and beauty, rooms lined with mirrors, masks from Venice, gold and silver wings suspended from the ceiling, a heavenly world out of Aladdin's Lamp.

The last time I saw Steven Arnold was at his studio about five years before he died. The place was in a flurry of activity for a photo shoot. Naked men covered in gold and silver glitter were preparing for Steven's camera. I always thought that was one place that would never change. Steven was a truly kind man, who cared so much about his art. I like to think of him lounging in a Heavenly villa with his mentor, Dali, laughing away and having the most divine time.

Chapter 3

Before Joni, After Fellini

Hiram Keller

I was introduced to Hiram Keller at one of Steven Arnold's salons, and for a time, I acted as his agent, though no real offers ever materialized for the star of *Fellini Satyricon*. Hiram had lived by his looks for most of his adult life. A self-proclaimed "hustler," he dabbled in acting as one of the founding members of *Hair*. Hiram was known far and wide as the guy who shed his clothes nightly on Broadway. He resembled Nureyev in a certain light, or rather, he resembled him enough to prompt Rudy to invite Hiram to join his tour for a few weeks until the novelty wore off.

Anne Rice's *Interview with a Vampire* was very hot at that time, and Paramount had announced that John Travolta would be playing Lestat. When Paramount made the announcement, Hiram became instantly obsessed with being cast in one of the remaining male roles as long as he could play a vampire. When Hiram was living in Rome performing in *Fellini Satyricon*, one of the more imaginative extras between takes told a haunting tale of ancient vampires that roamed the Coliseum at night preying on the unwary strangers that wandered in to experience a little history and instead was consumed by it. Hiram was amused that a city so full of light and optimism had such a passion for the supernatural and all things dark and mystical. "I was born to play a vampire, and what a hoot it will be to go back to Rome and watch it with the maestro!"

Steven Arnold had duly noted the possibilities, having already somewhat envisioned Hiram as one of Dracula's disciples from the first moment he heard about the film being prepped, offering his considerable talents to do some makeover stills for Hiram to send over to Paramount for an audition. A series of photographs were created. All the make-up and lighting were done by Steven, as well. The end result was "vampire heaven." Hiram was indeed to the coffin born.

What happened next convinced Hiram that film was to be his destiny after all. Hiram had come out to Los Angeles from New York with his adopted family from the Broadway production of *Hair*, which included best friend Paul Jabara, who was well on his way to becoming the king of disco in Hollywood, winning an Oscar in the process. Through Paul's connections in the music industry, Hiram was invited to a few of *Grease* producer Allan Carr's lavish parties in Malibu. During one of those decidedly decadent, *very* gay affairs, he apparently wasted no time in attracting the attention of John Travolta, the star of *Grease*. John immediately saw more than vampire possibilities in the studly persona of our Mr. Keller. Hiram was given a fast track thanks to John, though the casting process and the Steve Arnold stills were on Bob LeMond's desk that same week. At last, a break for our Mr. Keller! However, what Dracula giveth he can taketh away, and so it came to pass that within weeks of all that public relations media blitz, *Interview with a Vampire* all the sudden went into what they call in the business "turnaround," which simply means that the project was terminated until further notice. He did get an opportunity to meet with Bob LeMond at Paramount, but unfortunately a film of *Interview with a Vampire* would not be made for another decade or so. Soon afterwards, there was a parade of vampire films from Hollywood: John Badham's adaptation of *Dracula*, the Broadway hit with Frank Langella, and then George Hamilton, of all people, scoring his biggest hit ever with *Love at First Bite*, not to mention Werner Herzog remaking *Nosferatu* with his *bete noir*, Klaus Kinski

All of that bad karma was simply too much stress for Hiram, who quickly returned to his first career that was, of course, to hustle both sexes for another chance at the gold ring above the Hollywood sign. When I first came to know Hiram, he was being kept via long-distance by a Saudi Prince, who had given Hiram some amazing jewelry, but by then, was long gone. At one point, a group of us were at the well-known watering hole called Robert's in Venice one Sunday afternoon, when Hiram kept the house phone occupied for over an hour trying to get just one more advance from the Prince before his funds ran out entirely.

That way of life, however stressful, seemed to energize Hiram and he was good at it. He was the closest I would ever come to knowing a real *American Gigolo*, another film that ironically began with John Travolta. Hiram was the first person to describe himself as a hustler, and why not? His entire life was a series of encounters with the rich and famous of two continents. From the moment he stepped out nude on the Broadway stage in *Hair*, he was desired by both men and women. Hiram was also a true bi-sexual, as he could be attracted to anyone that acknowledged his beauty. While in Hollywood, he was attached to both Joni Mitchell and Carole Baker Sayer at practically the same time.

I entered Hiram's life one wild night at Studio One in West Hollywood during one of Neil Bogart's disco parties that seemed to go on forever. Paul Jabara was the star of the evening, and anyone who ever met that man was instantly won over by his charm and talent. That particular evening, he was very, very high, and there was Hiram Keller sort of acting as his escort, yet it was also obvious they were sisters rather than lovers and their connection was complex to say the least. Hiram was looking for an agent, and I just happened to have two clients up for parts in—of all things—*American Gigolo*, so things moved quickly. Once Hiram made up his mind that I might be of some help in getting him some film roles, we began a relationship that would be many things but never boring. I always will remember the way he would knock at the front door, and then before you could open your mouth, he would say, "Whatever you're doing, drop it. I have a plan."

Even without a John Travolta in the mix, the Paul Shrader film was going through transformations daily. At first, my client, Calvin Lockhart, was ready to sign on to play the evil pimp that places Julien in harm's way halfway through the script by involving him in a client's murder—a small but important role. The other part was the Malibu madam who is Julien's pimp at the onset of the film. That part was perfect for my other client, Barbara Steele, who had just been seen in Louis Malle's *Pretty Baby* a year before. Both of my actors would be replaced for one reason or another until my involvement in the film diminished altogether. Hiram had been counting on me to secure a part for him in one of those projects, and until I could make that happen, he made daily visits not just to my office in Century City, but home as well. He was the kind of personality who made himself at home. Whether he was in Saudi Arabia or West Hollywood, it made no difference, and for me it was worth it to have such a "living work of art" lounging about the place (as my pal, Barbara, would observe later on regarding my relationship with Hiram).

I knew my time in his life was just about up when no further offers came my way for Hiram, and after a time, he just ceased to call, and then, not unlike the Flying Dutchman, he was gone from my life just as quickly as he entered it. I guess life really had been a disco inferno after all. Hiram—being Hiram—wound up living with Joni Mitchell for a while before returning to Georgia, where he died some years later.

Time has not been kind to many that I knew during that time in my life. Steven Arnold, Paul Jabara, and Hiram have all since died, but they shall not be forgotten by those that knew them and were dazzled by their beauty and charisma.

When I heard of Hiram Keller's untimely death, I felt sad for just a moment, but then I remembered how like Dorian Gray he really was in his choices in life. He never envisioned himself growing old, nor more importantly, giving up his beauty, which was his passport to the bedrooms of the world. Hiram had cheated death: at least he left this mortal coil as he entered it, a beautiful creature transformed by Fellini into stardust, only to be made mortal again, and then disappearing beneath the Hollywood sign for eternity.

Chapter 4

Visconti's Widow

Helmut Berger

If life can in fact imitate art, then the notorious relationship between director Luchino Visconti and his protégé/actor Helmut Berger continues a tradition of older man/younger man mentor relationships. Consider Nijinsky and Diaghilev or, with more tragic consequences, Oscar Wilde and Alfred Lord Douglas.

In 1984, Helmut arrived in West Hollywood to begin a recurring role on television in the ABC mega-hit, *Dynasty*, which he hoped would give him a new fan base and a career boost. At that time, I was writing for John Russell Taylor's revamped *Films and Filming*, based in the United Kingdom. Helmut had been featured on its cover a few times in the past, giving John the idea of "bringing Helmut Berger full circle to where he is today." At Taylor's request, I began to actively entice Helmut into an interview for the next issue. Having heard different versions of what happened after Visconti's death and the profound effect it had on Helmut's life and career, I wasn't sure he would be interested in discussing the present, much less the past. Through contacts like Maggie Abbott, a former agent from Helmut's salad days in London, I tracked him down. I began a very complicated series of phone calls and missed appointments, yet I remained steadfast in my determination to have a "Helmut Berger cover" regardless of the obstacles.

Finally, we met at his rented flat on Larrabee Street in the heart of "Boys Town" to audiotape the glory that was Helmut. His legendary charm was very much in evidence that afternoon, as we began discussing his past life. When we reached the subject of *Ash Wednesday*, the film with Elizabeth Taylor, he laughed, "I like alcohol and so does Elizabeth. We had a great time except for her husband, Richard Burton, who became very jealous of me and behaved badly. The story of what went on off-camera was far more exotic then what was captured on film."

The conversation then moved on to his current status as a European trying the waters of American sitcom TV. Helmut, or "Muti" to his friends, thought the whole idea of *Dynasty* amusing as it was called *Denver* in Germany, and being Helmut, had no real concept of its importance to his career. Helmut felt like an outsider during filming because on his first day on-set, Joan Collins greeted him with great fanfare in front of the entire cast and crew, proclaiming, "Thank God, another European," isolating him from everyone in his mind's eye. Later on, Helmut bonded with co-stars Linda Evans and Pamela Bellwood, taking them to lunch and parties while he remained on the show. We talked for what seemed like hours in his apartment, taping the interview in-between bottles of wine and music. He loved The Rolling Stones, whose single, "Undercover of the Night," had just come out, so he played it over and over for the lyrics, "All the young men/they've been rounded up!" Helmut, at that time, was still a wild child in the city, moving fast and looking pretty.

Afterwards, we stayed in touch; I even ran lines with him for

Dynasty at one point. He would not play the Hollywood game and quickly soured on the idea of television, much like Peter O'Toole in *My Favorite Year*. After all, he was a movie star in Europe, so why be anything less in the United States? In spite of any advice to the contrary, Helmut's recurring role on *Dynasty* came to a premature end, and with it his time in West Hollywood. Helmut phoned a few times, and then he was gone. Once in a while, a stranger would arrive at my door fresh from the continent with a message from "Muti," such as, "Here is someone you should know," and usually they were.

Helmut returned to Europe to film a horror film entitled *Faceless* for Jess Franco and, lastly, almost unrecognizable in his role for *The Godfather, Part III*. In 1998, Helmut penned his memoirs in German. The result, simply titled *Ich,* candidly revealed all regarding his life and loves! In *Ich,* Helmut refers to himself at thirty-two years of age as "Visconti's widow," having been seduced by the great director during the filming of *Vaghe Stelle Dell'Orsa* in 1964. Three months later, Helmut shared Visconti's villa, embarking on a love affair that lasted twelve years. There is a wonderful site that is dedicated to Helmut on the Internet in English and Japanese called "The Salon of Helmut Berger." I highly recommend it to all readers for the wealth of information and images that explain why his personality is a unique and fascinating icon of that era of excess that gave the world Warhol and Studio 54.

Postscript: I was looking at www.youtube.com the other day, and quite by chance saw a clip of Helmut Berger in somewhat of a personal freak-out at a Swiss Air counter in the airport of some nameless European city in early 2009. He was dressed in flowing scarves, topcoat, and fedora, the very image of a Germanic Barrymore: grand, theatrical, and shit-faced. When I first began my recollections of Helmut back in the mid-1980s (when he was staying in a small apartment on Larrabee in West Hollywood), he still looked like the "movie star" Helmut Berger, although time was in the process of catching up with him.

As I was watching that video train wreck-in-progress, it triggered a series of images that were left out of my earlier recollections of the time I spent in the presence of the man who would always think of himself as "Visconti's widow." I shall begin by saying that interviewing Helmut was like trying to track a serial killer with little or no help from the police. Helmut began a series of phone calls with me that lasted for weeks before we finally set a date. After we had done that, he then proceeded to change the time and then the location from my house to his place half a dozen times. The only good thing to come from that madness was that my apartment was in a constant state of preparation for my celebrity visitor. The only other person to put me through such an ordeal was Rupert Everett—but that, as they say, is another story.

The thing about Helmut and the telephone is how much he liked to get on it when he was a bit high and just ramble on for hours until you would just hang up, only to have him call back and really let you have it for hanging up on him. My only defense that seemed to work with him was bringing up a mutual friend we shared: actor Hiram Keller. It seems we both had a relationship with the exotic Fellini star at different times, and I maintained that Hiram would never treat me that way, which, of course, was a lie. Helmut was always intrigued by my time with Hiram, and sometimes that would change the subject or bring it back around to making me choose who was the more attractive, Hiram or him.

Both Hiram and Helmut shared a world-view of fair exchange.

In other words, they had youth and beauty, which in turn connected them to wealth and power in the men they allowed to share their bodies and occasionally advance their careers. Hiram never felt he had a chance in Hollywood, since being exotic only got you so far, and hustling only got you that much further. Helmut was spoiled by Visconti, it was true, but he was also transformed by the great director, as well. Many who witnessed that firsthand were impressed with how quickly the young man caught on to camera angles and lighting, much like Marlene Dietrich must have done with her Svengali, Josef Von Sternberg—the irony of both Helmut and Marlene having played Lola-Lola in one form or another on screen. Fellini never did that with his protégés, and as soon as the film was over, so was Fellini's use for them. Hiram always made a point of that with the young actor in *Amarcord*, who was never heard from again.

Helmut and I finally sat down in his apartment with a tape recorder and committed his career for the ages. It became clear to me that a lot of what turned Helmut into the man I saw before me was his desire to distance himself from his early life. Helmut did not have a happy relationship with his father, who raised his son to be in the hotel business. Helmut never forgot being referred to as "a hotel clerk whom Visconti turned into a star overnight." The negative aspects of Helmut's behavior begin to make sense if you realize how all that must have played out on one so young and inexperienced. Helmut told me what an awakening it was to witness the lifestyle of a man like Visconti firsthand. Helmut was staggered by the luxury and privilege that Visconti simply took for granted. Helmut remarked, "I always thought Communists lived a Spartan lifestyle, but not Luchino."

As Helmut opened up, more and more became clear about how he turned his life over to his mentor and lover, and how he learned the art of film and film acting from a master. He confided to me that, although Visconti was a confirmed homosexual, he was also a nobleman and kept his sexuality private, although it was certainly no secret among the jet-set or the film community in Rome. Visconti had made lovers out of many of the men in his films. Helmut described the court-like atmosphere in Visconti's world: lavish parties with the Beautiful People, the cruel games Visconti played with young men and protégés, not unlike the way the gay aristocrats of the Russian court under the Czar toyed with male ballet dancers passing them about like objects for pleasure. Franco Zefferelli began his career as one of Visconti's lovers and frequently found himself the court jester when Visconti grow bored or found another more beautiful boy to play the grand *senor* with.

As these things do, it all came back to haunt Visconti in his last days. As his health declined, so did Helmut's attentions towards the great director, and the stories of abuse and screaming matches all created by Helmut in youthful spite and lack of sensitivity towards an old man facing his own Death in Venice are legion. One thing I have noticed about the Helmut Berger of 2009 is his genuine grief and regret at all of the remembrances of things past. Helmut is painfully aware that he had lost his soul-mate and all of Visconti's advice and concern for him was done out of love. Helmut Berger in his sixties has surrendered to the love that dared not speak its name and he will spend the rest of his life screaming it from the soundstages and TV shows of Europe.

The reality of fame is this: we all grow old, and yet if you created something worthwhile that stands the test of time, then all was not in vain. Helmut has lived long enough to fully appreciate his relationship with one of the towering figures of the cinema, and the films they made together will remain masterpieces long after we all have shaken off this mortal coil. In *Conversation Piece*, the last film Helmut made for his mentor, his character is simply an extension of himself in the eyes of Visconti. Burt Lancaster is Visconti's persona on film, an aging nobleman who dreamt of beauty in all its classical forms, only to be brought down by the realization that "conversation pieces, however beautiful, cannot substitute loving someone in one's own lifetime." As Visconti loved Berger, so Lancaster love Berger in the film as Helmut lies dying in the actor's arms.

Helmut Berger will always have a place in world cinema because Visconti's films will always have a place of honor in world cinema. The mere fact that Helmut has matured enough to know this is reward enough for those of us that have grown to admire them both as artists in a time when they are needed most.

Chapter 5

Icon of Cool

Terry Southern

In the 1950s and 1960s, one writer in particular represented the Iconoclast in American fiction and satire. He was the man immortalized on the cover of The Beatle's *Sgt. Pepper* album as "the guy in the sunglasses," the hipsters' hipster, Terry Southern. He was at the center of most all of the counterculture action in my lifetime. Terry wrote screenplays for Kubrick, gave *Easy Rider* the edge that allowed Fonda and Hopper to carry the torch for a generation, and later on made the scene with a younger band of rebels on *Saturday Night Live*.

Terry Southern was cool and he knew it! With novels like *The Magic Christian* and especially *Candy,* Southern excelled in sending-up our decaying Western society and all its sacred cows. When *The Loved One* was made into a movie that was universally panned by American critics, I was in the minority of moviegoers that thought it was way ahead of the game with that special brand of gallows humor only "Big T" could dish out with panache. Terry was a visionary genius creating his own brand of gonzo journalism in the early fifties long before there was a Hunter S. Thompson. My generation is indebted to writers like Terry for the creative freedom we pretty much take for granted in the new millennium.

Terry entered my life in the late 1980s thanks to his close friend, Nelson Lyons. Nelson had worked on *Saturday Night Live* with Terry and the two became soul mates from that time on. It was Nelson who organized the recordings Terry made during that period, as well as doing all he could to keep Terry working and productive. Nelson and I had much in common: we both loved movies and shared a similar sense of humor, so it wasn't long before he made me part of his scene, and that included getting to know Terry Southern in the flesh. Terry flew out to Los Angeles to work on a script, and Nelson decided to throw a party in his honor that very weekend. One thing that will always remain with me about that particular visit was how hard it had become for Terry to write new material that satisfied his own standards. I was asked to collect him at the Sunset Marquis the afternoon of the party. When I arrived, he was still not quite ready to come down, so I went up to his room. He had already made the place his own with a typewriter, various magazines, and books to refer to if needed. I could not help but notice that the wastepaper basket was filled with wadded- up paper and much of the floor around the typewriter, as well. He came to Los Angeles to polish up some script, or maybe tackle a work-in-progress. It was if the time and place were familiar territory for Terry since he had done some of his best work there, yet something had changed within Terry . . . perhaps his confidence had been shaken (but believe me, not his talent). Terry would always be tops in his field to admirers like me.

As I look back on it now, it seems like a surreal flashback that could have been in one of Sir Guy Grand's epic put-ons, yet it was real! "Terry," observed Nelson, "took to me like the fellow Texans we were," as I sat by his side the entire evening celebrating his "grand-ness." At the time, I was still doing my cable chat show, *Sinister Image*, taping one every two weeks with whatever celebrity I could convince to spend an hour or so discussing their careers for posterity.

Terry agreed to appear almost at once, signing my bound copy of *The Journal of the Loved One* with the following: "This copy here within inscribed for a certain ultra grand Dave Del Valle, tops in his field and the best dang Texas galoot to come down the pike in many a moon. Even as I inscribe this I am looking forward (indeed anticipating like a giddy schoolgirl) his so-called invite to be on his almost legendary Sinister Image!! Let's hope I'm not dreaming!! Anyhoo, here's wishing us a happy forever!! From his (or shall I say your) true friend Terry 'Big T' Southern."

To my everlasting regret, that was never to be, as Terry had to return to New York before I could get a date set for the filming of his interview. Months later, he returned to Los Angeles, and we had one last grand day together. Terry had not seen *The Loved One* in years, so I offered to show him my laser disc copy, which was the same version that played in theaters in 1965. Terry arrived at my apartment with ample supplies—a fifth of Bombay Gin and several ultra-fab joints rolled to perfection for our viewing pleasure. As a little surprise during the film, Robert Morse called to say hello, so I stopped the film for about forty-five minutes, while the two chatted away as if time had ceased to exist for the moment. Terry laughed about the dubbing of Bobby's voice as director Richardson thought him too American. The whole afternoon was magic, with Terry holding court as one after another of his ad-mirers dropped in to pay their respects. It was nearly midnight when I finally got Terry back to The Sunset Marquis, his favorite hotel at the time. I walked him up to his room and as I turned to leave he bowed from the waist saying, "Thank you, young sir, for your total grandness on this occasion. If I weren't so plum tuckered out, we might have caught the dawn." I shall never forget his charm and energy that eve-ning, nor will a day ever go by that I don't think of my Ultra-Fab friend, tops in his field, Terry "Big T" Southern, a truly Grand Guy.

They say hindsight is 20/20 and perhaps it is, but one nagging question that lingers with me as I replay that mystical moment in our time shared: watching Terry Southern swaying on the steps of the Sunset Marquis still marching to his own brand of cool as he bid me a foggy, fond farewell with no more cocktails to share, no more joints to roll, and no more yarns to weave regarding his salad days in Hollywood, when his phone never stopped ringing and the of-fers kept piling up by the typewriter. All that glory was lost in the faraway land of lava lamps and lapping tongues. Perhaps Terry's lost horizon was simply outliving the counter-culture altogether. The Pop Culture of the 1980s and 1990s recognized his place in the time in which he reigned as the Hipster Laureate of his generation; the prob-lem was there was no longer a culture to counter, not to mention his contemporaries (with the notable exception of Bill Burroughs), who were now part of the establishment.

So what is my question? Well, to put it simply: what happened to Terry Southern's place in our culture? Without him, we would not have, say, *The National Lampoon,* or satire as we now know it, or highly rated television programs like *Saturday Night Live*. I mean, that man wrote the legendary screenplay for *Dr. Strangelove*, one of the darkest satires ever to come out of 1960s cinema. He is on the cover of The Beatles' *Sgt. Pepper* album. He co-wrote *Easy Rider*—what more do you need to elevate him to Valhalla? The tragic reality of it all was that while Terry still wrote and was writing wonderful stuff including screenplays, Hollywood had simply chosen to ignore him, and that was the unkindest cut of all. For a 1960s icon like Terry Southern, to lose his mojo was to lose his rightful place in that time.

In the time since we lost Terry, much has happened, and I am proud to say that his archive has found a home at the New York Public Library thanks to director Steven Soderbergh. The best news yet is that Soderbergh is planning two films based on Terry's published and non-published writings.

While some of these lost horizons remain just that, we can at least take some consolation in knowing that while Terry's place in our culture was misplaced and seemed to stay that way at the moment of his death, time has been on his side after all. Like Terry's favorite character, Guy Grand, might put it, "The time to be ultra-fab is now upon us." Or better still, to take a line from his novel, *Blue Movie*: "Now, dig this!"

Chapter 6

We Sure Got High . . . Honey!

Timothy Leary

The other night on the Turner Classic Movie cable channel, a mini-festival of LSD movies was screening beginning with Otto Preminger's delightfully ghastly *Skidoo*, a film definitely ahead of its time and desperately in need of reappraisal; the end credits alone demand it. Afterwards, I stayed tuned in to catch another pop relic from the cinema of the psychedelic sixties entitled *The Love-Ins*. Even though I had never seen that film before, it became obvious to me within the first ten minutes that it was in fact a very non-factual Hollywood fantasy of the Timothy Leary story ripped from yesterday's headlines, as the studio press release might well have put it at the time.

I usually find any film that addresses the "peace and love generation" to be eminently watchable, especially those made while it was still happening during 1966-1971. It is quite a trip to see how dated those films tended to appear within days of being released, since Hollywood itself was clueless to accurately reflect what was really happening with the youth market they were always in danger of losing altogether.

The Love-Ins (1967) is ripe with guilty pleasures: a sincere performance from veteran actor Richard Todd (as the Leary figure), who was perhaps best-remembered as the killer from Alfred Hitchcock's underrated *Stage Fright* (1950), not to mention the unexpected hoot of witnessing a young Mark Goddard (the heartthrob from TV's *Lost in Space*) playing the evil hippie who helps the guru of LSD fleece the faithful followers of flower power with mind-altering drugs. Ironically, the actor also played a similar role a decade later in *Blue Sunshine* (1976), a cult horror film about LSD. American International Pictures somewhat cornered the counter-culture market on the subject with films like *The Trip* and *Wild in the Streets*, creating stars out of actors like Christopher Jones, Peter Fonda, and especially Dennis Hopper, in the process.

As I watched that Hollywood movie version of Dr. Leary's rise to celebrity, it released a flood of memories within me of the real Dr. Leary, or at least the one I finally got to know during the last two years of his life. The first time I ever saw Dr. Leary in person was in 1967 at the fabled Big Sur retreat of Esalen. That earthly Garden of Eden rests much like Mt. Olympus would in a movie in the clouds, on a cliff hanging over the Pacific Ocean. I can never forget how luminous Dr. Leary appeared on stage; he simply radiated superstardom in his bright orange robes looking more like a high priest in some Technicolor reenactment of Atlantis, than a Harvard professor gone native on psychedelics.

It rests with the historian—does it not?—to select and condense events as they come to mind. What I seem to remember about that first encounter was how much Dr. Leary lived up to his myth, which was that of being the empowering visionary that would eventually become his legacy at the end of his life. Dr. Leary was introduced that afternoon by Carlos Castaneda to a capacity audience of young, good-looking, and more than likely rich Californians that already seemed predisposed to the "doors of perception" as revealed by Huxley's book of the same name, the author himself having already experienced enlightenment through psychedelic drugs by the good doctor himself.

Dr. Leary was always an iconoclast from the moment he stepped onto the world stage, and in that moment, he initiated a renaissance that resonates most profoundly in our time now, this twenty-first century's brave new future world of cyberspace and virtual reality. Dr. Leary was most determined to acknowledge Socrates as his major philosophical influence ("I am a student of the school of Socrates.") adjusting one of the master's most profound observations, "Know thyself," into advising the audience to "Think for yourself, question authority; remember, thinking for yourself is dangerous, even blasphemous. Only devils and Satan himself, we are taught, ever practice such behavior—at least that is what they will tell you in this Calvinist version of America we are living in."

One thing I always remembered from that afternoon so long ago was Dr. Leary warning the audience that "Acid is not for every brain. Only positive, adventuresome, healthy human beings would truly benefit from the drug's infinite possibilities. The very word 'psychedelic' means mind-manifesting." Dr. Leary also possessed a healthy sense of humor as evidenced later in the same lecture. He speculated that, "If Aristotle were living in today's world he would definitely have his own television talk show." Dr. Leary was in the process of forming his "League of Spiritual Discovery" during that period. It was the Esalen lecture that first blew me away. Witnessing Dr. Leary's considerable onstage charisma coupled with his amazing, world-class verbosity spoken in that familiar, confident, awestruck voice of his made him quite irresistible, as my generation was about to discover for themselves.

Later on, of course, I would learn through the media of his exploits. I never once believed Dr. Leary was, in the famous words of President Nixon, "The most dangerous man in America." I always thought that was rich coming from the man that just bombed the shit out of Cambodia and then plunged this country into years of darkness and shame.

The fellow who was instrumental in my getting to know Dr. Leary on a more personal level was the ever-hip Nelson Lyon—so now would be as good a time as any to introduce some background about Nelson, as I already mentioned him briefly in my essay on Terry Southern called *The Icon of Cool.*

Nelson had been a staff writer for the wildly successful *Saturday Night Live,* at the same point in time that the legendary Terry Southern was installed there from 1980-1981, to make some serious money and try his hand at television comedy writing. Terry was having no luck in adjusting his gonzo wit to the fast pace of a show run by twenty-somethings, who were in the process of being born around the time Terry was already writing the screenplay of *Dr. Strangelove* for Stanley Kubrick.

Nelson became Terry's rock on that show, and they became life-long friends as a result. Into that relationship came the ever-mordant William S. Burroughs, and then Dr. Leary arrived, recognizing Nelson as a well-connected friend who was on his wavelength as well. Nelson produced and directed recording projects with all of them. The result for Terry was the audiocassette known as *Bring Me Your Hump* in which Terry reads excerpts from his short stories climaxing, as it were, with the title sequence from *Candy*. For Bill Burroughs, Nelson co-produced *Dead City Radio,* as well as other recordings later on. Nelson had appeared as an actor in *The Telephone Book,* a short but to-the-point grind house film that is now regarded as a classic underground film by those in-the-know.

Nelson, needless to say, is a brilliant man with many diverse interests, some of which we shared in common. When I first met him, he lived in a large upstairs flat on Orange Drive in that wonderful part of Hollywood between Third Street and Melrose, once the grand area where "old Hollywood " maintained large sprawling homes, most of which are now divided into duplexes. Nelson was a consummate collector in every sense of the word. He loved movies (vintage and otherwise), comic books (pornographic and otherwise), and anything related to pop culture.

His living room was dominated by four large Warhol silk screens of Marilyn Monroe, each in a different color. The black one, he told me, was the rarest of the four. He also had the famous Warhol of Garbo as Mata Hari. What bonded us straight away was his passion for films and especially collecting memorabilia from all the great films, which of course now are so expensive only museums can afford them. At that time, Nelson had the entire set of lobby cards from *Citizen Kane,* as well as Von Stroheim's *Foolish Wives,* with the three-sheet poster from the Film Noir classic, *Gun Crazy,* framed in his dining room. I felt a soul mate without question.

Unfortunately for Nelson, his real lasting claim to fame would not lie with icons like Terry Southern or Bill Burroughs, but in having the monumental bad timing of being one of just three people (later it would be revealed that both Robin Williams and Robert De Niro had dropped by, as well) of being present in the room with troubled comic genius John Belushi from *Saturday Night Live* on March 4, 1982, the night he overdosed at the Chateau Marmont.

Nelson was an eye witness to the woman who injected Belushi with the fatal dose of drugs that killed him. Cathy Smith was the former "back-up singer" for the rock group The Band, however her real talents lay elsewhere in the area of being a drug dealer and, more importantly, an addict herself.

In the end, Nelson gave his evidence to the Grand Jury, receiving immunity from prosecution, and knowing Nelson, he got no Schadenfreude from the experience either. As for Cathy Smith, she was eventually sent to prison for manslaughter. Nelson Lyon never really survived the notoriety from the press, and he fell from the heavens of Hollywood a howling devil not unlike another character we could name. That, followed by life-threatening health issues, took its toll on my world-weary friend, as time went by.

Nelson once proudly maintained a world-class book collection of the works of both his friends, Terry Southern and William S. Burroughs, most all of them first editions and signed to him with gratitude and humor. Most of those treasures were sold off in the years after the Belushi scandal.

I was fortunate to know Nelson at a time when he was relatively well-off and entertaining on a regular basis. It was during that time that Dr. Leary was a frequent visitor and confidant, who I believe was also involved in some of Nelson's audio projects. One must remember that Leary was as much of an entertainer as he was an academic. He had appeared on the Sunset Strip on a few occasions as a stand-up comic, or as an author reading from one of thirty books he wrote over the years, but it was his personality people came to see, as well as his notoriety as the infamous "Pope of Dope." Dr. Leary always laughed at himself first and made the best of whatever the fates decreed.

I, for one, could never stop the involuntary habit of always hearing that famous song in my head whenever Dr. Leary appeared, that ode to his fame that was done in the 1960s when it was all happening with the "summer of love": The Moody Blues were on the airways with that tune from their classic *In Search of a Lost Chord* album *Timothy Leary's dead* with that unforgettable refrain, "Oh no, he is outside looking in."

Sometimes I would be sitting on Nelson's couch when Dr. Leary would show up and we would wind up watching a film together while having drinks and some smoke. "This is as good as it gets" was my view—actually getting high with *the man*.

I remember watching (of all things) *Charlie Chan in Reno* on cable with both Nelson and Dr. Leary, when the whole Chan series was being broadcast on the old Z Channel, which, in itself, became quite the cultural phenomenon at the time among film lovers and hipsters in Los Angeles. For some reason (let's blame it on the quality of what we were smoking), I was at the top of my game that afternoon and provided a non-stop commentary for the film that really got Dr. Leary laughing and digging the film, which was a real high, believe you me. When it was over, he said to me, "David, you are a funny man and you should realize that you have a gift for interpreting films from the right side of your brain. You should do commentaries for all these films. That is your true calling, I believe." I never forgot what the good doctor said to me that day, and as of this writing, I have recorded nearly a dozen audio and video commentaries for films on DVD.

One of Dr. Leary's most endearing traits was his ability to remain non-judgmental of anyone who came into his orbit. He had a real talent for finding something worthwhile in everyone he met. He is one of a handful of people I have ever met where you learn something every time you are in their presence. If knowing Dr. Leary taught me anything at all it was to try and remember life's rich possibilities and take full responsibility to explore them the best you know how.

I did not see Dr. Leary again for a very long time after the party days and nights of Nelson Lyon, and I had practically lost touch with not only Nelson but a lot of other characters from that period. However, about two years before he died Dr. Leary was shining very brightly in Hollywood once more, and his hilltop home off Sunbrook Drive in the Benedict Canyon area of Beverly Hills was becoming a non-stop party attracting the young and hip crowd from the clubs on the Sunset Strip, as well as well-known personalities from the Art and Film worlds. Leary had always been part of that B-list of Hollywood's social scene, but now he was glowing on the Internet as the man who saw it all coming years before computers were the norm, and after his cancer diagnosis, he made up his mind to have a "designer's death" to show America how it is done with grace and good humor, and so he did.

My last memories of him were happy ones, of course, because he was a joyous man who savored every moment he had on this earth in spite of tremendous adversity with the Law, as well as the establishment he had once been a part of and then sought to ignore.

On one of my last visits, Dr. Leary was by then in his wheelchair with a pan of homemade pot-filled brownies sitting on his lap, which he was glad to share. Timothy loved to use his microwave to make snacks, and as you can imagine, he used his own special ingredient: several grams of his best pot to drop-kick any of his favorite recipes up a notch, always citing the microwave as a gift from the gods as it intensified the THC; it is safe to say that he enjoyed each and every day he had left with a childlike wonder at all that was around him.

After our kick-ass snacks, we sat there on his outdoor patio enjoying the spectacular view. I made up my mind to ask him to sign something for me as a keepsake. I did not have a photo or a book, so he took out an index card and asked me what I wanted him to say. I thought about it for a moment and then said, "Well, just sum up our time together, or whatever you want to say, Tim." He thought for a moment and then wrote, "For David, We sure got high, Honey!" It was so right on. As we went back inside, I saw his bedroom, which was by then filled with artwork and candles. It all resembled a well-thought out pleasure dome for the man who started it all and lived to see his vision justified, as well as having a legacy that will continue to lighten the path for all that will follow his example that began with "Tune in, turn on, drop out," and then on the very threshold of the twenty-first century became "Tune in, turn on, move forward."

As the good doctor was fond of saying, "We all will get the Timothy Leary we deserve." Cue The Moody Blues . . . .

Chapter 7

In the Mancave of the Acid King

David Jove

In a town that consists primarily of fruits and nuts with a liberal dose of crazy, to say that you met someone that exceeds previous descriptions of said characters, would be saying something profound indeed. However, in late 1996, I met perhaps the Mount Everest of madmen in the person of David Jove.

Who is David Jove you may ask? The descriptions vary depending on who you speak with. He was the co-founder (with the late Peter Ivers) of the New Wave Theater, which ended abruptly with Peter's murder, and which to this day remains unsolved. David Jove, who went by many names in his lifetime, was an acid guru. A cokehead, he carried a gun in his waistband and kept firearms on hand in his dwelling. In Los Angeles, he maintained a reputation as a video prophet and filmmaker of astonishing range and imagination. He pioneered new wave and punk in the Los Angeles club scene of the 1980s and could have been the next Phil Spector if he had not been so much of a latter-day Charles Manson. David was also drug dealer to the stars at one point, but most of all he remained a mystery to all of us, and now, he is, as they say, in a better place, so the speculation goes on.

I came to know him, as best I can remember, because of Maggie Abbott, who was working at a venue known as The Garlic Festival, held once a year in Los Angeles, and for some reason best forgotten. I was asked by the promoters to bring a Dracula-take on the proceedings, and under the name of "David Del Vlad" brought a Transylvanian twist on board with a guest appearance by one of Dracula's brides from the Coppola *Dracula* on the last night of the festivities. In any case, David Jove made an appearance that night, and as we were introduced he jumped on the fact that I reviewed films and asked if I would take a look at a film he had directed with a mutual friend, Mary Woronov, as one of the players. The film was called, at that moment, *I Married My Mother*. It was also known as *Stranger than Love*. In any case, it was unreleased, and he wanted my opinion. Almost at once, I was warned that he was a madman and also a suspect in a murder, so it might be best if I took a pass. I chose to take a chance and what happened next was my own fault, yet it worked out in any case. David Jove was like a latter-day Svengali—he simply would not take no for an answer and wanted me to see his film immediately if not sooner. The next thing I knew, I was on a "Mr. Toad's wild ride" in his vintage, convertible sports car, racing at breakneck speeds on the surface street of Los Angeles from Westwood to the Fairfax district, where he lived in (I kid you not) a makeshift cave around the corner from Canter's all-night deli in a back alley in what was once a storefront studio. David had at one time done much work in that place as a video editor, and he was an all-around genius of New Wave theater. Literally dozens of the greatest bands of punk and New Wave had walked through those doors, but now, much like Dracula's castle, it was a ruin as well as a madman's lair.

David Jove was a card-carrying psychotic, who was known to be violent on occasion, and there I was, his captive audience, yet somehow I was never afraid of him at any time during the two or so years we remained friends. I was one of the lucky ones he respected, and he was always a kind, if somewhat nutty, companion who left the violence to the hapless dozens that would come and go out of that realm of darkness in which he lived. It was a vampire-like existence to be sure, up all night on blow and booze until his body gave out and he would climb up to the loft he built above the front door, where he would then pull up the ladder, making his place of rest safe from harm—at least in his mind, his hands resting on a shotgun to finish off the pigs if they dared to try a bust, or perhaps an assassin bent on his destruction.

My first night at the cave was an all-nighter that surprised none of those who came before me. David is in total control of everything you see and do for the time you are his guest in his lair. The studio was pitch-black except for black lights in the walls showcasing his artwork, which consisted of Faberge eggs from Hell. He molded his creations solely from his wild imagination, adding world religion, the occult, and perhaps a dash of Scientology to the mix. They were all beautiful in a macabre sort of way. The high ceilings were riddled with bullet holes from random firings of the many guns and rifles he kept in the place. The front door to the studio was rigged with closed-circuit television so that David could see who came to the door. There was also a microphone installed so even the traffic noise could be heard just in case the police were alerted to all the drugs stored there from time to time. David was forever sending out for food and liquor late at night, and pity the poor slob who arrived at the door of that makeshift hideaway, only to confront David in attack mode, armed and extremely dangerous—at least to the general public.

David was determined to screen his film for me, and screen it he did, with a live audio track. There was much movement on his part, as he stood for almost the entire film and talked from behind my chair and many times in front of it. He sang along to the soundtrack and spoke much of the dialogue like a *Rocky Horror* vet on speed. The film was very weird and trippy in parts, and I found myself liking it, as if I really could have done otherwise under the circumstances. The film had been screened once before a live audience at the Gower Studios for one night only. David described the event as "positive," although I will always wonder how he could contain himself long enough to allow an audience to discover the film for themselves. I wrote a review for him the next morning, and he liked it so much that from that moment on we were blood brothers, and never did I ever experience a negative moment in his presence. Even when he was venting and threatening others in the cave, I was always exempt from his wrath. David was a verbal master, whose command of language and metaphor was impressive. Had I but known some of the famous people who had experienced it before me, I would not have been so surprised. David had the attention of the counter-culture greats of the 1960s from The Beatles to The Rolling Stones. David was a player in all their lives, sometimes in a negative way. For example, he was responsible for the infamous Redlands bust involving The Rolling

Stones, when he was calling himself David Schneiderman from Canada. Maggie Abbott actually brought Marianne Faithfull to the cave to meet David without telling her just who the man was and how he had affected her life at that time when the entire world was in on the joke. That was not too amusing at the time, as it caused legal hassles galore, considering that it was the end of the swinging Sixties.

David had so many names and personas that I doubt we will ever know them all. David Jove was obviously not his real name, as he even joked about the Roman mythology reference to the "King of the Gods," which was a title that suited him at that time in his life, and he held court in his own little kingdom of the cave, hiding from the reality of his past lives, staying underground in the city of night, which he chose to call home during his final time on earth.

David was also a father and husband. His wife, Lotus Weinstock, was a force of nature herself. At one time, she was the consort of none other than Lenny Bruce. Lotus was a very funny and gifted comic talent, and had at one time even worked for David Letterman. When Lotus died, David was in such pain and denial that I was concerned about him surviving the ordeal. He arrived at Lotus's funeral on a motorcycle, very high and with six-packs of beer. His presence was duly noted, but I believe he was allowed to remain, against the wishes of many mourners present at the time.

It is difficult to explain why any of us would endure those abusive and lengthy ordeals at his place, as you really could not just get up and leave as you never really knew what he might do. I had seen him almost hit people or threaten to kick their ass while sitting in that darkened space that was his universe to command. The real endurance test was his habit of playing certain videos or pieces of music, usually something of his own that he would begin to sing along with to the point of weeping uncontrollably at the conclusion of a particular tune or lyric that he found profound and sad. David would expound for hours on the futility of the Universe or conspiracies that our government was in the midst of committing, that we as citizens had but hours to expose or suffer the end of the world as we know it. We all had to be pretty agile as verbal ping-pong masters ourselves—or watch David just gobble you up, when he realized you were bluffing your way through one of the mazes in his mental mind games.

That is the reason I stayed when perhaps I should have just split. He was a sad, sad man who, like Icarus, had flown too close to the Sun and fell to Earth a broken man. Of all the characters I knew during my time in Hollywood, David Jove was the most talented to have let himself self-destruct in so colorful a manner. I did not know him when he was doing the New Wave Theater. I kind of wish I had. Several of my friends knew him then, people like Doug Knott and Tequila Mockingbird, who were more in the club scene than I ever was, which was minimal to say the least. I would have loved to have seen him working as a creative talent, which he was in those days, proving that even a lunatic can function, especially if he is also a *genius* lunatic and David Jove, for one golden moment in time, was such a force, and Hollywood did take notice, but as always all good things must come to an end. For David, it was just too soon.

At one time, I agreed to help him put his film out on DVD, but I made him promise to stay out of the negotiation process and let me be his agent. I even changed the title of the film that already had several to simply *Motherfucker*. I figured the time had passed to be subtle, and just to get the film out as a midnight cult film would be better than it just gathering dust on a shelf. For a short time, as the American Film Market approached, he was fine with it, but as push came to shove, David could not leave well enough alone, and the whole attempt was ended as quickly as it had begun. David could not leave anything in the hands of even his friends; he had to be on top of everything that was David Jove.

During 1996, we lost filmmaker Donald Cammell, who chose to take his own life after years of planning to do just that, and making his wife, China, and most of his close friends aware that it was just a matter of when and where. Donald shot himself at home in the presence of China, and since they lived on the top of a canyon, the paramedics could not get to him in time to save his life. That was the official story that went to press, but very quickly, another version of his death came to light, as in the old "print the legend," rather than the facts sort of thing we had from John Ford Westerns. I had done what was to become the last interview with Donald about a year before he died, and Tim Lucas of *Video Watchdog* decided to publish it. I decided to ask the permission of China before going ahead with any of it. We met at my apartment, and she told me that Donald shot himself in such a way that he was conscious and aware for nearly forty-five minutes and had asked her for a mirror in which to watch himself die, experiencing the whole death process like the filmmaker that he was. Anyway, that meeting and one other bonded China and I for a time during that period. I took her to visit Barbara Steele, who knew Donald well and offered a brunch to us both one afternoon. David Jove had also known Donald and Kenneth Anger for years both here and in England, so when the *Watchdog* came out, I phoned China and agreed to meet at David Jove's studio and give her the copies. For some reason, she did not show up, and so I left the magazines with David to give her the next day or so.

When China did finally arrive at David's, she came with her boyfriend, a musician who had known Donald and, as the legend went, was hand-picked by Donald to be her boyfriend when he was gone. Well, I will never really know what went down during their time with Jove, except that about four in the morning, I got a call from David, who was very hyper and excited. "Dave, I listened to the tapes and man, it is true they killed him, man." I still had no idea what he was talking about, so I made him start over from the beginning, and from what I could make out, China Cammell and her boyfriend went to David's, they all hung out for awhile, and the boyfriend played a tape of his latest songs for David's opinion. One of the songs, according to David Jove, was more like a confession of murdering Donald Cammell. Now there was never any reason to believe that any foul play was involved in the death of Donald Cammell, which was always judged a suicide. What was fascinating from my point of view was David Jove, of all people, who had been living as an outcast in Hollywood ever since becoming the number one suspect in the murder of Peter Ivers, making such an accusation. Knowing how one is judged in the public court of hearsay was just astonishing to me.

I never had a chance to discuss that with China, even if I really would have ever brought it up. Yet the magazines were left at David's. She never took them with her, and I never saw her again. I did mention it to Frank Mazolla, who thought it was just mad and said that I should just let it go. As with most of what David Jove would carry on about from time to time, just another of his many flights of fancy, no matter how destructive they might be.

I moved from Beverly Hills to Palm Springs in 1999, after living there for nearly twenty five years. While I was living in the desert, I heard from David Jove one last time. He was at that time heavily into the mystic powers of the crystal skulls that were purported to be buried in the desert near where I was living, and David called into my radio show, and then much later at home, asking me to join him at some secluded spot in the desert to await the aliens that were due to arrive and take us away to a better world than the one we were in. I have to tell you that I was ready to DO just that . . . take off for a new beginning with the mad prophet of Fairfax Avenue. Looking up at the black velvet sky, it seemed entirely possible that a mother ship was just out of focus, hovering over Palm Springs waiting for a bomber crew of Earthlings. I had to laugh, remembering the way David would offer coke to his friends. He nicknamed coke "blurr," so he would come up behind you while you sat in those makeshift lounge chairs of his and say, "Here, you need some more blurr." I am sure if we ever did get on one of those alien mother ships, David Jove would just have to offer those enlightened beings some blurr.

Chapter 8

Auteur of the Avant Garde

Robert Florey

In January 1978, film director Robert Florey inscribed the following dedication in the front piece of *Hollywood Annees Zero*, his book of memoirs published in French recalling the pioneer years in Hollywood: "To David Del Valle, This is a story of the heroic period of a Hollywood that no longer exists." Florey was indeed an artist from another era when Hollywood became the ultimate destination for talented Europeans eager to combine artistic ideas with scenarios for the general public. His was a unique talent that allowed him to keep his vision as an avant-garde filmmaker in a non-commercial sense, only to bring that same sensibility to mainstream Hollywood features.

During the last year of his life, I got to know him personally, visiting him several times at his comfortable home that was filled with the memories of a lifetime in the movies—not to mention a secret worthy of Bluebeard.

Robert Florey arrived in America in 1921 as a correspondent for *Cinemagazine*. By 1925, he was directing features, culminating in the extraordinary short, *Life and Death of 9413—A Hollywood Extra*. He remade that avant-garde work as a feature in 1936 entitled *Hollywood Boulevard*. He spent the next fifty years creating over sixty-five features and 220 television shows, not to mention books, articles, and essays about the nature and history of motion pictures as observed first hand from the silent era through the advent of television.

My admiration for Robert Florey as a director began with my first exposure to his expressionistic horror films of the 1930s and 1940s, especially *Murders in the Rue Morgue*, a Caligari-inspired reworking of Poe with Bela Lugosi as its star . . . the very same Lugosi, who was notorious for refusing *Frankenstein*, also scripted by Florey, as it was beneath him to play a role with no dialogue! Universal gave the pair the consolation prize of Poe's short story, with dialogue by John Huston no less. Surviving scripts indicate how different *Frankenstein* would have been—with Florey as its director, creating distorted camera angles, and with expressionistic décor establishing a truly Germanic nightmare—from what James Whale finally put on the screen.

Florey befriended as well as directed the great Peter Lorre in two of his best-remembered Hollywood films, *The Beast with Five Fingers* and *Face Behind the Mask*. Peter corresponded with Florey in handwritten letters, usually in French, throughout the 1940s, always beginning his letters, "Mon Cher Robert." It was obvious the two had enormous respect for each other as artists, especially since their relationship remained until Lorre's death in 1964.

My most vivid memories of that period with Florey were the afternoon visits at his home shared with his much younger wife, Virginia. He was painfully aware of the passage of time, keeping a rather macabre list of fellow directors who arrived in Hollywood the same time as he did. A red line was crossed through each name, as death claimed another in that elite list of Cinema pioneers. One day, he showed me the latest update. "Look, only King Vidor and William Wyler are left . . . soon it will be my turn."

Usually during those visits, Florey would bring out some amazing treasure to share with me, such as a matchbook advertising *Murders in the Rue Morgue,* or a window card from *Woman in Red.* One day, he brought out four incredible French posters for *Frankenstein,* explaining that Universal gave them to him to prove his screenplay credit was on all advertising in France! (After his death, I would own for a time the six-sheet for *Frankenstein.*)

However, one afternoon, Florey changed his routine, inquiring if I enjoyed history and, in particular, Napoleon. I must have looked a bit bewildered and said, "Yes, I find that period of history most fascinating." With that, Florey took me down a hallway to a large door with a special lock. When he opened the door, I was exposed to what had to be the greatest private collection of Napoleon memorabilia you could imagine! Florey had one of the coats worn by the little corporal in a glass case. There were priceless letters, medals, and paintings, even a cannon from one of the myriad battles during the Emperor's reign before Waterloo. I was completely unprepared for that and it showed. Florey explained that Napoleon was a lifelong obsession and his collection was the result! He also told me that very few of his admirers were allowed to see that room. I promised to keep his collection a secret and left that afternoon dazed by what I had seen in that locked room in what appeared to be a regular hilltop home for a successful man of his accomplishments.

A year later, Florey died, leaving his widow, Virginia, to sort out that mammoth collection of letters, photos, and material from a lifetime in the movies, not to mention the Napoleon collection. A few months ago, I had dinner with a colleague archivist and film historian Marc Wanamaker, who also knew the Floreys at the same time I did. He explained to me that a much younger Virginia had a lover during her last few years with Florey, a cameraman who knew them both as it turned out. The bulk of his letters and memorabilia went to a University in his name but the Napoleon collection was a mystery because Virginia did not really understand its value, therefore she did not contact the museums in France or in this country for that matter. The items were sold through auction, which was a shame, as I know he would have wanted the collection to stay intact.

Robert Florey was a true gentleman of the Cinema, who lived a long and charmed life, watching the art form he so adored turn decade by decade into what it has become in the twenty-first century.

Chapter 9

After Lunching at Baxter's

Les Baxter

One of the advantages of being a child of the 1960s was the thrill of attending each Saturday matinee to see for the first time films like *The Pit and the Pendulum* and *The House of Usher*. The atmosphere that Roger Corman created for those films was aided immeasurably by the music composed for the productions by Les Baxter. I knew nothing of that man's work beyond his film scores, which would number most of the American International beach party flicks, as well as the company's substantial horror output. For me, Les Baxter was *the man* . . . the musical equivalent for that magic period of films with Vincent Price and Edgar Allen Poe.

Flash forward to the early 1980s, when I began tracking down the survivors of those films, doing interviews with not only Roger Corman and Vincent Price, but also Daniel Haller and a host of supporting players. It was only after I got to know MGM photographer Ted Allan that Les Baxter became part of my inner circle of friends during those party days in Beverly Hills.

Ted introduced me to Les with the knowledge that he was "living out in Chatsworth in exile and rather lonely." One must remember that in the 1980s, interest in lounge music was non-existent, leaving the majority of Les Baxter's musical catalogue forgotten.

It did nott take long to see that Less was living in a very dark space career-wise, feeling out of touch with "today's music," overly conscious of his age, and carrying a serious weight problem, as well.

I recognized that malaise at once as part of the Hollywood obsession with youth affecting everybody in the business . . . actors, writers, and, yes, composers, as well. Les had once been the darling of Capitol Records until the advent of The Beatles and the British invasion left him feeling out of fashion. Not to mention out of work.

Les became even more isolated living so far out of mainstream Hollywood in the hills surrounding Magic Mountain and Cal-Arts. He was a composer in exile from the show business he loved. The young Turks that ran the music industry had turned their backs on the "King of Exotica."

When I came along, so in-awe of his film work, he responded warmly to my attention, and we bonded almost on the spot. Les really needed a friend at that time in his life, and soon we were going to films together, as well as many dinners in and around Hollywood, not to mention those poolside weekends with the mountains surrounding his house making you feel like you could be in Montana! Les loved to garden and raised many prized flowers in his home in Chatsworth, as well as having had a showplace in Hawaii for a number of years. I discovered that Les had a knack for selling his beautiful homes before they went up in value. Those losses were just another part of his depression.

He was still composing, even trying his hand at disco with a song entitled *I like Pretty Boys* with lines like, "I want to go with Rob Lowe." Les was so aware of his "non-hip" image that he hired a male model to take his music around town, pretending that the model wrote the music. All of that was way too "Phantom of the Opera" to bear, so I persuaded Les to get an agent to represent his work once more and deal with the age thing without ghosting someone else.

Looking back, I wish I had been more aware of the incredible reputation Les had in the world of exotic music. Had we but known that lounge music was just a few years away from making him a star all over again. Les had enjoyed so much fame and attention from people like Frank Sinatra and Mel Torme that the current rejection was making him bitter and unhappy. One of the things that apparently set off that negative feeling in the industry was when he sued John Williams on November 2, 1982, for lifting some of his music for *E.T.* The case was decided in Williams favor, causing Les to not work on a film for the rest of the 1980s. During that period, Les invited me and the Ted Allans up to his house. There, he would turn off all the lights and play a tape of the score to *The Beast Within*. Needless to say, the music was light-years away from the film itself, which was too grade-Z to ever bring him into mainstream film music again. All of those variables gave Les little to hold onto as far as the future. He loved the music of Carnival and the sounds of Rio, so for a time, Les worked on new music, allowing the Brazilian beat to reinvent his image and somewhat restore the master of exotic soundscapes to his rightful place once more.

Les was the kind of man you wanted to shelter from the unpleasant side of show business, as his talent made him at once child-like and

innocent, as well as destructive and self-pitying. The greatness that resided in Les would manifest itself whenever he chose to play his music
in public. Many times, he would have people over and play the piano,
making time stand still as his soundscapes swept over you, allowing
the listener to be a stranger in Paradise at least for an afternoon.

I had not spoken to Les Baxter in several months when I read in
the trades of his death. All I could think of was how happy little things
like a great meal or a well-tended garden could make him. We lost a
unique talent that day and one that we will not see the likes of again.

Chapter 10

Queen of Blood, Muse of the Space Boy

Florence Marly

Having the disposition of a true romantic, I wish my first celluloid encounter with Florence Marly had been *Tokyo Joe*, set in a smoke-filled cabaret somewhere in postwar Tokyo with a sultry La Marly dressed in a low-cut beaded gown seductively singing Cole Porter's *These Foolish Things Remind Me of You* to a world-weary Bogart. Instead, the first glimpse I had of Florence Marly was on film: she was mute, her skin bright Avocado green, not to mention her figure surreal, out of this world, in a skintight leotard that was also avocado green. For The Countess Florence Von Wurmbrand Marly, that character was tailor-made, allowing her a *tour de force* as Velana the *Queen of Blood*, draining her fellow astronauts (including a very young Dennis Hopper) of their red corpuscles as they journeyed back to Earth, not to mention laying her green eggs-in-aspic throughout the spaceship. The Countess created a unique character without dialogue, the centerpiece of Curtis Harrington's cult film, also known as *Planet of Blood*.

The film also created one of the most off-the-wall musical collaborations imaginable with The Countess joining forces with the great Frank Zappa to collaborate and record the song inspired by *Queen of Blood*, the infamous "Space Boy." There are two bootleg recordings of "Space Boy" with vocals by Florence Marly; one is *Mystery Box*, and the other *Beyond the Fringe of Audience Comprehension*, perhaps a good summation of the short film made by Marly and directed by Renate Dozuks, whose claim to fame was her performance as "Lilith" in Kenneth Anger's *Inauguration of the Pleasure Dome*. The lyrics, as sung by Marly, go something like this:

"Space Boy! Space Boy! Beware!
Velana is waiting for you out there!
Don't cross the parallel of time and space
or you'll die of love in a crueler place
Velana is the Queen and Fate is her code.
Velana the lover, sex without soul
Space Boy! Space Boy!"

The Countess made that short film in 1973, which incredibly found its way to a nomination for the Palm D'Or at Cannes the same year! To give you some idea of what that short was like to watch, imagine *Queen of Blood* meets "Vegas in Space!"

Curtis Harrington directed her one more time as a striking figure in his most accomplished feature, *Games*. Florence made a diva-like entrance during the party sequence at the brownstone abode of James Caan and Katherine Ross.

Florence Marly possessed a rather feline exotic beauty that could betray itself, creating a mask devoid of emotion, which made her appear ice-cold if misdirected. By the time Marly arrived in Hollywood to film *Tokyo Joe* with Humphrey Bogart, the studio was desperate to create another *Casablanca,* so *Tokyo Joe* was cloned to be just that, and it failed at the box-office. The fine work she created in Europe with films like *L'Alibi* for her first husband, Pierre Chenal, or the war film some consider Rene Clement's best work, *Les Maudit,* for which she received a nomination for Best Actress at Cannes, enhanced her reputation for the moment, yet her time in the spotlight was numbered by a shocking comedy of errors with mistaken identity creating a tragic waste of talent ... yet another example of the rise and fall of a glamour queen.

I came to know Florence Marly in what turned out to be the last year of her life. Curtis Harrington introduced us, as I kept after him until he made a call on my behalf (since I was still very much an agent then) for a film for which I hoped to submit her name for the part of the madam: *French Postcards.* At that point, I must stress that I assumed Florence still had that amazing figure from *Queen of Blood.* It was Curtis being wicked that he neglected to tell me that in the years following her work for him, she put on a lot of weight, and only her face and eyes remained recognizable. Florence had been barred from the United States from 1952 through 1956, as she was confused with another woman who was deported for spying or some crime, costing Florence her chance to remain in Hollywood, which killed her career. The attention she received making *Queen of Blood* gave her false hope for a second chance in Hollywood. As time marched on, her weight and looks began to fade, so Florence just let go of her lifelong routines and suffered the consequences. Unaware of all that, I was quite unprepared for what awaited me at the Marie Antoinette Apartment House in Westwood that summer evening in 1977.

The Countess was having a few people over for drinks, so she invited me to come and get acquainted. That was to be one of my first Hollywood parties. The Countess Florence Von Wurmbrand Marly greeted me at the door of her abode in a bright orange tent dress with a long scarf, also bright orange, with a bit of white fur trim. She looked nothing like her screen self, save for her bearing and attitude, which always remained that of a star, faded though she may have become. She had bags of charm, and took me by the arm into her living room, which was populated with characters bearing titles I thought had long ago passed into history. There was Prince Alphonse de Bourbon of Spain. He was a mere child being schooled in Switzerland when Franco took power, leaving him somewhere in line for the Spanish throne if such a thing still existed; Baron Eric Von Bulow, who was a special-effects wizard famous for creating the Pillsbury doughboy (not to mention the Zuni warrior doll that terrorized Karen Black in *Trilogy of Terror*); Alex De Arcy, the Egyptian actor and well-known procurer of girls during the days of the contract players; and a few other titles I no longer can recall from that 1970s time capsule. I do remember that there were almost no women there except for her best friend, the daughter of King Farouk, Princess Fawzia of Egypt. In time, I came to realize that Florence could not bear to be around working actresses, especially young and beautiful ones. I was prepared for a group of familiar character actors like a cocktail reception at the Academy, but not that travelogue of former rulers and their offspring! It seems that Florence kept in touch with many of the exiles from her glory days at Cannes, as well as the happier days as The Countess Von Wurmbrand. There was an atmosphere of failure in that room that was noticeable to even a novice at that kind of life-in-exile for people from the Golden Age, not only of Hollywood but the world stage, as well!

Florence was obsessed with her self-produced short film, *Space Boy*. "It was shown at Cannes, you know," so tonight she was planning to screen it especially for me from her own 16 mm copy. The film was avant-garde in style and concept, with weird electronic music on the soundtrack. I would love to see it again today as it might just merit a revival after all.

She still had her figure in the film, although I would have chosen a hairpiece a bit more in keeping with her *Queen of Blood* persona than the "Hot Voodoo" blond Afro wig she chose to wear for the camera! There was a rather cosmic portrait of her inspired by *Space Boy* that hung in her living room along with the Coat of Arms of the Von Wurmbrands. Florence longed to be back in the spotlight, dismissing all the reasons why offers ceased to appear, and my advice to forget the past and try for character parts like the one I suggested for her in *French Postcards*, a showy part of a once-glamorous madam who enjoys life in the present without regrets. I reminded her of actresses like Diana Dors and Shelley Winters, who let image and glamour go, only to have second careers in character work. All Florence could see was her former self, and she simply refused to face reality in the changing face of Hollywood. In the next few months, she tried, and she dieted to prepare for any chance at a comeback. I was still so naïve at that aspect of handling damaged personalities that I spent a good deal of time escorting her to various parties around town when I should have made her realize her health required more attention to her diet and less on entertaining ghosts from the past. She did introduce me to one lady that I will talk about in more detail in a moment—the fabulous Hermione Baddeley. As we got into the beginning of 1978, the dieting was not working, and Florence began to take trips to Mexico with Princess Fawzia and sometimes with Hermione to receive injections that were illegal in the states, since the FDA would not condone the dangerous effects such shots could put on the heart, especially in overweight people. Florence had just returned from such a visit, when she began to feel the results of those injections and was advised to check into a hospital immediately for tests.

Both the Princess and I begged her to listen to her doctors and prepare to be admitted. Instead, she insisted on having another one of those gatherings at her place as a kind of *bon voyage* to the hospital. I refused to go along with that and did not attend Florence's party. It was not more than three days later that Florence Marly suffered a fatal heart attack and died on November 9, 1978. At the funeral, Princess Fawzia showed Polaroid's of Florence from that final party, and for what it is worth, she looked like she had a great time.

I must be a romantic after all, as I now always think of her as she appeared in *Tokyo Joe*, singing "These Foolish Things Remind Me of You" to Bogart. The Countess was indeed foolish, yet she lived her life on her own terms, surviving after losing everything. She returned to Hollywood and partied to the end.

Chapter 11
Bedknobs and Gin Bottles

Hermione Baddeley

The only sour note in the celebrated careers of Angela and Hermoine Baddeley had to be the tunnel-vision of American casting directors, most of whom know little of the history of cinema and even less of theatre. They viewed the Baddeley sisters only as comic domestics on television. Angela received some of her best notices playing Mrs. Bridges for *Upstairs-Downstairs* on the BBC, yet she had worked with John Gielgud and Lawrence Olivier in many stage productions of Shakespeare. Television gave them both exposure, but not the respect they deserved as artists.

Hermoine, on the other hand, became a household name with American audiences, made serious money, and garnered raves for her work on *Maude* as the boozy Mrs. Naugatuck, yet few in Hollywood realized what a towering dramatic actress she had been in her prime. Tennessee Williams recalled in his memoirs the bravura performance Hermione gave as Flora Goforth at Spoleto of his play *The Milk Train Doesn't Stop Here Anymore*, where the great Anna Magnani, having witnessed her performance, insisted on going backstage, knelt down, and kissed the hem of Hermoine's dress—a tribute from one great actress to another. In her film work, Hermoine received an Oscar nomination for *Room at the Top*, losing the award, but acquiring the star of the film, Laurence Harvey, as a lover. She once confided to me that her relationship with Harvey was so intense that "there was a fire within Larry compelling him to work non-stop, he devoured life as if he knew it might be cut short."

Her time spent in Hollywood kind of set the stage for her image as a loveable domestic with roles in *Midnight Lace* for Ross Hunter and the two Disney films that created her image in the eyes of American audiences, *Mary Poppins* and *The Happiest Millionaire*.

It was Florence Marley who first brought me to Hermione's house, which, at that time, was high above Sunset Boulevard not far from George Cukor's busy address. We attended the first of many parties that Hermione would throw over the next eight years I was to know her. At that point in my life, I was always looking for personalities to represent. I had recently opened my own talent agency—Del Valle, Franklin, and Levine—which had just taken offices on the thirteenth floor of Century Park East. Securing names like Hermione made it possible to get lesser clients in the door of the major network casting directors. Those were the days of TVQ . . . all actors were rated on how much exposure they had on television in a given year, and having a regular from a Norman Lear production was pure gold.

The task of signing Hermione Baddeley as a client was a challenge to say the least! She would always say, "Yes, please take care of things, be my rock," then repeat the same gesture with the next agent that asked to represent her. I remember trying to negotiate her contract for a *Love Boat* appearance, only to have the casting agent ask me, "Why is Mark Levin submitting her as well?" It seemed Hermione met Mark at Bea Arthur's house and told him to see what he could do for her. When I confronted her with that, all she did was laugh and say, "Well, darling, let's see who gets the most money out of them." After a fashion, I decided it was far better to be her pal and not try to manage her career. She was highly sought-after to do voice-over work for commercials, and animated features, as well! Hermoine was in-demand till the end of her life, such was her talent.

Hermione always seemed to be at cross purposes with her life at home and what was required of her at the studios, yet none of life's realities seemed to matter much to her, as most of the challenges to be found in acting were behind her by then. Hermione wanted to party and have fun when she was not working. By the time I knew her, she had already stopped working on *Maude* and was freelancing on shows like *Little House on the Prairie, Wonder Woman,* and of course, *The Love Boat.*

Hermione's only constant companions during the time I knew her were a "summer stock" version of the charismatic young man. Enter Johnny Rebel, who was handy as houseboy and driver when needed. It was only later that I would learn he was much more than that! The other was a delightfully intoxicated English woman known as "Lady Jane." That woman was never, and I mean *never*, sober. However Lady Jane was a good companion for a character like Hermione, as she was loyal, howlingly funny, and dear.

I am blessed with so many memories of those two arriving at parties, watching Jane slowly gravitate to the kitchen or wherever the bar was set up, and remain near the booze until time to say goodnight.

Christmastime with Hermione could be considered the cocktail hour version of *A Christmas Carol*. (Remember, Hermione played Bob Cratchet's wife in what I consider the best film version with grand old Alistair Sim as Scrooge!) Christmas Day was always spent at the Cock and Bull bar and grill on Sunset Boulevard. A favorite watering hole for both veterans of Hollywood, not to mention the British film colony, the drinks were generous and the lighting as cave-like as possible. One could spot John Carradine in conversation with Murray Matheson, or see Natalie Shafer ordering more roast beef with Eve Arden. The grill section of the bar always prepared a Christmas buffet unsurpassed for brunch. Hermione would carry a large handbag, which she would fill with roast beef and turkey legs for her six or seven pugs she had waiting for her at home. Sometimes, we would arrive back at the house and before she could put the bag down they were off and running with it. I often wondered if the bag itself, having held so much food over the years, would be considered the first doggie bag.

Once, during one of my little parties, Lady Jane asked me to make Champagne punch, so I prepared a large punch bowel using her recipe. When they arrived, Lady Jane kept refilling one glass after another, finally telling Hermione to come into the kitchen as she could act as a waiter no longer! A few minutes later, I saw the two of them sitting by the punch bowl with two large milkshake straws draining the contents with schoolgirl abandon. Oh, for a photograph of that!

The best parties were the ones that Hermione organized personally to celebrate a friend's birthday or someone getting a job. On those occasions, she would cater the party and spend ample time up in her bedroom preparing her grand entrance after the guests arrived.

Hermione would come down the stairs with a feather boa around her neck and a large smoking cigar lit at full flame as she puffed her way down to her waiting guests. I remember meeting author Robert Nathan, whose work I admired, with his wife, the actress Anna Lee, a *grande dame* in her own right. The legendary Stan Lee was a regular at her soirées, and after a few drinks, would take me out on the veranda that overlooked Los Angeles and begin his speech to me about producing. "Remember, David, if you want to be a producer, start telling yourself that you are a producer; it is that simple . . . ." Stan always thought being an agent was not my cup of tea, and he was right on the money with that observation.

The divine Martha Raye came to many of those parties. What a remarkable talent she was, and so down to earth. One could see why Chaplin admired her work in comedy so much.

Martha loved to play off Hermione when they would get near a piano. They usually got Gavin MacLeod's wife, Patti, to play, while they took turns doing their favorite music hall ballads and randy tunes. Hermoine was a favorite with Sir Noel Coward, as well; he wrote several songs for her revues over the years. That evening, she sang two of them, "I'm the Wife of an Acrobat" and "Poor Little Rich Girl." The room burst into applause. That encouragement led to Hermione reviving her Music Hall act as a revue entitled *Why Not Tonight?* She worked very hard on that revue, the result being a *tour-de-force* for a woman of her advancing years. The material was a bit dated for the Los Angeles crowd, yet her humor and drive overwhelmed any real criticism beyond her choice of material. Hermione is credited with being the first to sing about a sex change in a revue. The song, entitled "I Changed My Sex a Week Ago," is still a giggle and a wink for Hermione and her legion of gay admirers, who were there on opening night to support that legend in English revue. She sang some of her old favorites like "Missing the Bus" and "Winter in Torquay," signing off with "Old Girls." *Why Not Tonight?* ran only for a handful of performances, as it was a trial run for a tour if she thought the show, as well as its star, would be able to pull off a long city-by-city tour. I have forgotten the exact reasons she chose not to tour—perhaps the expense, as well as being out of circulation for voice-over work, which was paying the bills at the moment, made her say no. It would be one of her last live appearances on stage.

Martha Raye would sometimes organize a visit to Laguna Beach for an impromptu songfest at a club called The Little Shrimp, where the two old-timers would pull out all the stops for a limited audience of admirers. My favorite experience with the two of them was not in Laguna Beach but right in West Hollywood at a tacky, dark leather bar on Santa Monica Boulevard called The Eagle. It seems the bartender there kept an autographed picture of Martha over the cash register, so one night, Hermione called me and said, "Darling, we are all going to meet Maggie over at this club to see why they don't have my picture up there as well." By the time we all converged on the club, it was wall to wall men. Never underestimate the power of celebrity. Both ladies walked in and owned the place, as drinks were on the house and Maggie got introduced to "poppers," a recreational form of amyl nitrate. From that night onward, there was always a vial in Maggie Raye's purse for a night out. After about an hour in the place a very rough-looking guy with a beer gut, leather cap, and pants walked up to Hermione and Maggie and said, "I want to meet you both." He looked at Maggie and said, "I watched you and Chaplin on tape back in Munich at our little film club." Maggie asked if he was in the business, and he replied, "Well, yes, I direct films. My name is Rainer Fassbinder." The name meant little to them, but I was stunned, until the bartender explained that Fassbinder liked the club so much that they gave him the back room to act as a sort of office whenever he was in Los Angeles. That moment was as good as it gets.

There were more good times with Hermione and Lady Jane, including a trip or two down to Newport Beach. I was in New York, when I heard that Hermione had suffered a series of strokes at home and was taken to hospital, where she was kept alive until her daughter could fly in from London to take charge. That was the end of an era in my life, for no matter how many stars or personalities I would come to know in this business, there would always be just one Hermione Baddeley.

Chapter 12
The Other Side of Midnight

Calvin Lockhart

No one could have imagined what kind of an impact the now-notorious film version of Gore Vidal's novel, *Myra Breckenridge*, would have on my future life in Hollywood or the career I would chose once I arrived in The City of the Angels.

During the long hot summer of 1970, *Myra Breckenridge* the motion picture became the ultimate celebration of pop culture nihilism, opening across the country for a fast Warhol fifteen minutes, leaving 20th Century Fox in a daze of bad counter-culture films made by suits without a clue what *Easy Rider* had done to the business they thought they were a part of.

I managed to see *Myra Breckenridge* in San Francisco at a midnight sneak preview with an audience of freaks that tripped through the whole thing, making it a "happening." My favorite observation regarding *Myra Breckenridge* was that her personality was really "Werner Erhard with a sense of Irony." Anyone familiar with EST knows what that means . . . naturally I will always love that film.

The following morning, I was off to Rome for a summer semester of college Italian style. *Myra Breckenridge* was also in Rome that summer, and the media hype was nearly that of *Cleopatra* in the 1960s: "At last, the book that couldn't be written is now a motion picture that couldn't be made." A huge billboard of Mae West as the statue of Liberty towered near the Coliseum. Regardless of the disastrous reviews, everyone wanted to know if Mae West was really a man or if Raquel Welch indulged in catfights between takes, as Rex Reed let it all hang out in his diary. Well, the scandal passed into legend with those diaries of Rex's locked away, never to be heard from again. However, the memory of Mike Sarne's third and last attempt at filmmaking would linger in the images of the amazing cast of actors that populated *Myra Breckenridge*. I would wind up representing at least three of them, as well as recording Mike Sarne's recollections of *Myra Breckenridge* on video tape nearly twenty years later for my *Sinister Image* series.

Calvin Lockhart, who was playing a cameo role as the very fey "Irving" in *Myra Breckenridge*, was on his way to becoming the cinema's Great Black Hope. The Nassau-born actor had once been a pupil of the legendary Uta Hagen in New York, where he caused a minor sensation on Broadway with *A Taste of Honey* with Angela Lansbury. His friendship with Mike Sarne began with *Joanna*, a strange 1960s mod time capsule that Gore Vidal would later say resembled "a collection of cigarette ads." Peter Max did the poster art, and for a time it seemed Calvin and Sarne had the best of everything. Calvin arrived in England to prove himself worthy performing at Royal Shakespeare Company at Stratford, as well as filming projects like *A Dandy in Aspic* for Anthony Mann/Laurence Harvey, and *Leo the Last* with John Boorman.

Calvin always maintained a kind of arrogance that was tolerated and somewhat balanced by his then-physical beauty. I would meet Calvin Lockhart during the first months of opening my own talent agency in Century City. My new assistant, Susanne Gordon, was an English blonde of great experience in show business, having worked for Shirley Jones and the impossible Jack Cassidy. Susanne had discovered through one of her contacts that Calvin was in town looking for a new agent, so she arranged for us to meet at La Scala Boutique in Beverly Hills for dinner.

That night in the fall of 1978 would remain in my memory forever as a favorite moment since Calvin would never again be so charming, and times would never be as glamorous as they were in Beverly Hills in those days before laptops, cell phones, and packaging for TVQ would render the business light-years away from the supper clubs of Beverly Hills and "Old Hollywood."

What made our first meeting work so well (looking back after all this time) was the fact that I knew next to nothing about Calvin except that he had been in *Myra Breckenridge* as a gesture to Mike, and had turned down the TV series, *Room 222*, after a rather unfortunate experience on a film entitled *Halls of Anger*, which in his view was directed by a racist and caused Calvin to walk off the film more than once.

Susanne and I arrived at La Scala that evening to find Calvin already seated at a table with a blonde actress he was ready to dispose of when we reached our appointed table. Calvin excused himself and moved over to our table, explaining that he ran into her while waiting for us to arrive. Before we could order our cocktails, the blonde came over, asking Calvin when he might be free later on . . . and she would not take no for an answer. Finally, Calvin looked at the water glass on the table and said to her, "You know, my dear, even this water can contain itself; why can't you?"

What became apparent during that first of many adventures with Calvin was the attraction my assistant held for Calvin and vise versa. So began the Susanne/Calvin affair that would, for a time, find Calvin moving into her apartment at the Chateau De Fleur on Franklin in the heart of Hollywood (the city that has no heart).

Calvin had been away from Hollywood for quite some time, living in Jamaica, after turning down the *Room 222* series, so the first order of business was to let the casting directors know he was back and ready to work. Tim Flack over at Fox called to offer Calvin a guest spot on the cop series, *Starsky and Hutch,* in an episode entitled "Cover Girl," with former model Maude Adams. He played a hired killer with a kink for model airplanes. While working on the Fox lot, Calvin arranged for us to screen the first film he'd made for Mike Sarne, *Joanna,* as well as the still-unreleased *The Baron,* also known as *Baron von Tripps.* That oddity boasts not only Calvin in his usual cad mode, but a star turn from actor Richard Lynch, who pretty much walks away with the film as Lockhart's adversary, with a great death scene to boot. The wonderful Joan Blondell is in it, as well, always referring to Calvin as "Hotdog." It seems all the women in this film are under his spell in one way or another. To this day, *The Baron* has yet to turn up even on DVD! After the Fox show, we needed some new photos of Calvin to send around town. Calvin insisted he knew just the right photographer, and the results are here for the record . . . Calvin dressed up like a pimp, complete with hat and cane! As sophisticated as Calvin Lockhart could be as a personality and world traveler, he still saw himself in Hollywood as a pimp.

I represented Calvin from the end of 1978 through the first part of 1980, during which time we attended many parties with amazing guys like the late Lawrence Cook (*The Spook Who Sat by the Door*), Roscoe Lee Browne (a hoot!) and Brock Peters. It was a difficult time for Calvin, since his return also brought him face to face with how much it really cost him to leave Hollywood in the first place. He left on the verge of stardom, and then he saw co-stars like Richard Pryor and Bill Cosby already major stars while he had to struggle all over again, all the while getting a bit older and more desperate. We found him a pad in the Barham Apartments, overlooking the Hollywood Freeway yet close to the studios in Burbank, an ideal location. The only scare Calvin gave me during our working relationship was his heart attack brought on by the news that both of his sons had lost the use of their legs, one from jumping under a train and the other from some kind of drug-related incident. That news, along with the pressure of trying to make it in Hollywood, put Calvin in intensive care at Cedars-Sinai. Brock Peters took care of particulars at the hospital and got him admitted, even though his Screen Actors Guild insurance had been in doubt since he'd left town so many years before. We left Calvin on the mend, and within days, he was back at his apartment and ready for work.

On Sundays, I would organize a brunch for some of my clients at a popular eatery in Venice known as "Robert's," positioned directly in front of the Pacific Ocean on the Santa Monica Boardwalk. It was there that Roscoe Lee Browne made his now-famous remark when asked if he was an Afro-American. Roscoe replied, "No, Honey, I'm an Aphrodisiac!" Later, Roscoe tapped Calvin on the shoulder and the two had an impromptu waltz; such was the atmosphere in "Robert's" after a few mimosas, with the likes of directors Paul Bartel, Paul Mazursky, novelist Christopher Isherwood, Fellini star (and hustler) Hiram Keller, Bond girl Martine Beswick, and Viva, a real mix of Warhol superstars and 1960s icons. Also in Robert's that afternoon was actor Monty Landis, who also had a small role in *Myra Breckenridge* as a wacko acting coach who clutches a tree, saying the immortal line, "A tree God-Dammit." Monty became a client that day, and later he and Viva would be cast in *Love at First Bite*, only to wind up on the cutting room floor, or, in Viva's case, fired over a long-standing problem regarding *Cisco Pike* (she had flown to New York to promote the film and just kept on going to Paris).

There were more good times during that period, with Calvin introducing me to the great Hugh Masekela (South Africa's musical ambassador to the world), who kept a bungalow at the Chateau Marmont to receive friends after a gig. Khaliah Ali, the amazing daughter of "The Champion," was a good friend of Calvin's, as well. I will never forget meeting Hugh Masekela's mother that evening, a very funny lady, who tragically was killed by an elephant while in South Africa a few months later. One incident stands out from that evening as an example of what might have been had Calvin become the star many thought he should be. We left Hugh and started toward the driveway at the Marmont, when a young man who worked as a valet in the garage recognized Calvin and insisted on locating his car. Calvin chose a white Rolls Royce that was sitting near the lobby archway. Within minutes, we were all in a stolen Rolls driving down Sunset, Calvin laughing his head off at the absurdity of it.

Calvin Lockhart will always be a Casanova best remembered on the silver screen, who stepped down from it occasionally to have a few laughs with mortals like myself, only to reappear perhaps in Jamaica on the arm of another man's wife.

Chapter 13

The Breast of Russ Meyer

Russ Meyer

Having focused on Myra Breckenridge, I thought it appropriate to discuss the other film being shot simultaneously on the 20th Century Fox lot that year: Russ Meyer's *Beyond the Valley of the Dolls.*

One can only imagine what it must have been like to wander away from Mike Sarne's druggy, laid-back sound stage over to Russ Meyer's set—brimming over with size double-D breasted ingénues decorating the director's vision of Hollywood. After all, any film that would cause Jacqueline Susann to tell the press it would damage her "reputation" as a writer must be allowed to unspool nationwide! Russ Meyer, an artist of such independence that he photographed, directed, and distributed his own films for years (possibly Hollywood's only true *auteur*), was given a budget of $1.5 million to create his masterpiece, one of three films to be made at Fox under his new contract. Like *Myra Breckenridge, Beyond the Valley of the Dolls* had a movie critic in tow—namely Roger Ebert—only that critic actually wrote the screenplay, and what a ripe screenplay it was! I don't think a week goes by that someone doesn't bring that fact up to Ebert, or at least, I hope they do! Never was there a more vanilla film critic in America than good old Roger Ebert, yet for Russ Meyer, he let alcohol take over long enough to pen some of the most quotably outrageous dialogue ever!

What took the Fox front office by surprise was that the film-going youth of America, who wouldn't be caught dead at a screening of Susann's *Valley of the Dolls*, rushed to make Meyer's epic a financial success, something *Myra Breckenridge* failed to do at the time.

Russ would appear on two half-hour segments of my *Sinister Image* cable program years later to discuss his films. He told a great story about Miriam Hopkins, who worked on his *Fanny Hill* in Germany: he liked her a lot and laughed about her getting on a train with a famous director like Fritz Lang, who convinced her they were going to get married and even had a minister perform the ceremony on the train. After a "honeymoon," the director revealed that the minister was an actor and the whole thing was a joke! Russ also recalled driving Hopkins around Berlin looking for women for *her*!

After we shot the first half, my crew, which consisted of two overweight girls from the AFI, refused to tape the second half (that would have been all about *Beyond the Valley of the Dolls*) for fear of "God's wrath" (I kid you not). Russ thought it was very funny, especially since we were in Santa Monica, of all places. Russ explained that "Jesus freaks" had been the bane of his existence ever since he started making films back in the late 1950s.

The night before our taping, Russ took me out for dinner and regaled me with stories about his life in show business. He was what they call "a man's man," a combat veteran of the Second World War, where he began using his camera to take photographs and later news-reel footage of what was happening in Europe, not to mention as many busty women as he could get in front of his lens! Russ would take re-sponsibility for coining both the phrases "soft-core" and "hardcore" to describe the kinds of films he liked to make. I remember that at dinner he ordered tonic water, and as soon as the waiter left, he fished two small bottles of gin (from a recent plane trip, no doubt) out of his pocket and made a good old Gin and Tonic! "Waste not, want not" is my motto," said the director of *Mudhoney* under his breath. One thing you realized in talking with that man was his total knowledge of the filmmaking process, yet he was so down to earth about Hollywood . . . a charming guy that Russ Meyer was!

After dinner, Russ drove me by his house up in the hills, which was a virtual museum of Meyer memorabilia! He had bronzed and mounted on the wall some of the giant bras worn by his leading la-dies. There were awards, photographs, posters, and props from his en-tire *oeuvre* proudly displayed for all to see. Over a brandy in his living room, Russ waxed nostalgic about his success: "At my age, I have noth-ing to complain about. There's a forty-year-old gal from Finland who is built like a brick shit-house, who comes over once a week and kicks the shit out of me, so I'm not what you would call frustrated." Russ was very proud of his connection to young filmmakers, telling them not to give up on their dreams. "I've made films all my life, whether the money was there or not; don't let anyone get in your way." Russ always signed autographs "I was glad to do it!" Believe me he was!

Russ Meyer passed away recently at the age of eighty-two, and had not enjoyed good health in the years since we taped my show. His aesthetic is admired and copied by directors like John Waters and Quentin Tarentino. His films will continue to inspire the young Turks of Hollywood, and perhaps in time, his place in film history will be properly recognized beyond the valley of the dolls.

Chapter 14
Taste the Black Sperm of My Vengeance

John La Zar

When I first saw *Beyond the Valley of the Dolls* way back in 1970, it was John Lazar as "Z-Man" who had all the great lines. His was the persona that best represented just how far-out this film could be! This character was so over the top in terms of performance, especially armed with Roger Ebert's mix of faux Shakespearean verse with 1960's hip phraseology, that it was understood John Lazar was the "Man"—it was his happening—and it freaked us all out, baby!

As with my recollections of *Myra Breckenridge*, I was fortunate to know on rather personal terms the directors of both films, as well as cast members, some of whom became clients during my time as an agent.

Unlike Calvin Lockhart or Monty Landis, my experiences with John Lazar were decidedly not positive. The majority of my adventures with the cult figures of Hollywood have been fun, some more than others, and yes, there have been situations where I wished I had kept my naiveté regarding how certain actors can be so unlike their screen personas. Sometimes, it is better not to meet those you admire on the screen because they can bite you.

After the Russ Meyer, interview I felt compelled to meet the rest of the cast of Russ's own personal favorite of his films, *Beyond the Valley of the Dolls*. Originally, I asked Russ if he had a phone number or a way I could meet John Lazar; I recall asking why that obviously talented man never made more films or, more to the point, whatever *happened* to John? Russ said at the time that he did not know how to reach John and had been out of touch after casting him in his last film, *Ultra Vixens*.

For the record, Russ never said anything negative about John as a person or as an actor. Russ always felt that the very nature of the character forever typed John in a category where he would never work again. Russ said, "I ruined that guy's career!"

That character, "Ronnie Barzel," known to all *Beyond the Valley of the Dolls* fans as "Z-Man," who behaves in the film like a gay man, then abruptly reveals he is really a hermaphrodite who likes to dress as "Superwoman." Once in this pseudo Wonder Woman attire, "she" devotes the better part of last reel of *Beyond the Valley of the Dolls* beheading the object of her desires, "Jungle lad," aka Lance Rock (Michael Blodgett), to the fanfare of the 20th Century Fox theme music! Once you saw that performance, you were never likely to forget it.

There was one point during John's time with me when I was able to ask some questions regarding the filming of *Beyond the Valley of the Dolls* and especially about his relationship with actor Michael. I confessed to John that I, like many others, found Michael to be very sexy with that killer physique matched with movie star good looks. John reacted to that by telling me what rivalry they had from day one on the set.

"I had my ladies on one side and Michael had his on the other. We had a lot of sex on the film, but not with each other, if that's what you were thinking. I remember at a line reading getting so intense with him that I blew my top at one point and threw myself across the table, grabbing him by the throat. We had to be separated by the crew. Afterwards, once we became aware of each other's power, we got along okay. I will tell you one funny incident during our bedroom scene. I was in bed with Jungle Lad as Super Woman, and between takes, Mike said to me, 'You know, John, I have done two really hot make-out scenes with the ladies in this film with not one rise of a hard-on, and now with you and me in bed, it would be just my luck to get a hard-on with you.'"

Michael certainly held his own with John's flamboyance, and would go on to make at least two more cult films of note, *The Velvet Vampire* and *There Was a Crooked Man.* He would remain beefcake material throughout his acting days and was lucky enough to discover his writing talents early enough to have a second career. His friends called him "Mookie," and from all accounts, he lived a very happy life in Hollywood right up until his death in 2007 from cancer.

So what really happened that prevented the actor who could conjure up such a performance from never making more than a handful of films? Other gender-bending performances come to mind, such as Tim Curry in *The Rocky Horror Picture Show,* or Chris Sarandon in *Dog Day Afternoon,* where talent is recognized regardless of the role that brought that actor to attention, sometimes even establishing a career. Consider Boris Karloff in *Frankenstein.* Well, I was about to find out the answer to that question in spades.

That brings us to 1995 and preproduction for a film called *Night of the Scarecrow*. One of my good friends is director Jeff Burr, who shares my love of old movies and the people who made them. Jeff is very talented, not to mention a great guy with a big heart. Jeff was also the director of the aforementioned film. One afternoon, I got a call from Jeff asking me to meet him at Café Figaro on Melrose, which was, at the time, a couple of blocks from my then-apartment in Beverly Hills. Jeff had a surprise waiting for me there. The great Z-Man himself was sitting at a table with Jeff waiting to be introduced to his number one fan! Jeff was prepping a film, and John was very interested in being a part of it. We had a super time together sharing anecdotes about films in general and *Beyond the Valley of the Dolls* in particular. I left the restaurant knowing I had made a new friend.

For nearly a year John Lazar was enjoyable to be around. By then, I had met his wife and three kids who lived in the valley. John was really concentrating on his craft, working out, and taking classes. At that time, Jeff had given John the part of the warlock who curses the town in the film's flashback, explaining why it all had to be and so on. It was a small role, not more than a cameo. John had auditioned for the larger part of the scarecrow killer, however he was cast in the cameo instead. That was most likely the beginning of his problems with Jeff. John had prepared a scene from *Macbeth* to secure the scarecrow role. I remember him calling me afterwards thinking he had just blown everyone away with his reading. That should have been a warning all was not well, but at the time, I just wrote it off to an actor ego tripping. John was an expert swordsman and should have been teaching fencing for the movies. I suggested on several occasions that ability could be a very lucrative second career and would have also taken some of the pressure off his wife in supporting the children. During the filming, I got a call from John, who was irate because Jeff wanted to film him semi-nude at one point in an orgy sequence where, according to John, you could see his ass. That was a breach of contract to John, who wanted me to step in and do something. Looking back, it was beyond absurd, as John wound up showing his ass to everybody in any case!

Fred Olen Ray, known far and wide as a mega-fan, not to mention a producer/director of exploitation films, had put John in a couple of his films with titles like *Attack of the Fifty-Foot Centerfold.* John was starting to get noticed by the baby-boomers in the business who, like myself, were mesmerized by the Z-Man back in 1970.

During that time, Fred had a birthday party at his home, and John and his wife took me with them. We met some great people there, such as Russ Tamblyn, France Nuyen, and lots of actors from old Hollywood. During that evening, John started talking about his career and how he was about to break out to super-stardom. He was really tripping on it, but in a cool way, or so it seemed at the time. I want to emphasize that John did not drink during that period and was the picture of health, at least physically. He worked out everyday and it showed! He was buff and tanned if not a little hyper, like a man with no time left to waste.

Several months went by, and then I heard that John had left his wife and kids and moved in with a middle-aged school teacher who better understood his need to "get his career on track."

I spoke with John a few times on the phone, sensing a growing desperation in his voice about how the next year would see him in major acting roles, and if their had been any justice, his role in *Beyond the Valley of the Dolls* would have brought him the Oscar, stardom, etc. About two weeks later, I got another call from John asking me if he could crash at my place for a few days since I lived near the production office that was about to employ him for a low-budget film. When I asked where he was at the moment, he said, "I'm staying at Jeff Burr's place, but he is out of town scouting locations and we are just not getting along."

That should have tipped me off that something was terribly wrong, however I told John to come on over and I would fix a place for him in the living room for a few days. I left a message on Jeff Burr's answering service for him get in touch since I had John as a house guest.

What happened next was like outtakes from *Beyond the Valley of the Dolls in Hell.* John arrived at my place close to midnight with the middle-aged school teacher in tow, and he was demonically drunk. He tore into that woman with abuse you had to witness to believe, yet she took it for about forty-five minutes before leaving in tears. I had never seen John like that and still could not reconcile the man I was staring at with the man I thought I knew over the last year who was a fitness freak.

I really needed to speak with Jeff Burr, and to decide what to do with Mr. Hyde! The next morning, John was up at six o'clock in the morning doing push-ups, and then announced he was off to a gym in Beverly Hills that was about half a mile from where I lived. He left before I could really have it out with him about his behavior the night before. Around noon, he returned with a six-pack of giant beer cans, two of which were already gone. *This was how John Lazar capped off a workout?*

I have had more than my share of encounters with alcoholics, including having the most notorious drinker of all, Lawrence Tierney, stay with me for days, yet he never drank in my presence, lucky for me! John was just such a shock because I was completely unprepared to see him in such a state. Finally, I got Jeff on the phone, only to find out that when Jeff returned to his apartment, he found that John had taken all the food Jeff had left for the week—around $300 worth of goods—back to the market for a *refund*! Then, John proceeded to buy booze with the money, spending the remainder of his time at Jeff's trashing the place before coming over to me.

For the next three days, I lived like someone from *The Lost Weekend*, or some weird variation of a TV movie-of-the week about alcohol abuse, or more like hitting rock bottom with Linda Blair!

At one point, I gave my heartfelt salvation speech to John and I really did emphasize how he had let his family down, as well as any fans he might have in the future. John would have none of it. He said that he was going to be a star and that a year from then we would be sitting at the Oak Room at the Plaza Hotel in New York toasting his new-found success with champagne! He told me he had a grown son in San Francisco from his first marriage, but they were estranged, which is not hard to believe under the circumstances. I soon began to see what happened to his acting career—the one film I looked up between *Beyond the Valley of the Dolls*, which had been directed by another friend of mine, Jim Wynorski, who later told me the same sad story of alcohol abuse on location.

Finally, I simply had to put an end to his staying in my apartment, so he began his search for another person to take over. It didn't take him long for him to locate Sage Stallone, the son of Sly Stallone. Sage is a nice guy who loves films, even creating a company to distribute cult titles like *The Beyond*, and not surprisingly, he also wants to be an actor. John had him dazzled, I guess, because the next day, Sage arrived and took John to a motel, renting him a room for a month. I was so grateful to Sage I that felt guilty not telling him right off what he had in store. Jeff and I left messages with all the facts we thought he needed to know, yet Sage never returned one call. Later on, I met the ladies from *Beyond the Valley of the Dolls*, as well as other journalists, who unknowingly tried to take John to a restaurant or a coffee house for an interview, only to have their own horror stories regarding Z-Man's antics that always began with a drink.

I will always admire John Lazar *the actor,* who gave me such pleasure with his talent in Russ Meyer's masterpiece, which is being rediscovered all over again and again with the release of the film on DVD. All I can hope for is that John finds a friend or lover who can lift him out of his addiction because the talent has always been there, but he just needs to believe that as much as I do. *Bon Chance,* Z-Man!

Chapter 15

Big Noise from Winnetka

David Bradley

Since we were discussing the late John Kobal, another name from the past came to mind: that of the also late David Bradley. If you want to talk about a character, look no further because that man was a hoot and a half!

First of all, David was famous around film circles for having collected a staggering collection of silent films, the only existing prints of many of them left in the civilized world. David was also infamous for "discovering" Charlton Heston and putting the young actor in the first of two 16mm features: Ibsen's *Peer Gynt* and *Julius Caesar*. Charlton appears bare-chested in the first and with that famous jaw in place in the second.

Those films opened doors for both men in Hollywood. David went into a director's training program, where he managed to direct his only decent film, *Talk About a Stranger* (1952), starring two actors destined for California and Washington politics, George Murphy and Nancy Davis (later known as Nancy Reagan, wife of President

Ronald Reagan). That was a minor Film Noir that benefited greatly by having the great John Alton as the cinematographer. Charlton also advanced with a few small but showy roles, and the rest is, shall we say, history.

David was already becoming well-known around town as a major pain in the ass to work with. He was so opinionated with just one minor film to his credit that his reputation for being "difficult" was beginning to be set in stone. His next film, *12 To the Moon* (1960), was dreadful, and David made a lot of enemies over the re-editing of it. That proved to nearly be his undoing as a director except for one more turkey that was yet to come to roost.

In 1963, David Bradley made his masterpiece of utter crap with *Madmen of Mandorus*, or, *They Saved Hitler's Brain*. That film is beyond *Plan Nine from Outer Space* and yet it dares to be dull even as grown men drive around with Hitler's head in a glass case between them in the back seat of a car! You may ask, with those credentials, how could that man be arrogant and self-important? Well, wait and see!

What makes all of this so bizarre is that David Bradley had the attention of a lot of intelligent, well-known people in Hollywood, who would turn up once a year for a New Year's Day party to watch David and his live-in boyfriend, Ken Du Main, film the guests as they arrive, after which they would see a film from his vast collection, usually starring one of his guests from the silent era. David's crowning moment came with the attendance of born-again Mary Philbin to one of those clambakes, where he made her recreate the unmasking scene from her 1925 classic, *The Phantom of the Opera*, however in Hollywood the monsters just come as themselves, so it was decidedly anti-climatic to unmask David yet again! Dare I say, the crowd went wild (pacemakers not withstanding).

After having lived in Beverly Hills for over a decade, John Kobal told me about David and his parties, suggesting that I go at least once just to say I'd been there. How could I truly have arrived in Tinseltown without having been to one of Bradley's New Year's Day soirees?

The problem was getting invited to such a party, since David was mad or feuding with just about everyone in the field of film history. He especially hated John, so when I finally got the phone call from David himself, he went on a rant for over an hour with a list of people not to bring if I were to bring a guest. I finally convinced him I would bring no one that coming New Year's Day.

Well, the auteur who directed *Hitler's Brain* lived way up in the Hollywood Hills in a faux Greco-Roman area called Mt. Olympus, which was off Doheny and Sunset Boulevard. The house itself was nothing too elaborate, but it was large enough to accommodate a crowd and featured a back patio for those who smoked or wished to relieve themselves. The crowd was defiantly older, befitting the silent era David so admired. I met Madge Bellamy, who David introduced cruelly as his "Baby Jane," and indeed, the poor lady looked very much like Bette Davis in *Whatever Happened to Baby Jane.* His "friend," Ken, had a camera mounted on his shoulder and went about the house filming whatever David told him to film, actually barking orders like someone sent from Central Casting to impersonate Cecil B. DeMille!

Out on the patio stood a frail Sam Jaffe and his wife, Betty Ackerman, and next to them was Rouben Mamoulian and his wife, Azadia, who was getting bombed. I knew Rouben slightly by that time in 1983, so I spoke with him, but he did not introduce his wife, who was moving further away as I approached. A few minutes of small talk and I headed back into the parlor, where more waxworks were chatting away as David and Ken captured them all on celluloid. "Don't move your head!" he shrieked to Jetta Goudal as she pushed her sad, browbeaten husband aside for a close-up. As I opened the door to enter, you could hear Rouben at the top of his voice saying to his wife, "Enough Azadia, you are disgracing the name of Mamoulain!" Funny, I thought she was right on!

I discovered later that David would always tell new-arrivals that Charlton Heston was on his way to the party and would be there shortly, but to my knowledge, the one-time "Peer Gynt" was always a no-show. One can only wonder what exactly young "Chuck" Heston had to endure for that first break on the silver screen; something not dreamt of in your philosophy, no doubt.

David Bradley died December 19, 1997, leaving nearly 4,000 films as his legacy to film history. So after all, David managed to save more than Hitler's brain.

Chapter 16
Marked by the Devil
Michael Armstrong

This is a cautionary Hollywood tale of a screenwriter/ director fighting to stay visible while hustling for projects in a town where failure can gather like a cloud until there are no career choices left at all. At the very beginning of 1985, I received a phone call from my friend and client, actor Reggie Nalder, who informed me that he just confronted one of his former directors at the corner market and it turns out he was living right across the street from me.

Michael Armstrong is best remembered today as the director of *Mark of the Devil*, a decidedly infamous film banned in several countries due to extreme violence. When that film arrived stateside, it made a fortune on the drive-in circuit with the ever-tasteful gimmick of a vomit bag given to each patron just in case the visuals proved too much. Sadly, Reggie's image was on every one of those bags, a constant reminder of a youthful accident that scarred his face forever, typecasting him to a lifetime of playing villains and monsters.

Mark of the Devil was filmed in Austria with an international cast headed by Herbert Lom as the Witchfinder, a very young Udo Keir as his assistant, not to mention our dear Reggie as Albino, who relishes the torture of innocent maidens in the most appalling ways imaginable.

Since that was Michael's first film abroad, he spent the first day of shooting looking through the wrong end of the camera. By the second week, things were in such a state that Adrian Hoven took over the film, relieving Mike of any more embarrassment with a predominantly German crew. Michael's screenplay was left alone except for two very important details: first, Herbert Lom's character was to have been a latent homosexual, whose desire for Udo Keir makes him torture the young women of the village out of frustration. That was removed by Hoven, which unfortunately took away any real motivation for the lead characters.

Michael had also dreamt up a nightmarish ending, where all the dead come to life and rise up at the film's conclusion to torment the survivors. That ending was actually filmed, but then cut from the final print. The experience traumatized Michael; he still had not been allowed to finish a film by himself either in London or abroad.

Michael had been in Hollywood a little less than a year, when Reggie brought him round to meet me. He had sold all his personal belongings in England and said a momentary farewell to his parents, as he made his way to Hollywood to finally justify the hopes and dreams that had evaporated in the changing climate that ended the swinging '60s scene in London, and with it, his self esteem.

In the late 1960s, he had enjoyed a bit of attention with a small independent company called Tigon who, except for their involvement in Polanski's *Repulsion*, were known by their output of sex comedies and horror films. Michael had been an early supporter of David Bowie's career, casting the then-unknown singer in his first screen appearance as "The Boy" in the experimental short, *The Image* (1967), a study of illusion vs. reality and an artist who destroys his creation.

Michael hoped to star Bowie in his first horror film, then known as *The Dark*; however, by the time AIP got involved, the pop star role was recast with Frankie Avalon. Neither the film nor the director survived the result, which became *The Haunted House of Horror*. The head of Tigon, Tony Tenser, hired Michael to direct his dream project, and then allowed the American distributors to re-cut the film and add scenes that rendered the finished product unwatchable. One should mention that Michael's original screenplay was quite avant-garde, with a strong sub-text of homosexuality involving the Bowie character, so chances are that would not have gotten by Tenser in any case.

In just the last couple of years, a boxed set of Tigon horror films was released in the UK with an audio commentary from Michael, who gloomily sat through the film explaining that perhaps three scenes remained that were actually directed by him.

Michael was a riot, a real funny, charming guy, as I got to know that personality of his over the course of the next several weeks. Perhaps a bit camp at times, especially after a few drinks, yet it was obvious that the fellow had a heart of gold, not to mention bags of talent. Michael was also a man-child who, like Peter Pan, refused to grow up. He was terribly in touch with that inner child of his, but rarely did we ever get to see the man, if he was really there at all.

He was very bright and well-read in the classics, and he adored Opera, especially Puccini and Wagner. Michael loved to create miniature theater sets that he made in great detail by hand. He made me a three-act recreation of the Edward Gorey *Dracula*, which I have to this day.

One of the things that bonded Mike and I at once was our connection to *Films and Filming* magazine. Mike had written for it early on, creating a very close and personal relationship with then-Editor

Robin Bean. I, on the other hand, came on after Robbie had left, with John Russell Taylor, the art and film critic from the *London Times*, taking charge as Editor in 1979.

I must explain just what was going on with *Films and Filming* under Robin's editorship, which represented the magazine at its peak in popularity. Originally, *Films and Filming* was highly regarded as a serious film journal, with such respected critics as Raymond Durgnat or Sheridan Morley turning in essays and reviews with substance and style

Robin saw an opportunity to create within the magazine a gay agenda that was obvious if you looked for it, and believe me, the readership looked for it as sales increased with every new issue.

Profiles on Warhol films, underground films like *Pink Narcissus, Fortune in Men's Eyes,* and even the *Royal Hunt of the Sun* became a film about Leonard Whiting's codpiece. If I could count how many covers were devoted to Helmut Berger, Joe Dallesandro, Alain Delon, and especially Udo Keir, (who lived with Robbie at different stages of his career). The conga line of pretty boys and studly ingénues seemed never-ending. The scholarly approach quickly went out the window, which does not mean it was any the less a film journal; it just became a bit more like an American Theater and Arts magazine called *After Dark,* which followed the same line of thought in New York.

One of the saddest memories of Mike's stay with me was the unraveling of Robin Bean over many trans-Atlantic calls, as he descended into madness with drugs and alcohol. Michael tried so hard to get Robin out of his flat, which was in ruins, and into a hospital.

It was obvious to me that seeing his friend slide into self-pity and substance abuse was a bit of a wake-up call for Mike. Robin had been a sought-after photographer and film journalist with a successful film magazine when that darkness just took it all away. We never discovered what became of Robin, and his disappearance is still a mystery.

Michael was, at the time I first met him, working for a producer named Sandy Howard, who was full of beans most of the time. No matter how often you would meet the guy, he would never fail to grasp your hand and say, "Hello, Sandy Howard here." Always hustling, never listening, that was the Sandy poor Mike had to deal with. We did go to the wrap party for *Vice Squad* in Hollywood, where Michael ran into fellow Brit, Malcolm MacLaren, who compared notes after both had their day with the Sex Pistols. Quite an evening with Carrie Fisher, Wings Hauser, and Nina Hagen all shaking hands with—who else?—Sandy Howard.

During that time, Mike lived across the street from me, and he soon became a fixture at my place, as he was lonely and loved to drink and chat the night away when he wasn't rewriting some of Sandy Howard's crappy screenplays. Once that job ran its course, Mike was in dire need of money, so it was not long after the Howard gig ended that Mike was evicted from his flat and was sitting out in front of the building on Doheny Drive with all his belongings in shopping bags and him in the center suffering a raging head cold. I finally gave in to the inevitable and invited him to stay with me until he could get back on his feet.

I knew that going into an arrangement such as that would not be a walk in the park, since Mike had displayed a dependence on drink, as well as delusions of grandeur regarding his career. His one cherished dream was to see the realization of a screenplay he had been working on for years, a stalk-and-slash epic he called *Orphanage*. That was the tender tale of a sad group of under-age boys being preyed upon by a serial killer. The killer, it seems, was a bit of a pervert, who masturbated over the lifeless bodies of the boys after killing them. Well, if David Bowie having it off with a lad was a no-go, you can imagine how much of a chance that had in the market place of 1985.

After reading *Orphanage*, it became rather obvious that all of Mike's adolescent sexual yearnings were in full flood since they had been to some degree in all his screenplays as far back as *The Image*. It is a shame that one project could never come together since it was no worse than most of the slasher films of the era in terms of violence, or Mike's kinky sex killer for that matter.

Michael spent nearly all of 1985 with me, and we had some great times going to parties, screenings, and at one point, reading scripts together for Cannon Films under the supervision of Chris Pearce, who would produce a number of titles for the company.

Michael had written the screenplay for *House of the Long Shadows* for Cannon, which boasted the only screen pairing of Vincent Price, Christopher Lee, Peter Cushing, and John Carradine. That historic moment was held together by a revamping of the old warhorse, *Seven Keys to Baldpate*. Mike wanted to create an homage to that 1930s-style thriller with Dick Powell trapped in an old dark house with Joan Blondell. What he got was Desi Arnaz Jr., who performed with grace under the circumstances. The legend goes that Cannon head, Menahem Golan, told producer Jenny Craven he wanted to make a horror film with all the horror stars. "Now get me Boris Karloff and Vincent Price!" When Jenny told him Karloff was dead he said, "Well, get him anyway."

House of the Long Shadows was not a success in spite of the dream cast. Michael blamed Cannon for not promoting it, and especially Jenny Craven for tampering with the final edit without director Peter Walker in attendance (something she apparently had done on another Cannon release entitled *Ordeal By Innocence*). We were friendly with Jenny at the time, since she lived in Venice by the beach, and even had her birthday party at my house that year.

One assignment Michael worked on while he lived with me was trying to polish an anti-war script written by TV star Richard Hatch (*Streets of San Francisco, Battlestar Galactica*). The story was meant to be a showcase for Richard as a soldier caught up in the Vietnam experience entitled *The Man with the Broken Gun*. Richard was a soft-spoken guy, who lost his TV fortune by trusting an accountant that made off with his earnings from both hit shows. That script was one of his last attempts to get back in the mainstream, and the pressure was on Mike to deliver the goods. I drove Mike up to Richard's house in Benedict Canyon for endless rewrites. Eventually, Richard had to let go of the house and move into smaller quarters. They then met at my apartment, and to help with his tan, Richard insisted they work on my sunny back lawn. I would look out my window to watch poor Michael, white as a snow and roasting in the sun, while Richard tried in vain to get in touch with this tormented character. I don't believe the project ever took off, and years later, I saw Richard, a trifle long in the tooth, playing his old character "Starbuck" on the retread of *Battlestar Gallactica* as a special guest to bridge the connection from the old to the new space opera.

It was an experience to watch him network around town, doctoring other people's scripts, and at one point, ghost-writing *My Jewish*

Vampire, a dreadful play done in Long Beach. Through the entire experience, he remained in high spirits, actually living in Long Beach for the duration. The only perk was using the director's phone to call his mum in the UK to tell her the latest plot twist on *Dynasty* so she could impress her neighbors who were all hooked on the soap opera, as was most of the United States at the time

After Michael returned from Long Beach, it was time to face up to what was not happening in terms of his chances of making a go of show business in a town that had pretty much written him off. He gave it his best shot with the likes of Sandy Howard, and experienced a bit of hope with actor Kristopher Tobari, who tried to fashion a screenplay about hookers. It looked promising for a while, but then no money could be raised, so that went by the wayside, as well. Michael also had a green card problem to add to the confusion, so his moment of truth arrived.

For a few weeks, Michael wandered around the Hollywood area, staying a while at the seedy motel where Jim Morrison supposedly wrote "L.A. Woman." Finally, Michael became truly homesick, not to mention concerned about his parents' health. So with lots of wine and tears, I got him to Los Angeles International Airport and walked him personally onto a jet heading back to the UK. For a while afterwards, I received drunken calls from Mike at midnight, still reeling from his "Hollywood nights." Later, he traveled to Paris to do a rewrite for some small film company. After three months, that, too, ended badly, so once again, he went back to his parents for a rest and to rethink. The last time I heard of Michael, he was giving an acting workshop for those wishing to toil in theater and film. Remembering the old axiom, "Those that can, do; those that can't, teach," it seemed life had finally come full circle.

Yet there was one more glimpse before Michael's final oblivion, and that would be receiving a review copy of Tigon's boxed set of horrors in PAL editions, where Michael Reeves' now-classic *Witchfinder General* stood alongside the company's real miscalculations such as *The Beast in the Cellar*, the mind-rotting *Virgin Witch*, and yes, *The Haunted House of Horror*, with a commentary by a rather lathered Michael Armstrong.

There he was, a full two decades later, explaining the obvious regarding his lost opportunity to direct that film. As the film revealed itself, Mike said things such as, "Well, this bloody thing has been at it for twenty minutes and there is not one scene that is directed by me." I did enjoy his recollection of Karloff being offered by AIP to appear in the film, only his ill health got the best of him and he was replaced at the very last minute by Dennis Price, who was just about to die himself. The saddest moment came at the end of the commentary, when Mike spoke about his screenplay of *Orphanage*, which he hoped to see on the screen before his sixtieth birthday. In a perfect world, he would do just that

As Clint Eastwood was fond of saying in his "Dirty Harry" mode, "A man has got to know his limitations."

Chapter 17

From a Whisper to a Scream

Vincent Price

*"It's though the very foundation
of the place was human suffering."*

—Vincent Price as Julian White

Towards the end of the 1980s, Vincent Price was hosting *Mystery* on PBS, touring the nation as Oscar Wilde, and occasionally acting in motion pictures. After the lack of distribution for *The Monster Club* and *Madhouse,* it seemed that his last real horror film would be *House of the Long Shadows.* However, he made at least one more before his official swan song in Tim Burton's masterful *Edward Scissorhands.* I had been planning to write about my experiences on that film and just never seemed to find the time.

I wish to rectify that right now with my recollections of being the casting director and unit publicist on *From a Whisper to a Scream*

(1986), one of the last films Vincent made before his health began to fail, resulting in his death a few years later from lung cancer.

Let's begin by first explaining how Vincent came to be involved with that project that was created by four young film buffs with no connections to speak of in Hollywood (and not a lot of development money, either). Yet they all shared a unique vision and a childhood passion for the Horror genre.

At just twenty-four years of age, Jeff Burr, a recent graduate of USC Film School, directed all four segments, working in concert with his brother, William and Darin Scott, as producers. Courtney Joyner, also from USC, completed the ensemble, putting together the wraparound material that featured Vincent as the librarian, Julian White.

Those guys had been sharing a house in Tujunga, struggling as a team in breakout mode with the four episodes already in the can. Their primary goal for months was looking for more backing, sending out screeners to most of the usual film companies, but even with veteran actors like Cameron Mitchell and Clu Gulager in the cast, they still could not find a distributor to release their anthology project.

Jeff raised most of the money for what they had so far by returning to his home town of Dalton, Georgia. Dalton is known locally as "the Carpet Capital of Georgia," not too far from Atlanta. Jeff had the movie bug bad enough to ask the local residents for money to help finance the screenplay. That included asking girls he went to high school with, and even his dentist was hit up for cash. From all of that, came the independent film company known as Conquest Entertainment.

I think it was my friend, filmmaker Dan Golden, who first put Jeff Burr in touch with me regarding getting Vincent to look at one of the segments and chat him up about appearing in the film as a kind of avenging host, lending his legendary reputation to get off the ground yet another horror film that otherwise might wind up unseen and forgotten in some straight-to-video release.

At the time, I had an impromptu houseguest in the person of British director Michael Armstrong, who, as fate would have it, had written the screenplay for another one of Vincent's later horror films, *House of the Long Shadows*. The reason Mike is of interest to this situation is that every time Jeff and Bill would come over to discuss the project, Mike was there gloriously unemployed and preparing endless cocktails to fuel things up a bit. Needless to say, the end result was that the two of us drunk out of our skulls while chatting the night away about Hollywood and now and then, as well as how to convince Vincent to do the film.

Since those guys were dyed-in-the-wool horror fans, the notion of having the director of *Mark of the Devil* on tap for advice seemed like a no-brainer. However, the advice of a man whose own career was in dire need of a transfusion was not always prudent, to say the least.

I mentioned Michael to Vincent at one point during all this, and he recalled one incident in particular. "I remember waiting in London for the rewrites for *House of the Long Shadows* to turn up. One afternoon, they arrived hand-delivered in the person of Mr. Armstrong. The script, front cover, and some of the pages were somewhat soaked in gin." I had been wondering all along why Michael had never sought Vincent out while he was in Hollywood, so Vincent's comments kind of explained why, and it made me sad because Michael should have had more of a career than he did with all the talent he possessed.

After several meetings with and sometimes without Mike being present, it became my mission in life to help Jeff convince Vincent to act in *From a Whisper to a Scream*. Vincent asked to see some of the film, so Jeff sent him a tape of the Cameron Mitchell segment, which was similar in tone to *Children of the Corn*, only darker. After seeing the footage, Vincent agreed to act in the new wraparound material and create a central theme to link the stories together.

The film was also known as *The Offspring*, when it was first released theatrically, but then reverted to its original title for the DVD release a few years later.

As the 1980s came to a close, Vincent had been married for nearly two decades to his third wife, the celebrated stage and film actress, Coral Browne. Their life together had been intensely magical from the beginning. Vincent confided once, "I always knew something wonderful would happen to me when I turned sixty-five." Both of them gave up considerable lifestyles to be together. Coral left her London flat and friends of a lifetime to come to Hollywood and become Mrs. Vincent Price. Vincent divorced Mary Grant after three decades of marriage and even risked the relationship with his daughter to be with Coral. The glory of their union was the realization that they were soul mates, and more blessed they were to discover that even late in life rather than not at all.

By the time of Jeff's film, they had weathered some rough spots in the marriage with Coral resigned to living in Los Angeles—a city she really detested—just so Vincent could be close to Hollywood for film and TV work. When he was touring in *Diversion and Delights,* he gave perhaps his greatest performance as Oscar Wilde, a role he did over 800 times in nearly 300 cities over a period of five years. Vincent was so proud of that, he told me, "It is an enormous challenge to get out on a stage, and I did it sometimes in front of three or four hundred people, talking about a man who was dandy, who was probably the greatest wit in the world. I did it first in towns and big cities, New York, Chicago, and then I started taking it to colleges. I was really worried that maybe they wouldn't get the full impact of his wit. They got it in spades. The show ran sometimes ten minutes longer because they not only laughed harder, they clapped." I asked him if he would ever just stop working. He replied, "Now I go mad not doing things. Sometimes, this makes me do things perhaps I should not have done; regardless I do try and make them work the best I know how to. I mean unemployment? I would have to cut my throat, so I am always employed."

While the Prices were staying in San Francisco for a limited run, lo and behold, Coral fell in love with the city, and for one fabulous moment thought of what it might be for them to forsake Hollywood with all its vulgar glamour and thoughtless friendships and reside as a golden couple in that Baghdad by the bay.

One of the perks of being Mr. and Mrs. Vincent Price was, of course, endorsements for television commercials, and especially pleasure cruises to exotic locations. The Princess Line was proud to announce the Prices were in residence to offer seminar screenings of their films with question-and-answers afterwards, as well as hosting the opening and closing night parties for the cruise. In return, they were handsomely rewarded with first-class accommodations, not to mention a fee.

Vincent and Coral were on a Caribbean cruise half-way to Aruba, when it was decided by committee that since Jeff had Vincent's services, he should take full advantage of them and rewrite his wrap-around material. Courtney Joyner worked on the new material, producing a camp send-up of all that was Vincent Price Horror Star, at least that's what they hoped for in theory.

The new script was duly sent to Vincent while he was at sea. It took only one day for his response—which came in the form of an angry ship-to-shore call to me. "You tell those guys that I signed a contract for the script I was given, and if they expect anything else, they can deal with my lawyers!"

Now that time and death have intervened, the reality of that situation was why at that particular point in time and with that particular picture that Vincent decided to exert his grand senior prerogative. The time had passed to question the screenplays he was allowing his name to exploit. As his friend and admirer, I wish that he had been more selective over the years. Vincent seemed to be always living in fear of not working because of his bout with "gray listing" in the 1950s, the result being that he took most anything that was offered if the money was right and the property was not too out of control.

The truth of the matter is quite simply that *From a Whisper to a Scream* was one of his last decent roles at a time when he still looked like Vincent Price, with his ability to invest a line of dialogue with panache remarkably intact. Julian White, the haunted librarian of Oldfield, Tennessee, complete with a serviceable southern accent, suited the Vincent Price persona like a glove.

Looking at this film today, you can appreciate the difference between it and, say, *Creepshow*, which is much brighter like a comic, yes, but *From a Whisper to a Scream* is more like a DC comic, darkly gritty and sinister with very little brightness to it at all. The late Rosalind Cash noticed the rather groundbreaking use of Black characters in the film. "The Black roles are more knowing about the future, more resigned to fate. You don't see parts like this in most films in this genre." Years later, Jeff Burr would return to that atmosphere in his next to best film, *Straight into Darkness*.

The settling for all of this would be a lumberyard in Venice (the scene of many a classic film, especially Orson Welles' *Touch of Evil*) that is actually a film studio owned by Roger Corman. Behind parked cars near a side street was one large trailer. There was a smaller group of low-level buildings, and in between them were tables filled with junk food and coffee urns. Past all that there was a door. Through that, and finally you were on the soundstage. One corner was devoted to the *From a Whisper to a Scream* set. The area was filled with cartons and cables that led one down to the brightly lit library room set. Paint was peeling off the walls, decay and sinister shadows lingered, and the ambience was vintage Vincent Price.

Roger Corman came down to the set the second day of filming. I will always remember standing next to Roger, as Vincent rehearsed an exchange of dialogue with actress Susan Tyrell: "There is a corpse under these floorboards. The whole house is a morgue." Roger almost stopped breathing, as he watched his leading man of over three decades ago stand on his mark and still be as magnificent as ever after six decades in the business. When Jeff finally said "Cut," Roger looked at me and said, "Beautiful work. He is an original. There is no one else that can create that particular atmosphere as well as Vincent." There are some fantastic stills of the two of them taken during the filming. They reunited as if time itself had just stood still since the golden days of their Poe films at American International Pictures.

Vincent shared his trailer with actress Susan Tyrell, who was a bit eccentric to say the least.

"SU-SU," as her friends call her, had been a working actress since the late 1960s, when she caused a sensation on Broadway. She quickly made her way to Hollywood, where she got nominated for the Oscar on her second film, *Fat City*, one of John Huston's best films made late in his career. Vincent was amused by her at first, but then later becomes concerned. "That girl is disturbed," he said. Apparently, Susan was reading a very explicitly sexual book and just loved reading passages from it to Vincent as he was lying down between takes. At one point, she began to speculate whether or not Vincent was "getting enough at home," referring of course to his sex life with Coral. That just drove Vincent around the bend since he really didn't know what to do with her. Was she kidding or what? The last day she worked, she came into the trailer to say goodbye, and I will never forget what happened, as Vincent and I were walking toward the set.

Susan was walking the other way to the parking lot, and she turned around and yelled for the whole crew to hear, "Hey Vinnie, you give a big one to Coral tonight for me, baby!"

We just waved and kept walking.

Vincent looked over at me and said, "You know she is completely mad, but I kind of like that about her."

I then related the story I knew about when Susan met the great playwright, Tennessee Williams. After a while, Tennessee took stock of the young actress and summed her up by saying, "My favorite actors are 50 percent male and 50 percent female. You, my dear, are neither!"

The laugh that brought out of Vincent was worth the whole exchange because it was heard by the whole crew.

The next day, I decided to bring his co-star from the Poe films, actress Hazel Court, onto the set for a reunion. I had called Hazel the night before and asked if she could come down and give Vincent a little support since he was surrounded on the picture by kids, and with Su-Su being so wild and disrespectful, I thought Hazel could bring some welcomed nostalgia into play. Hazel was just about to go into hospital for some routine surgery, yet she dropped everything and made herself available for her co-star and friend.

Hazel is just about the happiest person you could hope to meet in life. Her marriage to actor-turned-director Don Taylor was one of Hollywood's happiest, and her painting and sculpting are well-received among the critics, so life is good. Vincent had been a little grumpy when I left the set to collect Hazel, and I was counting on her presence to cheer him up. Her arrival did just that, and soon, the two of them were laughing and finishing each other's sentences like two old friends tend to do. After about an hour or so, it was time to take Hazel back to San Vicente, which was what she and Don called their Tudor-style house. It also happened to be located on San Vicente, as well. On the way, Hazel was concerned for her friend, as she noticed he was thinner than she remembered seeing him in a while. "I know Coral frets over his health. I just hope he will take it easy now and not work himself to death."

During the few days Vincent worked, I had a chance to speak with Coral on the phone. One of the things about her I miss to this day are the phone calls with that archly funny woman, whose Australian accent gave every line an off-kilter kind of zing. One morning, she called and began with, "Oh hello dear, how is Vinnie today? You know, dear, he going to come home in a box one day if he does not let up a bit, don't you know? Did you happen to catch Hayley Mills on the telly last night? Well, I mean, she looked 500 years old, dear. I mean, lit from the bloody floor with every line in her poor face glowing out of the screen. It was just fucking awful, dear . . . ."

When Vincent was doing *The Whales of August,* the company was named Alive Pictures. When Coral heard this she replied, "They should call it 'Just Barely,'" referring to the age of her husband's co-stars in that film, all of whom were over eighty.

Among the cast members for the wraparound shoot were Film Noir icon Lawrence Tierney and Hammer Queen Martine Beswicke. Courtney Joyner was responsible for Lawrence being in the picture because they were very close friends and he played the warden for a change after a lifetime of playing killers and con men. There was a great moment during the shoot, when Lawrence was sitting around the donut and coffee table a little too shy to go up and knock on Vincent's trailer to say hello. They had, of course, met many times over the years at various studios, as their careers crisscrossed. Finally, I went in and asked Vincent if he would mind saying hello to an old friend. Lawrence went into the trailer, and they must have chatted away for an hour before he finally emerged. He came over to me and said, "You know, kid, that Vincent Price is an okay guy."

Later that evening, as I was driving Vincent back to his house off Doheny Drive not far from my own, I asked him about his chat with Lawrence. It obviously had an effect on him. Vincent began talking about his brother, Mortimer, who was a bit older than he. "You know, David, I have had more than my share of experiences with alcoholics, and Larry Tierney was one of the most notorious in this town during and after the war."

I explained to Vincent how the guys on the film felt about Lawrence. He was kind of their mascot. I mean, they worshiped that guy. Vincent then remarked, "Well, first off I was shaken at how bad Larry looked. I mean, he was such a handsome guy, and to see what the effects of years of drink and hard times can do to a person. It is encouraging to see young filmmakers like Jeff appreciate actors with a history like Tierney and help them get back to work.

"My brother Mortimer was a brilliant man and, for the most part, an honorable one, yet he had the same vice as Larry. Mortimer always had a glow about him and when I was younger I simply did not realize he was drinking, and he remained a drinker for the rest of his life, yet I loved him just as much drunk or sober. After all, he was my brother."

I had brought Martine in to play the pivotal role of Vincent's niece, Katherine White, a mass murderer, who puts the stories in motion. It is her execution that brings in Susan's character and thus her visit to Vincent's library in Oldfield, the town that has a reputation for breeding killers, or, to quote Vincent's dialogue, "The history of the town is written in blood on pages of human skin." Martine was still a beautiful woman and made a great addition to the cast. Vincent just fell in love with her the first time they met. I drove her over to see the set and do some wardrobe tests for the dream sequence where she wears a white evening gown. Vincent was there and they posed for some group publicity stills with Rosalind Cash, and Clu Gulager with Jeff Burr. That was the absolute best time on the shoot since everyone was so upbeat and Vincent just enjoyed people so much he just radiated that day and everyone loved him.

As the weekend rolled around, I got a call from Jeff telling me that they still needed to do some pick-up shots of the front of Vincent's house in the imaginary town of Oldfield and they found a perfect location near Santa Barbara in the small town of Carpentaria. He wanted me to pick up Susan Tyrrell and bring her to the location. That could well be an all-nighter. Jeff also decided to confide in me that Su-Su was in Alcoholics Anonymous, and not to stop at any bars on the way. I was a little surprised at that, yet with all the drinking that had been going on at my pad with Mike, I should have expected it.

I called ahead to Tyrrell's abode in Santa Monica to let her know I was on my way, when a man answered the phone, who was kind of not with it at all. I found out later that he was Susan's latest boy toy, all of nineteen years old and very hung up on our Miss Susan. When I got to her front door, she was still getting ready and was having a time keeping her guy from having her right on the spot as we spoke. It is funny to me now, but then I must have looked like a square, as I tried not to notice that they were in heat, baby . . . .

Finally, she grabbed her tote bag and French kissed him goodbye for the umpteenth time. With kisses in the air, we made it to my car, which had my friend Alan in the driver's seat since I did not want to cope with alone with what was to happen. Heading for the freeway, Susan surprised me yet again by telling Alan, "Stop at the next 7-11 and pick up some beer." Well, I know I should have said something after Jeff mentioned Alcoholics Anonymous, but I was not her sponsor or her baby sitter, so we stopped and got a 12-pack of Bud and off we went. Susan is a blast, don't get me wrong, and the ride to the location was a hoot. She brought her Aretha Franklin tapes, so we played "Freeway of Love (Pink Cadillac)" more than once before arriving at the mock-up for Julian White's foreboding library. Jeff was not too pleased to see that all of us except for Alan had a heat on. I foolishly thought that the more of those twelve beers I drank, the less there would be for Su-Su. Well, forget it, we were high and that was the name of that tune. Fortunately, Jeff did not require any dialogue from her, so it worked out, but somehow, I felt like I let him down a bit. I was determined to make up for my slip, so I worked on that location till daylight and got back in his good graces before returning my crazy lady back to her sex-crazed boyfriend—just like in the movies.

The last day of filming was particularly poignant for me personally, since I had spent more quality time with Vincent than ever before. Also, I could not help but notice that he was beginning to show his age somewhat, yet he was still Vincent Price and his wife, Coral Browne, had not shown the symptoms of cancer that were to follow, so I could take some comfort in the knowledge that he might make some more films. His death scene in the film involved putting a rubber knife in his neck, and the afternoon when that was done, I remember they got blood on his shirt. When I drove him that night, he had that shirt in a plastic bag so Coral could soak it out. It struck me that what other wife would have blood to deal with instead of lipstick? Only the wife of Vincent Price was the reply.

Jeff and the two producers bought him a large basket of goodies with wine wrapped in plastic with a card. They had placed it in his trailer as a gesture from a grateful crew. He came in a few minutes later to collect his things, and then we were off. A journalist from *Variety* had come out that morning because Otto Preminger had just died and they wanted Vincent to comment since he was one of the surviving cast members from *Laura*. While they were setting up, someone asked him about how he felt working with a director like Jeff, who was only twenty-four years old.

Vincent gave the reporter a glare, and in his most imposing tones replied, "I was directed by Orson Welles when he was twenty. I think the fun is really being directed by young people because the old ones get stuck unless they're terribly good. Billy Wilder doesn't get stuck, as well as a few others."

With that, they brought up Orson, to which Vincent observed, "Orson and I have discussed what an actor must do to survive. If you look at, say, Kate Hepburn, she is one of the very few women who still have a career as important as it was at the peak of her career. Look at Welles for a moment; no one had such potential. He was the greatest director I ever had. He could have been the greatest theater and film director in the history of the American stage or cinema, *yet he blew it.* He did not have the discipline. I think it was a terrible frustration to him. He became fat, he became unhealthy, he became a caricature of himself, and he knew it. In my work, I have perhaps fulfilled most of my potential, certainly more than Orson at this point. My wife, Coral, has brought me back into the theater and bless her for that. Still, all in all, it has been a life well lived."

I was preparing to take Vincent home that night, when he explained that he was being picked up that evening to begin yet another film, a comedy about zombies. He was laughing that one of the leads, Joe Piscapo, was a bodybuilder now, so he wouldn't have to really act like a zombie, just be himself. I then said goodbye, although we would still work together at least once more when he appeared on my *Sinister Image* pilot a few months later. When I got to my car, I realized I did not even bother to lock it all that day. Sitting in the passenger seat was the basket of goodies that had been given to Vincent by the crew. He had placed this hand-written note on top:

"David, you were super on this shoot.
I hope you stay in this business where you belong.
Love, Vincent."

I drove from the lumberyard and down to Pico, where I turned right off to Beverly Hills like I had done all week with Vincent. As I kept driving along, all at once an overwhelming sense of loss came over me. I burst into tears. It was only when I managed to pull over to compose myself that I fully realized how much that man meant to me over such a period of time and always will.

Chapter 18

Hamlet Meets the Wolfman

John Carradine

By the time John Carradine came into my life, he was coming to the end of his own mortal coil. Fortunately, John lived to see his considerable talents as an actor appreciated by a new generation of admirers. His sons all became actors with varying degrees of success, and John basked in their reflected glories. Today, John has his star on the Hollywood Walk of Fame and a legion of fans thanks to DVD and cable television making his nearly 300 performances on film available to fully appreciate his versatility.

One of my favorite celebrity haunts in the "good old days" when I was still a working theatrical agent was the now-legendary Cock 'n Bull pub at 9170 Sunset Boulevard, where many agents and their clients would met for lunch. In the evenings, show-biz types made the pub sparkle with *rendezvous* aplenty involving starlets as well as just pretty girls anxious to be part of the Hollywood dream.

On one particularly hot afternoon in 1977, I decided to cool off in the air-conditioned darkness of the Cock 'n Bull's pub before the evening crowd filled the establishment for dinner. The pub was nearly empty except for a trio of character actors getting rather stiff in the corner of the bar. The trio was instantly recognizable from a lifetime of working in TV and films. First there was Frank Ferguson, a character actor from Westerns such as *Johnny Guitar*, yet for me Frank would always be Mr. McDougal, who bosses Lou Costello around in *Abbot and Costello Meet Frankenstein*. Next was the Maytag repairman himself, Jesse White, with his ever-present cigar, who starred with Jimmy Stewart in *Harvey*. Rounding out the trio was Alvy Moore, a regular on *Green Acres*. I sat opposite those guys and listened to the conversation. It seemed Frank had the nickname of "Fartface," and the guys joked about that for a bit until I had had a couple of drinks and felt comfortable enough to join in their fun. I asked Frank about the *Frankenstein* film.

"Lou played cards all day long," he said.

"What it was like to act on a Joan Crawford set?"

"Joan terrified everyone but Nick [Ray]."

He was a good sport, as were the others, and just as all this was moving into a late afternoon of gossip and booze, in walked the unmistakable John Carradine.

John found himself a stool several seats away from us, and after ordering his "usual," he acknowledged the presence of his fellow actors by saying to Frank, "Greetings Fartface."

By that time, I was fearless enough in my confidence to hold my own among those tipsy thespians, so I moved over to the stool next to John and asked if I could buy him a drink.

John replied by saying, "Young man, the seat is not my property. By all means, sit, however I like to buy my own libations if you don't mind."

At that point, Jesse White came to my rescue by saying to John, "You know, this kid knows his stuff about our business."

"Indeed, well what do you know of the theater or my work in it?"

There was my opportunity to shine, so I mentioned his Shakespeare Company that toured the California coast during the war.

John smiled, and then reminded me that the tour was kind of a bust. "I could not for the life of me get my troupe out of Los Angeles, so the tour ended right there at Union Station around 1943. I always wanted to do Lear, but that requires a certain age I was not at the time. Shakespeare also requires the actor to utilize a certain amount of anemometry in reciting the text successfully."

We talked at length for the rest of that afternoon until nearly midnight. As the pub began to fill up with customers, John was easily recognized. He was by then used to attracting attention and seized the moment to recite from memory The Gettysburg Address, which was so moving the room burst into applause when he finished. One tends to forget what a magnificent talent John could be as he continued to play in mediocre films and television just to keep the wolf from the door.

It seemed that John came to the Cock 'n Bull to meet his son, David, who never showed up. There was still a rift between John and his boys regarding their past history, with John absent for much of their upbringing. The pub closed at midnight. The bartender, a real pro, knew John's habits by heart. For one thing, all evening he drank what looked like large glasses of water, which turned out to be vodka with a little ice. John advised, "Never pollute the beverage with tonic or soda; it causes nasty hangovers."

As last call was announced, it became clear that John would have to make his own way for what was left of the evening. "There are *other* establishments. *Perhaps it is time to locate one?*" said John, slightly irate.

The bartender told me that when that kind of situation presented itself in the past, it was best to steer John to the old Hyatt House up the street on Sunset. It seemed that the hotel allowed the veteran actor to stay in one of their rooms free of charge as long as he slept on top of the sheets, leaving little for the maids to do after he left. (Who says there are no perks for movie stars?) I was more than happy to help John to his well-worn Mercedes complete with a few dents from other nights on the town. He bowed in a courtly manner before settling into his car for the short drive to the hotel. His parting words to me were, "It is too bad that you are not amenable to finding another establishment that would allow us the more traditional last call, rather than this *witching hour* conclusion to a fine evening!"

Looking back, that was one of my favorite moments in Hollywood, to have spent the entire afternoon and evening with that great man. We had exchanged phone numbers, making sure our paths would definitely cross again.

A couple of years later, I became involved with PBS and a very nice couple named Gene and Susie Feldman, who were preparing a documentary on horror films entitled *The Horror of It All*. I not only appeared on-camera on that show, but also helped the Feldmans locate some of the subjects for the broadcast. I called John Carradine and convinced him to allow them to film an interview at his home in Montecito near Santa Barbara. They photographed John as he sat in front of a magnificent painting depicting him as Hamlet. It was one of the highlights of the program. John displayed great dignity, as he reminisced about his admiration for—who else?—John Barrymore and what John felt about acting the title role of Bluebeard for Edgar Ulmer.

During that time, I was having a lot of parties at my place, and at one of them a rather derelict actor named Hy Peak arrived with a very fun lady in tow, who he introduced as his "girlfriend," claiming to have met her wandering in the desert near Hemet, California, alone and a bit out of it. She was a former actress named Sonia Sorel. Hy had just appeared in Ridley Scott's *Blade Runner*, and was on a bit of a roll. He reminded me of another boozy eccentric actor, Fox Harris, who I've mentioned earlier in my recollections of Elizabeth Shepherd. Sonia had also been the second wife of John Carradine during his salad days in wartime Hollywood, playing one of his victims in *Bluebeard*. She had been the leading lady of John's Shakespeare Company. Sonia was the mother of actors Keith and Robert Carradine, as well as actor Michael Bowen (*Kill Bill, Part I, Less Than Zero*) from her marriage to world renowned artist Michael Bowen.

From what I was able to discover that evening, John had been her soul mate in life, and his departure was something from which she never fully recovered. Eventually, they divorced in 1956. Sonia had fallen on hard times, living a life of poverty.

When I had asked John about her he replied, "I heard she was a bag lady in Hollywood," yet that evening in my home, she laughed and seemed happy in spite of everything. Her sense of humor was intact: listening to a song that was being played at the party, she turned to me and said, "I wish someone would write a song about me."

I replied, "Honey, they did. It was called "I'm Easy," the song her son, Keith, had won the Oscar for composing. I said that without really thinking about the ramifications, but nonetheless, she roared when she heard it. I liked her instantly, and regret that soon afterwards she disappeared from Hollywood altogether. I learned recently that she died in 2004 on my birthday, September 24.

After all that, I decided that it was time to do my own interview with John, and enlisted my friend, photographer Dan Golden, to drive me up to John's house to do an audio recording and prepare him for taping my cable television show, *Sinister Image*.

The trek from Los Angeles to Santa Barbara is always fraught with delays, since the coastal highway is crowded no matter what time a journey begins. I had called John late in the afternoon, telling him we should be with him in a couple of hours. Unfortunately, we arrived sometime after nine o'clock that evening. John was waiting with the patience of Job and immediately offered us drinks and a little tour of his comfortable home nestled in the hills between Santa Barbara and the sea.

The interview began with John laughing about the film he had seen earlier in the day starring his son, Robert: *Revenge of the Nerds*. John said, "You know, I've been around nerds for years and never knew what to call them until today." Then he said, "I am very proud of all my sons, as they learned their craft from me." John had appeared in a number of shows with his sons, on stage as well as being on David's *Kung Fu* television series.

I asked him about turning down the role of Frankenstein's monster in 1931, and he explained that it was Cecil B. DeMille who discouraged him by telling him that "your face is too thin and narrow, and the camera won't record anything from your face." I listened to every word he said at that moment. "I was working around Hollywood full-time as a sculptor and sketch artist. During that period, I sculpted a magnificent bronze bust of DeMille, which he had on display up at that house of his on DeMille Drive for years. I also did one of John Ford, who is still my favorite director. I've done ten films for him in my career, including some that are now considered masterpieces in the art of filmmaking."

We made plans that evening for John to tape a segment of my *Sinister Image* show in Santa Monica. He was having a great deal of fun speculating about what if John Barrymore had played Dracula instead of Lugosi. John felt Barrymore could play any role placed in his path, not to mention he had a real fascination with the macabre.

By the time I had reserved studio space, John Carradine was off working on films all over the world. I regret that Fate decreed that we would not document his long career and especially preserve that amazing stentorian voice of his that made any line of dialogue memorable just by the sheer power and range of his talent.

John was a unique figure in film history, who could have achieved greatness if he had not followed the example of his idol, John Barrymore, allowing his career to lapse into self-parody or, more so in John's case, descend into grade-Z horror films, until his reputation could never fully recover from it. However, unlike Barrymore, he lived long enough to create some memorable moments in television, as well as on film. John had been a memorable Dracula over at Universal in the forties, and even managed to play a werewolf towards the end of his life for director Joe Dante in *The Howling* (1981). In that film, John managed something even Lon Chaney, Jr. could never do: pathos and humor at the same time. Who can ever forget John's retort to Patrick MacNee's therapist werewolf, "Screw all this 'channel your energy' crap! You can't change us Doc. It just ain't natural. We gotta eat meat!" I will always remember what his co-star in that film, the late, great Elizabeth Brooks, said to me right after it came out: "It looks like Hamlet met the wolf man after all."

Chapter 19
The Auteur on the Hill
John Brahm

One of the most memorable films of the 1940s has to be *The Lodger*, with a tour-de-force performance from that underrated character actor Laird Cregar. That was the second and perhaps definitive adaptation of the famous novel by Marie Belloc Lowndes about "Jack the Ripper." The first was, of course, directed by Alfred Hitchcock in 1927 with Ivor Novello, but the version with Cregar was directed by John Brahm, whose Germanic background proved invaluable to the Victorian melodrama. The film was a huge success, and Brahm was asked to follow it up with yet another shocker entitled *Hangover Square*, also starring the obese Laird Cregar. That film proved to be Cregar's undoing, who was by all accounts a "tormented homosexual," who, right after filming ended, dieted himself to death in a desperate attempt to consummate his first heterosexual relationship.

Today, both of those films are highly regarded by the critics and most especially by yours truly. When I first came to Los Angeles and started making the rounds, my friend, Reggie Nalder, took me to afternoon parties at the beach house of Stuart Whitman's father, Joe, who in turn introduced me to Baron Eric Von Bulow, the special-effects wizard who designed the Pillsbury Doughboy for television, as well as the terrifying Zuni Doll that terrorized Karen Black in Dan Curtis's memorable *Trilogy of Terror* TV film. The Baron, it turned out, was great friends with the very man who brought my favorite Jack the Ripper film to the screen, John Brahm.

Brahm lived in a modest (by Malibu standards) beach house high on a cliff overlooking the Pacific Ocean. By then, he was in his mid-eighties, confined to a wheel-chair, and yet fiercely independent. He created and designed his home to include a living room where everything was level to his chair and could be moved or pulled out of the wall. He still loved to entertain, and weekends were always filled with a variety of writers, actors, and artisans making the conversation always interesting. James Mason was a close personal friend and always saw Brahm when he was in Los Angeles. One of my favorite memories of Brahm was actually kind of scary. Brahm loved the sun and sat out on a veranda all day long. One afternoon, he was dozing in his chair and some strands of his hair actually caught fire. Fortunately, we saw it in time and no harm was done except to freak me out, since I never have before or since known that to happen. Needless to say, Brahm was very tanned indeed.

The most amazing coincidence was yet to reveal itself since one of my close friends at that time was Barbara Steele. In 1978, Barbara divorced from screenwriter James Poe, and they had a young son, Jonathan, who was about seven years old at the time. Brahm had sublet his guest house to Poe, and in the months that followed, I sometimes drove the boy to see his dad on weekends. That enabled me to do Barbara a favor and also see Brahm, as well. Sadly, Poe died quite prematurely in that very same guest house several months later, upsetting all concerned, as you can imagine.

Sometimes, Brahm could remember his career in great detail, but then on other days he went for hours without saying much at all. He had in his personal library the Filmbook adaptations of both films with Laird Cregar, and those were the only film-related things he had in the house. I was fortunate to catch him on one of his good days and taped what was to be his last interview. I later published that interview online with Brahm's daughter, Sumishta Brahm's, amazing website, Sumishta's Universe (www.thirfg.demon.co.uk) Please do yourself a favor and have a look as you will find a uniquely gifted and spiritual person whose interests are universal in every sense of that word.

Brahm was part of the Golden Age in Hollywood, and his films at 20th Century Fox will stand the test of time as we are beginning to appreciate not only his thrillers but his work in Film Noir and his overwhelming amount of work in television on such classic shows as *The Twilight Zone* and *The Outer Limits.* My personal favorites of his were the hour-long episodes of Boris Karloff's *Thriller* series, where he created some mini-masterpieces of the macabre from screenplays by such authors as Robert Bloch.

When I think back on John Brahm, I always seem to conjure the voyage up that dirt road until finally reaching the top of a crest looking down on the ocean, and there was his rambling house. Once inside, I can still hear his Germanic voice asking me what I wanted to drink, or asking me to examine his latest invention to make his environment even more compact and modern. He was such a vital man and a brilliant craftsman. Just watching one of his films like *The Lodger* will make that abundantly clear.

Chapter 20

The Happy Cooker

Monique Van Vooren

Monique Van Vooren was a scene stealer ever since she appeared in *Tarzan and the She-Devil* (1953). As Lyra, the "She-Devil" of the title, Monique made a spectacular villainess, although Raymond Burr kind of steals the show as a vile creep who finally gets his just desserts in the last reel by being trampled by elephants. Monique had already made her film debut in an Italian film entitled *Domani E Troppo Tardi* with Vittorio De Sica and Pier Angeli in 1950. The Belgium-born entertainer arrived on the planet earth in 1933, and has been trying to figure a way to blast off of it ever since.

Monique always turned heads with her ample figure, and later on by the sheer power and determination of her need to attract attention, which she craved like a drug. Long a front page fixture in New York club life as a society icon and jet-setter, Monique hit her peak during the "Warhol years," when she managed to capture the imagination of the world's most famous ballet dancer, Rudolf Nureyev. Rudolf stayed for weeks in her New York penthouse posing for *Interview* and *Vogue*, while nightclubbing at Studio 54 in the company of Halston, Liza Minnelli, and Andy Warhol. In that period, it was impossible to not see Monique in total diva mode, dressed in the latest by Georgio Sant'Angelo, a "late night fantasy," as the disco song goes.

Monique tried to encourage an affair, especially for the tabloids, but alas, Rudolf was just too gay to think of her in such terms. Later, Monique got her revenge by penning a veiled account of their relationship in her book, the gossipy *Night Sanctuary* (1981), a promised glimpse into the boudoirs of the rich and famous. Unfortunately, that attempt at prose, purple though it may have been, was decidedly dull and lifeless upon execution.

Monique's claims to fame have almost always centered on someone just a little more in the limelight than herself. For years, she dined on the story of renaming a young dancer (who was hoofing in one of her early reviews) Christopher. His last name was Walken. Thus, Christopher Walken was born and went on to a lasting career in films. However, it was her relationship with Rudolf Nureyev that provided her with a blueprint for a lifestyle that could have only existed in that particular space and time.

While all that drama with Rudolf was spinning, she ignored her husband, the long-suffering Gerard W. Purcell, by whom she had her only child, a son named Eric. The marriage lasted until Mr. Purcell died in 2001 at the age of eighty-six.

Monique would on occasion do her "act," a Cabaret revue involving her life as a socialite, as well as a confidant to the rich and famous. She tried to do a bit of Dietrich by way of talking her way through songs including "La Vie a Rose" and, of course, "Falling in Love Again." Rudolf was a part of that act whether he liked it or not. She provided a slide show during her revue that included photos of him, and she asked very loudly to her audience, "Is this *my* forbidden fruit?" That always got a laugh, since her audience was usually a combination of gay men and fans of her Warhol tour-de-force, *Flesh for Frankenstein*, which most of us saw in 3-D. I could never forget seeing Monique Van Vooren as the Baroness Katrin Frankenstein slurping madly into Joe Dallesandro's armpit with such abandon that it quite simply stopped the show, and in 3-D no less. Monique earned her place in film history right on the spot.

My Monique experience took place around 1978 at the infamous Studio One (formally the old Factory) at 652 N. La Peer Drive in West Hollywood in their equally famous Backlot cabaret directly behind the disco. In that hallowed space, I saw and mingled with Bette Davis, Geraldine Fitzgerald, Eartha Kitt, Sally Kellerman, and the fantastic Francis Faye. Monique was quite the rage that week: she played the club and I was taken to opening night by her *Flesh for Frankenstein* director, Paul Morrisey, and Tab Hunter. Paul laughed at everything she did that night and promptly took us backstage afterwards to congratulate the diva, who managed to keep her wig on throughout the evening, when everyone about her was losing theirs.

Paul, it appeared, had an ulterior motive in inviting me that evening: Monique needed an agent in Hollywood. I could say nothing but yes, and then found myself at her hotel the following afternoon. The Westwood Marquis was the perfect setting for that encounter, since it possessed a certain glamour and Monique was nothing if she was not glamorous. She kept me waiting in her suite for about an hour, as she adjusted her appearance just for me. Soon, she appeared all in white, complete with a matching turban and a large "MVV" embroidered on her silk blouse. All she lacked was a long cigarette holder, and within seconds she had that, as well. She waited for me to light it for her, and asked, "Can you get me the same parts Faye Dunaway is offered?"

After pondering that concept for a moment, I replied, "Anything is possible. Let's give ourselves a few weeks and see what happens."

She had yet another surprise for me in that she had just written her first cook book, *The Happy Cooker*, with such recipes as "Spanish Fly Burgers," as well as "Stoned Chicken" made with a generous helping of marihuana in the stuffing, and so on. It was very clever and fun, so I agreed to try and book her on the Dinah Shore morning chat show a few weeks later. Within days, I received a box of cookbooks with a note: "Get Cooking, Love Monique."

As hard as I tried, I could do nothing for the bombshell from Brussels. Dinah said no and would not change her mind, since Monique was on Burt Reynold's shit list and I never found out the reason, so that dashed what would have been a classic encounter with those two divas in the kitchen cooking with dope!

During that time, I was seeing quite a bit of Hiram Keller (as was everybody else in Hollywood, apparently). When he discovered I was representing Monique, Hiram began laughing about her famous "quickie facelift" that was demonstrated to him one evening when they were club-hopping in New York with ever present Rudolf, of course. It seemed that Monique had a trick she learned from the divine Marlene Dietrich: if she pulled her skin tightly around her hair, it would act as a lift, if only for the evening. With her trademark hauteur, Monique pulled both slides of her face up at the same time, but did not tighten one as securely as the other. During the evening, one side dropped dramatically—unbeknownst to Monique—but it certainly caught Rudolf's attention and soon the whole restaurant. They howled at the poor woman, as she ran to the ladies room for an adjustment. That gave Hiram and Rudolf a chance to depart on what would prove to be a momentary affair, since they did resemble each other in more ways than one. Much like Rudolf, the highly-sexed Monique did like her "boy toys," even if they, for the most, part fancied each other. *Amour, toujours, Amour.*

I still have my inscribed copy of *The Happy Cooker* and fond memories of that one-of-a-kind celebrity, the kind they just don't seem to make anymore. However, the story does not end there. As luck would have it, several years later in the middle of 2000, I was doing my radio show in Palm Springs and who should walk in, chic as always, dressed in white and yellow with a large hat decorated with yellow roses? Monique Van Vooren, who was there to promote her appearance at a small venue known as The Rock Garden Restaurant and Grill on Palm Canyon Drive.

We embraced after nearly two decades, and she told me she was living at her country estate in Bayside, Queens, with her son, Eric, not far away. *Good for her,* I thought, and we chatted away about her revue and her amazement at the following that *Flesh for Frankenstein* had with kids. Later that night, I sat once again in the audience, as Monique stopped her singing long enough to bring out her well-worn slides and ask that famous question just as Rudolf Nureyev's image passed the though the lens: "Is this *my* forbidden fruit?"

Chapter 21
The Queen Mother

Isabella Telezynska

In the early 1970s, there was no greater director working than Ken Russell, and like Eric Von Stroheim before him, Russell flaunted convention and especially his critics by creating one masterpiece after another, first on the BBC, and then with his first wave of films.

At one point in London, Russell had three films playing at the same time. His greatest film, *The Devils*, had just opened, while *The Music Lovers* and *Women in Love* were already running in the West End cinemas.

My admiration for Ken Russell knew no bounds, thus I saw those films over and over again until I knew cast and crew alike. I am telling you this, dear reader, as an explanation for why a few years later I would take into my life the actress known as Izabella Telezynska. You see, Izabella acted the role of Madam Von Meck, the wealthy patron of Tchaikovsky, as played by Richard Chamberlain in Ken Russell's film of *The Music Lovers*. She had also made quite an impression as the "Queen Mother" in Visconti's film, *Ludwig*, with his amorata, Helmut Berger, in the title role.

By that time, I had already met several of Russell's stock company through his close friend, designer/photographer Leonard J. Pollack. "Lennie" was, and still is, a great friend of mine, and through him I would come to know many of Ken Russell's band of players.

Lennie had photographed most of my clients, when I still had the agency, and he delighted in sharing the "Russell" contacts with me when they came into town.

In meeting the fabulous Madame Von Meck, there came a warning from Lennie: "She is a royal pain in the ass, so proceed at your own risk." At that point, fools rush in, as the saying goes, so I went ahead and invited the "Queen Mother" to my apartment for cocktails. Just to make the evening as regal as possible, I asked Elizabeth Shepherd to join us for what I imagined would be a subdued evening of conversation with insightful glimpses into the world of Ken Russell.

Izabella Telezynski, the patron of the arts and Queen Mother to Ludwig of Bavaria, arrived at my apartment dressed like the gypsy queen Maria Ouspenskaya from *The Wolf Man*. She stood framed in my doorway in a blouse pulled off her shoulders to reveal a silver necklace made of stars and moons around her neck. "I am Izabella Telezynski," she announced as she came through the door. "I work for Visconti and Ken Russell. You got any whiskey in the house?"

I did not have any whiskey, and after giving her a large glass of Champagne, I introduced her to Elizabeth, who broke the ice by telling her that she had indeed seen the full three-hour version of the Visconti film in London and thought Izabella exquisite in the role of the "Queen Mother." From that moment on, Izabella felt at home and proceeded to enlighten one and all about her glory days in Rome with Helmut and Visconti.

"Helmut gave me a golden phallus on a gold chain that I treasure to this day! Visconti spoiled any actress that ever worked for him because his standards were that of a nobleman, which, of course, he was in life." On Ken Russell she had praise, but also a sense of loss, since he did not find enough work for her to remain in the UK. Russell had put her in *The Devils* as one of the mad nuns. She also has a fleeting moment in *Lisztomania*.

One of the last things she did in England was a cameo in *Count Dracula*, the Louis Jourdan version, as the woman in the coach that gives Harker a cross to wear. Izabella had a much better part in the last Hammer film ever made, *To the Devil a Daughter*. As Margaret, she bears the child of the demon, Astaroth, having been impregnated by evil defrocked priest Christopher Lee, of all people. I was on the phone with Lee at some point during her time in Hollywood, and when I told him of meeting her, he replied, "I know this woman, and no, you may not give her my number!"

The evening was not what I had expected, but I certainly got an earful. Having adjusted my conception of Izabella-the-person from her screen persona (something I needed to learn in dealing with actors), I discovered that I liked her, and a friendship was born.

Izabella had made only one film while she was in Hollywood, a comedy that started out being called *Saturday the 14th*, and which starred Tommy Smothers and Carol Kane, and was directed by the very strange Alfred Sole. Sole was known as the director of Brooke Shields' first film, *Alice, Sweet Alice*, where she is killed off in the first reel in a very unpleasant manner. The film's title was then changed to *Pandemonium,* and ironically, she played a parody of the Gypsy in *The*

Wolf Man, appearing during the film saying, "Beware the full moon when the pom-poms are in bloom." The plot, such as it was, involved a serial killer on the loose around sorority girls in college. The film was a disaster, and I don't think Alfred Sole made many films after that.

One evening in particular will always stand out when I think back on my memories of her: the night Izabella acquired her nickname, "Iza Duck." As usual, she proceeded to take over a dinner party I was having in which a theme had not yet been decided. One of my clients had given me a present of several ducklings to cook, when I received an impromptu visit from Izabella. She took one look at the ducks and said, "Now David, the point is this: in London, we have a tradition called the 'bottle and dish' party. Everybody brings a bottle or a dish, and if you have enough of the right people, you have a fine party. After all, nobody in London can afford to have parties anymore unless you do it this way. These ducks must be cooked with lots of potatoes to absorb the grease. You leave it to 'IZA.'"

So, I immediately got on the phone and invited Antonia Ellis and her boyfriend (they were both dancing in the road show of *Chicago*, which was downtown). Antonia was very dear to me, since she played in both Ken Russell's *The Boy Friend*, as well as *Mahler*. Her scenes with Robert Powell are simply jaw-dropping. Waris Hussein was also invited and chose to bring Elisabeth Shepherd. Martine Beswicke and her latest young man, Dmitri (who was building a dream house in Laguna Beach for Robert England at the time), rounded out the guest list for the evening.

After all was said and done, Iza had her own special way with the ducks and created a splendid dinner for one and all. Afterwards, we had our drinks in the living room, enjoying the fire and conversation that went from Ken Russell to out-of-body experiences. In the meantime, chef Iza had been sampling generously of all the whiskey and champagne in the kitchen, therefore she felt no pain as she sat down next to Martine's boyfriend and began her monologue about "Hollywood," or as she was fond of calling it, "Hollywooding."

"The point is this: I don't understand this place at all…I go to posh dinner club and meet man who was playing the violin for everyone. After he meet me, we talk and I think he likes me, so I invite him around to my flat the next evening for a drink. He arrives, and after a drink or two, tries to kiss me and then asks if I could give him fifty dollars. I don't think Izabella going to meet a man in this town. They all on make or fancy each other."

Since none of us could add to that line of thought, the evening came to a well-deserved finale. From that night on, she was always our own "Iza Duck," if not a lonely one. Lord love an "Iza" Duck!

Izabella's time in Tinseltown was not a happy one, since work was nearly impossible for someone as exotic as her, and with that accent. Her age presented yet another woe, since all the parts were for the young or well-established character actresses. Izabella lamented that "I do all this Hollywooding and still can't work or meet a man!" She had a daughter living in South America, and they jointly began corresponding about working together in television. After a very stressful year, that is exactly what happened, and indeed Izabella wound up on a soap opera in Buenos Aires until she and her daughter could stand each other no more. The "Queen Mother" then resided in London, where she did an occasional television show. I can still hear that distinctive voice starting every sentence with, "The point is this: I play the Queen Mother for Visconti!"

Chapter 22
Marsha Loves to Cook

Elisabeth Brooks

Elisabeth Brooks caught the attention of the film world with the portrayal of "Marsha" in Joe Dante's *The Howling*. Her performance of a nymphomaniac who also happens to be a werewolf was as unique as it was sexy; she demonstrated strength of character proving once again that a woman can be tough without relinquishing her femininity. That performance should have catapulted Elisabeth into a long career as a B-movie queen, especially with dialogue by John Sayles, no less. Why it did not is a story in itself.

I got to know 'Lisa,' as she liked to be called, in the late 1980s and did my best to help jump-start her career until she began to get very ill from a procedure that proved toxic, giving her cancer. She was as remarkable a woman in real life as she was an actress.

Lisa was blessed with a son named Jeremy, who was around twelve when we first met, and she adored him with all her heart. She was a single mom trying hard at a show business career in a town that was as tough as it comes to break into and succeed.

During her notoriety in *The Howling,* she was tested several times for the *femme fatale* in *Body Heat,* losing out finally to Kathleen Turner in the role that made her a star. Lisa worked at odd jobs during that time, including working as a hostess at the Roxy on Sunset Boulevard, where she encountered superstar Jack Nicholson, resulting in a six-month affair that brought her into the supernova of Hollywood high rollers. She emerged a bit shaken, but still the same level-headed woman she would always remain.

Lisa was living in the valley with a guy named Ernie, who was also as good-hearted as they come, and he loved her without question. Lisa and Ernie had a small business they called "Schlep-a-ride," which provided a service for show folk by taking their kids to school or getting actors to their auditions on time: in other words, getting people from one place to another. They even had tee shirts that said "Schlep-a-ride" on the back. I wore mine a lot and was always surprised when someone stopped me so they could jot the phone number down. The business was making a living for them, and for a while, Lisa got her share of interviews. Well-meaning Ernie sometimes found out where she was going to read and called with messages such as "Please tell Elisabeth to call Universal— very urgent," leaving her more amused than angry, since his heart was in the right place, after all.

The other important person in Lisa's life was the young movie star, Kristy McNichol, who Lisa met years before her stardom while she was babysitting on a film set. They were as close as sisters, with some of the same ups and downs. Kristy could be the most wonderful person to be around, and then her mood could swing into a total depression, making it unclear when to visit or when to stay away.

Kristy was living with Liberace's niece at the time I got to know her, and the two girls seemed to have an endless flood of houseguests and pool parties. During that time, I was representing a script that Lisa was convinced would be a sure thing for Kristy to star in, so she persuaded me to pitch it to Kristy right away. Well, trying to talk shop at Kristy's house was never going to happen with all the traffic at the pool, so we agreed to meet at the local Denny's, which I will never forget. Even seated way back at a dark table, people still came up to Kristy for autographs or just to say, "Aren't you Kristy McNichol?" I could see that all the attention was not happening for Kristy, and I wasn't surprised when, within a few years, she retired from acting.

Lisa was the main cheerleader for Kristy's career and worked on her sets as a helper, as well as to be there for Kristy. In 1984, I remember going to a private screening of *Just the Way You Are*, a charming little film about a handicapped girl (she had a lame leg), who finds love at a ski resort, pretending her leg is in a cast from skiing. Throughout the screening, Lisa cheered and laughed because she was so glad to see her friend on the big screen. Lisa had no feelings of bitterness at Kristy's success. She was a special kind of lady, no doubt about it.

Lisa made only one film with her friend, the 1990 ghost story, *The Forgotten One*. She gave a good account of herself, making the poor distribution of the project all the more tragic, since Lisa deserved a career more than most, in my opinion. All she ever needed was another show-stopper like the Joe Dante film.

Throughout the 1980s and up until the ghost film, I arranged meetings and suggested auditions for plays in and around Los Angeles. Lisa was always upbeat and excited. Nothing brought her down, including the shadow of cancer that hung over her during the late

1980s and early 1990. She appeared in a play in Hollywood, and I took every director I knew to see her. She gave a raw and emotionally charged performance, but it just was not seen by that one person who could have made the difference. We stayed in touch, usually on the phone, keeping track with late night calls. I loved hearing her whiskey-rich deep voice laugh about whatever caught her fancy during the day or something Jeremy did. Soon, there were fewer calls, and then she just withdrew from her Hollywood friends. I learned that she'd taken a place down near Palm Springs to sort things out and try alternative healing methods for the cancer that was sapping her energy.

I learned the circumstances of Elisabeth's last days when I chanced upon a website devoted to her memory by her friend Gigi Porter, the wife of actor Reggie Bannister from the *Phantasm* films. It seemed that we lost forty-six-year-old Elisabeth on September 7, 1997, in Palm Springs. Her son, Jeremy, was present at her bedside. In accordance with her Comanche heritage, a ceremony was performed to release her spirit.

Of all the actors I have known in Hollywood, Elisabeth Brooks was one of the most deserving and talented ladies of them all, and rarely does a day go by without me remembering that she is gone, yet my heart is not saddened because she is free of pain and must be aware how much she is missed by those she left behind.

Chapter 23

Werewolf Bitch: The Making of The Howling II

Sybil Danning

In the not-so-distant glory days of picture making, if a film was a financial success at the box office, not to mention garnering impressive reviews from the nation's critics, a sequel was more often than not a slam-dunk. The sequel would try to copy the elements that made the first one work and sometimes even surpass it in one way or another (think *The Bride of Frankenstein* or *The Godfather, Part II*).

Granted, director Joe Dante struck gold with screenwriter John Sayles' witty and humorous script that sent up *The Wolf Man* and genre films like it. *The Howling* was a box office hit in its day and received raves from fans and critics alike, so when the time came for a sequel, what happened?

I am going to tell you exactly what happened because I was there from the time the late Elisabeth Brooks received her first script until the film premiered at the American Film Market at the Beverly Center's multiplex with the amazing Sybil Danning standing bravely at the back of the theater enduring the catcalls of the press, rabid horror junkies, and her fans, as the end credits rolled underneath the image of Sybil ripping her bra off, revealing her two best assets over and over again (a total of seventeen times!) before the lights finally came up. By then, mercifully, Sybil had left the building. This is the story of *The Howling II,* or *Your Sister is a Werewolf,* or my personal favorite, *Stirba: Werewolf Bitch!*

In 1977, author Gary Brandner penned the first of what became a trilogy of werewolf novels, all of which have found their way to the big screen. *The Howling* was made into a film by Joe Dante in 1981 and would have been a mega-hit instead of just successful if it had not been for *An American Werewolf in London,* which made for just one too many werewolf transformations in one season. What made the Joe Dante film work as a send-up thriller is entirely due to John Sayles' flair for genre-friendly humor and his understanding of genre lore, whereas the Landis film recreated the village atmosphere and folklore of *The Wolf Man,* and then betrayed it with jock humor and a lame subplot redeemed somewhat with big bad wolf effects that impressed fans at the time. Be that as it may, the Landis film softened the blow for any werewolf film that followed, even a superior one; plus we had a double dose of the same transformation effects from Rob Bottin and Rick Baker in back-to-back releases, and nothing says "jaded" to a horror fan faster than a double-dose.

In organizing a sequel, it was always understood that the character of "Marsha" as played by Elisabeth Brooks would be the carryover from the first film, as well as being a lead character in the continuing saga as the "Queen of the Werewolves," and there was the franchise for all the *Howling* films to come. However, from 1981 until the cameras started rolling on *The Howling II,* Brooks received no less than a half-dozen scripts of varying quality (not to mention continuity) from the first film. By 1983, Elisabeth began to experience the oncoming effects of the cancer that eventually took her life. The final script that she received in 1983 was more or less the one that was filmed the next year with Sybil Danning as the werewolf queen.

Elisabeth had real misgivings from the first film regarding the nudity that was required in the sequence where she and actor Chris Stone shed their clothes and make love in the woods by a roaring fire, as their lovemaking triggers a full transformation into werewolves. The set was closed for filming that sequence, yet photographs leaked out to the media and resulted in an unwelcome appearance in *Playboy*. Elisabeth was a mother and she did not want her son to see that aspect of her work turned into what she considered pornography. Her displeasure did nothing towards ensuring her participation in a sequel, especially one without Joe Dante as the director.

The arrival of the script for what became *The Howling II* (1985) was a major disappointment for Elisabeth because it contained "a three-way sex scene" of transforming werewolves, as well as a number of questionable "improvements" to what came before. In spite of her desperate need for work, Elisabeth said goodbye to the role that brought her so close to stardom, yet sadly not close enough.

Enter Australian auteur Philippe Mora, who had to his credit a sleeper cult film with the great Dennis Hopper called *Mad Dog Morgan*. Mora is a very charming man with a knowledge and appreciation of Hollywood history to the point of being a fan. The casting of Christopher Lee for a lead in *The Howling II* seemed to establish an aura of classic horror in the grand tradition, as well as keeping true to the spirit of the original film that boasted a classic star-turn by veteran horror star John Carradine in a key role. The character of "Marsha" was dropped from the script and the continuity from the first film to the sequel became the resurrection of Karen White (Dee Wallace) as a werewolf. Since she was to be dispatched by a monster hunter played by Lee (in the Van Helsing tradition), Dee decided not to appear. The sloppy transition of creating "new" footage of Karen being shot at the television station without the original actors such as Kevin McCarthy or Dee Wallace made the production begin to appear like a high school play version of the original—or worse, something thrown together at the last minute after the real stars said no.

Instead of "Marsha," the nymphomaniac werewolf from the first film, we are treated to "Stirba," the blonde bisexual queen of the werewolves, who lives in a castle in the "dark country," in other words, Transylvania. The actress chosen to play that character was the incredible, outrageous-looking Sybil Danning. Sybil had achieved major cult recognition in a low-budget Roger Corman-produced space epic entitled *Battle Beyond the Stars,* and she cemented her cult queen status by appearing topless whenever possible, and for a time seemed to be channeling Jayne Mansfield in the sense that, like Jayne, she bought a classic Hollywood mansion that had once belonged to Jean Harlow (a gift from Howard Hughes), and she made the scene in a series of outlandish outfits that gave her breasts star billing at all times. Her relentless campaign to play the title role in the James Bond film, *Octopussy,* is legend; unfortunately she did not get the part, and to her credit, has never given up the quest for her rightful place in the lights of Los Angeles.

My involvement in the proceedings was the direct result of working with a really fun and hip PR firm known as The Michael Dalling Company, which had a funky floor of offices above a popular British pub/restaurant on the sunset strip. As correspondent for *Film and Filming* magazine, I had covered a few films they were promoting, and my friendship with Christopher Lee made me a natural to cover the making of *The Howling II.* A delightful young woman named Jane Covner was placed in charge of the Hemdale production, and she began getting the word out. I was given the task of interviewing the director and all the lead actors for the European market. Jane had a great sense of humor, and I am happy to report that she went on to bigger and better things, and today, she is an executive at the prestigious PR firm, Rogers and Cowen.

What I remember most about that stage of the promotions was a tall, pale young man (forever sporting pastel-colored sun shades), who called himself Scott Constantine Dacy. That would-be hustler gleefully appeared to be living on-and-off with Sybil Danning as her manager/lover/press agent. He had the nickname around the office of "Dribble," as in "Sybil and Dribble." Scott turned out to be a predatory sociopath, who stalked strippers and models when they arrived in Hollywood looking for that all-important break.

Of course, none of that was readily apparent at the time. We were just very aware that there was something not right about his handling of Sybil's affairs. Scott bullied people on the phone (I once heard him tell a producer "You have three strikes and then you are out!" Then, he screamed, "One, two, and three! You're out man!" and banged the phone down, ending any chance of her calling back. He routinely kept tabs on Sybil and her appointments, always placing himself in the way of interviews and photo shoots. He tried to be the producer/manager on all her projects, and within a couple of years, virtually destroyed her career. Scott was a budding pornographer, who prided himself on his ability to take nudes not only of Sybil but anyone he could lure off the streets.

The afternoon I finally interviewed Sybil was thankfully free of Scott and proved to be one of the more relaxed and enjoyable interviews I did for the film. On her own terms, Sybil was charming, funny, and a refreshingly modest woman, who raised herself from humble beginnings to a self-made celebrity with a certain amount of success, all of it well-deserved. Sybil was proud of her physique, and she should have been. I personally have never seen anyone who could equal her almost-perfect body that had a face and personality to match.

After nearly two hours of conversation, the last hour of which we sat by the fire in her massive living room drinking champagne and enjoying Viennese chocolates (she had just come back from Vienna), she realized she had to prepare for a dinner party. As I headed for the front gate, my luck took a turn for the worse. Scott made his way into the house, stopping me as I was leaving and asking "just what was I doing there" and so on. He was impressed enough that I was with *Films and Filming* to ask me back in the house to collect some of his own personal slides of Sybil that he had taken of her in full costume for the film. I remember feeling rather uncomfortable when he insisted we go upstairs, and as we passed a bedroom with the door slightly ajar, he pushed it all the way back to show me the mirrors over the bed. The room was rather disorganized with clothes lying about, however I looked over to the unmade bed and noticed a large, opened, well-used jar of Vaseline on a nightstand. Scott caught my eye and read my mind. He stated, "One day when I know you better, I might show you the results of the photo shoot we did in here." By that time, I just wanted to get out of the house as gracefully as I could without letting Sybil know what I had seen. Scott and I had made it back out to the front of the house when Sybil came by and reminded me to call her about the Christmas party because she would do her best to come. Scott knew I had invited her to my Christmas party, so I also had to extend the invitation to him. They both walked me to my car, leaving me with an overwhelming sense of foreboding for what was to come.

During that time of year, just as the Christmas holidays began to take hold, several outlandish tales from the Czech Republic location where most of *The Howling II* was shot began circulating around the Mike Dalling office regarding the wholesale fights between Sybil and "Dribble" that went on during filming.

Scott apparently hit Sybil in the face, resulting in a black eye that could not be covered with make-up, so in the film, when you see Sybil wearing Ray-Ban shades, that is what she is concealing behind them. The crew spent their evenings sitting by the hotel pool listening to them argue and throw things at each other. At one point, Sybil threw a television out the window, trying to brain Scott for some terrible thing he had done or said during the day. Why a beautiful woman like Sybil would endure that relationship is one of the great mysteries of my time in Hollywood. Scott made enemies almost daily, while we were preparing the press materials for the film. The day of my Christmas party, I had invited what I thought were too many people, and I spent the day buying more supplies to prepare for the Walpurgis Night to begin.

The party was quite a lot of fun, and all my favorite mates showed up in fine form. Martine Beswicke came with her current young beau; Arthur Hiller and his lady arrived full of Christmas cheer. Reggie Nalder came with a small gift for Sybil, since she nearly worked on a film with him, and they were old friends from Vienna. By ten o'clock, the place was filled to capacity. Sybil arrived with infamous Scott at about that time. She looked terrific in a black-and-gold outfit, but she always looked like a movie queen. In my bedroom, there was a television, and at half past ten o'clock, Scott asked if he could watch a show on HBO that had Sybil as a guest star, an episode of *The Hitchhiker*, a mystery show with a supernatural twist. That evening's segment featured Sybil and guest star Robert Vaughan in "Face to Face." In the show, Robert played a plastic surgeon that spends the night before an operation snorting coke off one of Sybil's breasts (in other words, the perfect show for a Christmas party). Most men at the party squeezed into my bedroom to see that, while Sybil remained in the kitchen having conversations and champagne with the rest of the guests.

All seemed to be at peace with the spirit of Christmas until we neared the witching hour. At that time, someone came up to me and said that I better have a talk with Sybil's agent, since he was getting heavy with some of the guests about something. I walked into the bedroom and Scott grabbed me by the collar and started raving about me trying to take Sybil away from him. He quoted some things I suggested to her during our interview, twisting it all around like the paranoid bastard he was. Within minutes, a couple of my friends pulled him off of me and marched him to the front door. I ran back to the kitchen and told Sybil that I had to ask Scott to leave. In tears, she said that if he went, she had to go, as well. I got the impression that was something of a habit in their relationship. I also got the feeling she was afraid of him. Later, I was told that Scott sometimes threatened to throw acid on a woman's face if she crossed him.

The next day at Mike's office, I was told that Scott went utterly berserk on the phone demanding that I be fired, and he was busy letting all Hollywood know that I was out to steal his star and place her under contract to me. Jane was laughing it all off and she tried to tell him that I could not be fired because I was a freelance journalist and was not an employee of the Dalling office, end of story. Scott still demanded I return the slides he gave me at Sybil's . . . but I still have them to this day.

At that point, none of us had seen the film, only stills, but we had heard first-hand accounts of mishaps and so forth while Philippe Mora was in the Czech Republic filming. My conversation with Philippe led me to believe this the film might become a real classic, since he openly admired Tod Browning and James Whale as directors, and he was a total film buff, to boot. I loved the fact that he kept a prop severed hand in the fruit bowl on his coffee table. It wasn't until I visited the prop and make-up department out in the Valley that I began to wonder if that project was indeed a return to classic horror or even as good a film as Joe Dante's.

The guys who created the make-up had spent days packing the props and werewolf gear to be sent overseas, and they had a different tale to tell. "This film is really gonna suck, cause the gargoyle on the staff cannot be animated properly and they are going to try painting beams of light onto Sybil's fingers for the conjure stuff cause there is no money to do it right."

Apparently there was a cash flow problem over at Hemdale, and the special effects were the first to feel the pinch. "Look at these masks; they'll rot before they arrive and there's no one at the other end to fix them properly." One of the make-up men related how Scott had threatened to kill the guy who was applying werewolf hairs on Sybil's body (and I mean *all over* her body). At one point, Scott was barred from the set until they wrapped the three-way sex sequence. By that time, the whole crew knew about me tossing Scott out of my Christmas party, so the stories flowed about his abusive behavior.

My old friend, Ferdy Mayne, had a small but showy part as a werewolf at the film's beginning and is fatally staked by the hand of his old mate, Christopher Lee. Ferdy remarked about the make-up being "all rubber and teeth," and also expressed concern for Christopher, since he was not feeling well during the filming. Later, he discovered that he had to have open-heart surgery soon after the film wrapped, and that the Lee family made the decision to return to England for good. Ferdy wanted to play Christopher's part and felt he could have really given it a bit more life, since his pal was under the weather. Christopher did remark soon after I saw Ferdy that the scene in the graveyard where Ferdy used his feet like an animal "was absolutely on and so right for his character."

The other werewolf bitch in the film was played by the fantastic Marsha Hunt, who appeared with Christopher in Hammer's *Dracula*

A.D. 72, one of their very last Dracula film's, one that has since become a cult favorite. Marsha became world famous for having a daughter by Mick Jagger (legend has it the stones hit single, "Brown Sugar," was all about her). Marsha was the third sex partner in the werewolf three-way, and had hoped it would "rock." As she explained, "You can never tell about how this shit will look until they fuck with it." Somehow, I knew just what she meant by that. You go, girl!

As more information began to mount, so did anticipation to see the epic as soon as a print could be made. The answer to everyone's wish came in the guise of The American Film Market, which was the venue Hemdale chose to screen *The Howling II: Your Sister is a Werewolf* for foreign distribution, but not for reviewing. There was no release date for a Hollywood premiere and there never would be.

Nothing could have prepared me for the film when I finally sat down to experience the wonders of Stirba and her three-way for myself. There are many who, after seeing *The Howling II: Your Sister is a Werewolf* that day, felt it was the *Plan Nine From Outer Space* of werewolf films, or better yet, the worst film ever made in the Czech Republic. For me, it was just a total mind-fuck as to what on earth could have made an intelligent, sophisticated gentleman like Philippe Mora make such a sloppy, incoherent mess. The make-up and lame effects were the worst I have ever seen in a horror film, even worse considering the budget the film was supposed to have had. The best thing about it was Sybil and her fantastic body. Even Christopher Lee, with a voice like God, seemed lost in the sea of celluloid despair. The film was shot in such darkness that, mercifully, you could not make out whether the werewolves were really men in fur coats, but I swear that is what they looked like. The infamous werewolf three-way proved not to be very erotic, unless matted hair turns someone on. It was, in fact, downright silly. Marsha and Sybil growled and clawed at their male companion as if they were all infested with fleas.

The film, as it stands today, is a catalog of bad moments, some rather camp, but not enough to create a midnight cult film. Perhaps it is, as I feel my unique experience with it disqualifies me from an opinion, although now that it is out on DVD from MGM, viewers can decide for themselves. The disc offers a widescreen presentation, or you can flip it over for full screen. Either way, it won't get any better, I assure you.

Since that fateful 1985 afternoon, Christopher Lee went on to become an icon in the business and worked more than anyone else from the film. Sybil broke away from Scott, got married, and continued making films. Her website became filled with information just for her loyal and diehard fans.

Philippe Mora returned to Australia, where he made oddball little films that sometimes showcased Barry Humphries, better known as "Dame Edna Everage." Mora even went back two years after that film and made another *Howling* film, and that one came off a bit better because it was supposed to be a comedy, and we all know now that Mora works best down under.

As to what became of evil Scott Constantine Dacy, he finally got his comeuppance as one would-be actress too many got fed up and turned him over to the police for stalking. He was under investigation later, after being exposed on a nationally televised crime show about celebrity stalkers. Scott was eventually found dead in a rooming house in Hollywood where he had been living alone.

Perhaps the film will find a life after all in the weird, wacky world of "so bad it's good" films that grace our screens at midnight on Halloween. Shall we let our in house punk band"Babel" speak from the track that opens and closes the film *The Howling II: Your Sister is a Werewolf*:

"In the pale, pale light
pale pale light of the moon glow,
I've got an emotional hunger,
a hunger I cannot control.
I'm alone now, in my room again,
on the prowl now, through your dreams again,
howling, howling, since the world began,
and the forest looks so green again,
and I worship at your feet again,
howling, howling,
since the world began."

Chapter 24

The Spider Woman Strikes Back

Gale Sondergaard

I first became aware that the legendary Academy Award-winning actress, Gale Sondergaard, (first recipient of the Best Supporting Actress award) was indeed alive, well, and living in Los Angeles, when the late Ron Haver screened the Bob Hope version of *The Cat and the Canary* at the Los Angeles County Museum of Art in the summer of 1980. At that time, it was nearly impossible to see the sound version of the silent classic unless a screening like that was arranged. Ron was a tireless champion of film preservation, as well as the guiding light behind Filmex in Los Angeles, a festival that brought international attention to Hollywood, as well as the art of cinema. The night of the screening was a sell-out with many celebrities in attendance, but none was more welcomed than Gale Sondergaard, who played the sinister "Miss Lu" in the classic horror comedy.

Gale was seated in the front row with Ron, as the house lights dimmed and then went up again to reveal a still striking Gale, who then introduced the film with humor and grace, remembering the cameraman and director for special praise, while modestly accepting a standing ovation from the audience.

What she left unsaid that evening was her personal dislike for the star of *The Cat and the Canary,* a man she acted with on four occasions, the powerful comic icon Bob Hope. It seemed that Hope had become so right-wing and narrow-minded that he held a personal political vendetta against his former co-star until her death in 1985.

Almost all of the Hollywood community is of the same mind in condemning the infamous blacklisting that destroyed lives in the 1950s, when Senator Joe McCarthy and Congressman Richard Nixon persecuted many of the most respected Hollywood actors, writers, and directors in their communist witch-hunt. Sadly, many equally well-known Hollywood professionals such as Ronald Reagan, John Wayne, Cecil B De Mille, and Adolphe Menjou turned against their own, fanned the flame of suspicion, and named names before the House and Senate committees during that time of shame. Even worse, those committees took what the men had to say as true. Those men also helped create lists in shades of gray and black to make sure that anyone under suspicion never worked in Hollywood again.

After meeting Gale that evening, I asked Charles Higham, who escorted her, to introduce me properly, and we began a friendship. A few weeks later, I was invited to her "compound" (as she called it) in the Silver Lake district, an area of old Los Angeles that became trendy and expensive. Our friendship endured until 1984, when Gale retired to The Motion Picture & Television Country House and Hospital.

Gale was never bitter or resentful of the past. She had a sharp and clever mind, and did not suffer fools gladly. She was a very accomplished actress on both the stage and screen. She understood her limitations better than most directors and never thought in terms of stardom since her goals were always to perfect her craft rather than bask in the glow of her own publicity.

Gale was the widow of Herbert J. Biberman, a producer/writer/ director, who achieved national attention as one of the infamous "Hollywood Ten." His refusal to testify led to him being blacklisted. He was sent to jail for a year and fined $1000. Gale also refused to testify, and her Hollywood career ended. She relied on the stage after that and worked right through the blacklisting until she and her husband worked together once more on a retelling of *Uncle Tom's Cabin,* which became the film, *Slaves.* Herbert Biberman died of cancer in 1971.

Herbert also designed furniture, and his artistry was in abundance, in Gale's home. When I entered, she announced that all the furniture in the living room and hallway was pure "Biberman." In an alcove sat her Oscar for *Antony Adverse.* I had the thrill of holding the statue, which was my third time to hold an Academy Award. The other two included Groucho Marx's honorary Oscar and James Poe's Best Screenplay award.

Gale was a practical woman, and her home reflected a deep love of gardening and an appreciation for art. She was a survivor and she knew every day was a blessing. She also had her sister living with her, who was suffering with poor eyesight and stayed upstairs most of the time.

During my visit, I attempted to ask about her film career, and she did her best to make me understand that living had very little to do with studying old films, and I could better serve myself learning more about life and less about Claude Rains! Gale did tell me that she did not get along with Gloria Holden, the actress who I admired so much from *Dracula's Daughter*. Gale was also with her in *The Life of Emile Zola* (1937), the Paul Muni film. She felt that Gloria was a snob and a bit too grand for her own good. Gale loved working with Paul Muni and especially Claude Rains, who she described as "one of the best actors Hollywood ever had."

"One of my best friends in the early years in Hollywood was Luise Rainer. She was just a lovely person and very sensitive. After I made *The Letter*, people often confused us and complemented me for my work in *The Good Earth*, and I always had to say, "No, that was my good friend, Luise Rainer."

When we got around to discussing the film she made unforgettable with Bette Davis, where Gale has no dialogue, yet speaks volumes with her eyes and body language (I am of course referring to William Wyler's film of Somerset Maugham's *The Letter*), this is where Gale began to talk about her distaste for Bob Hope. During the celebration of Adolph Zukor's 100th birthday on the Paramount lot, where all the surviving stars of Hollywood made the mogul's affair an event never to be equaled for the gathering of more stars than there were in the heavens, Gale was greeted by many of her former players, and none as warmly as Bette Davis, who said for all to hear, "Oh Gale, you were luminous in *The Letter*," and with that, planted a kiss on Gale's cheek. As the two actresses walked up the ramp to the main table—the one just before the guest of honor, Mr. Zukor—Bette said to Gale, "I hope you are sitting with us. Let me see where they have seated you." Apparently there were several chairs yet to be occupied. However, when Gale asked to be seated, the ushers told her to come with them back down to the bottom of the stairs. All that confusion occurred because seated very near to Zukor was none other than Bob Hope, who, after co-starring with Gale in four films, demanded she be removed from his table and placed in dishonor with a table at the bottom of the stairs for the "Commie pinko traitor" she was to him. An angry Bette Davis let her feelings be known, and Gale was placed at Davis's table away from Hope, but that was really the last straw. Gale could never forget his treatment of her that evening, nor the many things he did during the blacklisting to see that she never worked anywhere in Hollywood. As Gale told me this, her face grew dark with anger and her fists were tight around her chair. "There is nothing in politics that surprises me anymore, not even a man like Nixon taking the Presidency, or Reagan! People must stay informed about their leaders."

Gale recalled for me the breakthrough that jumpstarted her career, even though the threats still arrived via the American Legion to stop her from appearing in *Anastasia*, a summer theater production, but the publicity over her being cast as the Empress became news on a national level.

"Each performance was sold out, and that opening night was the most exciting of my entire career. Everybody of importance from government to the American Legion was in the audience that night to see if I would have the guts to appear. Well, my entrance in the middle of the second act was positively electric, a moment in time that brought me full circle after all those terrible years of being denied the right to practice my craft. All that disappeared the moment I walked out on that stage and stopped the show for an ovation the likes of which I never knew could exist outside of a movie script.

"Yet the blacklisting was imposed on Hollywood, and especially the studios. It would take the independents to start rehiring those who could not work for so many years after the blacklisting finally died away. There were other actors like Hope, who believed we were a threat to the American way of freedom; men like John Wayne and Ronald Reagan. The one we all remember was Adolphe Menjou who hated communism more than anyone else in Hollywood and would go out of his way to act like the witch hunter he was in private life."

Gale managed to laugh at one point and told me she got along famously with Hope in their films together. "I remember coming home from the set aching from laughter because Bob was so funny, always full of quips. Bob began to change the richer and more Republican he got."

The afternoon wore on and Gale began to tire, asking me if we could perhaps talk more at some other time. The whole experience was so overwhelming. To be in the presence of such a commanding lady, much less having her full attention and trust, was more than I could ever have bargained for from a chance encounter—thanks, oddly enough, to a Bob Hope movie.

At the beginning of 1981, Curtis Harrington and I escorted Gale to a screening of what was supposed to be *Sherlock Holmes and the Spider Woman* for a group of Holmes scholars at the motion picture academy who called themselves the "Non-Canonical Calabashes." At that point, I should explain that Curtis had asked especially for Gale Sondergaard when he was directing a made-for-television horror film called *The Cat Creature*. While Gale was working one afternoon, the Academy presented her with an Oscar statuette for Best Supporting

Actress, because in 1936, they only had plaques to give out in that newly-created category. Ever since then, Gale and Curtis had a special bond of friendship.

A print of *Sherlock Holmes and the Spider Woman* could not be found for that evening, so *Sherlock Holmes Faces Death* was quickly substituted. The program was sold out, and as Gale rose to her feet to introduce the film, the audience gave her another ovation and the rush she needed to get through it all. She spoke with genuine respect for Basil Rathbone, calling him "a dedicated actor who treated Holmes as a real person, making the audience also believe he was Sherlock Holmes." Gale handled the questions about her characterization of the Spider Woman with humor.

"I was asked to play this evil yet powerful woman. This Spider Woman character, as scripted, had no hint of background or motivation, if you will, and no concept of how to play her as a three dimensional character. I mean, what kind of a childhood could she have had? Ultimately, I chose to play her as Holmes' equal and allow their battle of wits to be played out much like a female Moriarty. Both Nigel and Basil were so dear together, as they enjoyed those tea breaks at four every afternoon that they worked at Universal, and I was honored to be in their company."

At the end of that evening, I suggested to both Gale and Curtis that I was planning a very special going-away party for someone they both would enjoy seeing off. I kept the name a surprise, and I told them both to come to my place the following weekend for an afternoon to remember—an understatement—that will be proven in the next chapter.

Chapter 25

The White Flame Meets the Spider Woman

Gloria Stuart

Gloria Stuart is totally unique in show business history in that she survived beyond even her wildest dreams all the way into the twenty-first century and was the oldest person ever to receive an Academy Award nomination in 1997 for *Titanic*.

Gloria began as a former contract player with Universal Pictures in the early 1930s, when she captured the imagination of James Whale, the most successful director on the lot, after the overwhelming public response to his masterpiece, *Frankenstein*. Whale cast Gloria in three of his films, the most famous being yet another masterpiece, *The Invisible Man*, and the other two being the nearly forgotten *The Kiss Before the Mirror*, in which she is killed off at the film's beginning, and her own personal favorite of the three, *The Old Dark House*. That may have been Whale's favorite, as well. It had long been regarded as a lost film until Curtis Harrington made it his business to find it while directing *Games* on the Universal lot. The film survives on DVD as the prototype for all "old dark house" films that followed in its wake.

Gloria once told me that Whale instructed her to behave "like a white flame that dances about the old house much like a moth." He made sure her costume was a white clinging silk *décolletage* gown that did give her something to be a flame with. I owe my introduction to the remarkable lady to a fellow artist, Don Bacardy, who had done several portraits of Gloria over the years. I wanted to introduce her to Curtis Harrington, since they both knew James Whale at different stages of the great director's life.

Gloria was never what you would think of as a "conventional" lady, and age never diminished her energy or zest for living. While she was at that time well into her late seventies, Gloria Stuart was about to take an adventurous vacation to Morocco by jeep with another girl-friend for a month. I decided, upon hearing about that, to throw her a going away party and allow some of my friends to experience the ageless wonder for themselves. My guest list was made up of actors who might know her or would like to, and of course, Curtis and my new friend, Gale Sondergaard. Both actresses worked at Universal at different times and in different roles, and both were known for their horror pictures.

As far as I knew, the ladies had never met or worked together, since most of the forty films Gloria made were in the 1930s, and she retired on at least two occasions to devote more time to painting (and had the shows to prove that it was time well spent). Gloria had been one of the founding members of the Screen Actors Guild in 1933, and was also known as a "liberal" when it came to politics. I just knew the gals would hit it off. I decided to make large punch bowls of sangria for the party, since it was summer and it seemed festive for the occasion.

Gale arrived with Charles Higham, and she wore a brown and white two-piece summer outfit that showed off her amazing figure—the spider woman struck back, and how!

The room was filling up, soon spilling out onto the back patio, and the party was off and running. At some point, Curtis came up to me and said that Gale wanted to speak with me in the kitchen. When I went in and saw Gale was waiting rather nervously, I asked if anything was wrong. She told me that her late husband, Herbert Biberman, was a bitter enemy of Arthur Sheekman, who was married to Gloria Stuart. Gale had forgotten that little tidbit until that moment when the two were about to be introduced. I pondered the situation and decided to simply go over to Gloria and explain what was going on with Gale. As I had hoped, Gloria could not remember if her late husband had a problem with Biberman or not. You see, Gloria was a very liberated woman, and after Arthur died, she met a man who was more involved in the arts, and they lived together until his death. I knew that Gloria was not one to hold on to the past. Once I made her aware of the situation, she went into the kitchen and embraced Gale, telling her "that the past was just that" and that they had too much living to do to worry about what their husbands were up to in another life. With that, the two became friends for the rest of the afternoon and beyond.

The other moment I remember well was when Curtis Harrington, who needed a place to sit in order to be closer to Gloria Stuart as they compared notes regarding dear "Jimmy" Whale, went out on the patio and brought in one of my metal folding chairs and seated himself right by the pink flame. I was in the kitchen, when I heard a loud crash. Curtis and his chair had collapsed, and he spilled sangria on Gloria as well as himself. I was very naughty and could not stop laughing because Curtis, in those days, was accident-prone. He had, in fact, walked into a fountain at another party a few weeks before, getting soaked once again. Knowing me as he did, Curtis was angry at first. He thought that I might have given him a trick chair or something. In time, he forgave me since I reminded him that he picked that chair himself. I think he also made up with Gloria for the sangria-dousing, and she later attended some of his parties, as well.

Gloria and Gale locked arm in arm and walked out to the patio area, laughing about how they survived the "Universal horror factory" in the eras in which they worked. I asked Gloria about *Secret of the Blue Room*, a 1934 film she made with a favorite screen villain of mine, Lionel Atwill. She began to laugh at the mention of it, saying to me, "You know everyone called Lionel 'Pinky,' and he was quite a womanizer in his day. He was playing my father by day, but when we were not on camera, he was very flirtatious, and I remember one afternoon my husband was away on business and I was not on call at the studio. The doorbell rang around lunch-time, and who should be standing in my doorway but "Pinky," dressed immaculately in a gorgeous three-piece suit with a monocle, no less. His first words to me were 'Gloria, you are such a beautiful creature, let me spoil you with lunch anywhere you like.' I was taken back for a moment, but I quickly let him know that I was happily married and wished to keep it that way. He never wavered, but removed his monocle and bowed, saying, "Well in that case, it is my loss," and departed with grace and style. The next day, I was playing his daughter again in Universal city.

Gale had a much different experience with Universal when she played the title character in *The Spider Woman Strikes Back*, a spin-off to her star turn as the female "Moriarty" in the Sherlock Holmes film. It was not up to her standards, but work was work. There was a union dispute going on at the time they shot the film, and no one was supposed to cross the picket line to work at Universal on the first day of principal photography. Gale had to make a hard decision, whether to refuse to cross that line and lose her job, or go to work. To her lasting regret, she chose to work, since her family sorely needed that paycheck.

Gale remembered that afternoon like it was yesterday. The first setup was in a hot-house full of deadly-looking plants filled with poison, and she and Rondo Hatton (a tragic figure in horror films since he was genuinely disfigured) were to extract the poison with a hypodermic needle. On the first take, Gale burst into tears, since her mind was still on those men and women she had to walk past to go inside the back lot to work. "I was ashamed of myself and vowed I would never do such a thing again in my life."

When I asked Gale about working with Rondo Hatton, she surprised me by being totally unaware of Hatton's suffering with acromegaly, which caused his features to distort, creating a monster without makeup. Universal shamelessly exploited him in half a dozen pictures. Gale was in shock and told me, "I would have spent more time with the poor fellow if I had known that. I was led to believe he was just another of Jack Pierce's masterful creations."

The afternoon began to fade, as my guests left one by one, with only a handful remaining in the living room. As Charles and Gloria started to leave, she gave me a kiss, thanked me for a wonderful party, and especially for relieving Gale Sondergaard of any more guilt involving her late husband. Gloria remarked how much Gale had suffered in Hollywood, and yet she remained as free of bitterness about her career as Gloria had by leaving the business to pursue her bliss with painting. Both ladies represented a spirit of personal freedom and strength of character that was unique in Hollywood. Years later, Gloria Stuart achieved even greater recognition with the world-wide success of *Titanic,* and she is still actively painting. Gale lived to see her work recognized and appreciated by film historians and fans. In 1985, she passed away at The Motion Picture & Television Country House and Hospital.

Chapter 26

Gooble Gobble
One of Us

Angelo Rossitto

One of the most unsettling and celebrated moments in a pre-Code Hollywood film occurs during a vicious thunderstorm as a circus caravan moves through a forest at night. The film is Tod Browning's infamous *Freaks* (1932). The events that follow that climatic thunderstorm, where circus freaks armed with sharp objects crawl through the mud to enact a shocking retribution for the poisoning of one of their own, has been the subject of scholarly debate for decades. The comeuppance of Cleopatra (Olga Baclanova) and her lover Hercules (Henry Victor) was deemed too strong for audiences in that Depression era, leaving MGM to withdraw the film and remove their company's logo from all prints. The film was reissued by a different company in 1949, and then disappeared until its legend overcame any obstacles to prevent modern audiences from appreciating what is now an acknowledged classic of surrealism, unique even in the realm of the horror genre itself.

I was privileged to have known two of the performers from that film, Angelo Rossitto ("Little Angie" to his friends) and Johnny Eck (John Eckhart), the "Human Torso." Angie was the only actor from that bizarre ensemble to have an acting career in Hollywood following the disastrous initial release of *Freaks*. By the summer of 1986, I was working as Unit Publicist for a portmanteau entitled *The Offspring*. Since one of the stories took place in a carnival, the director, Jeff Burr, had but one actor in mind for the role of the front man who lures customers into the tents to see the special attractions, and that of course was Angelo Rossitto. To be honest, I think Jeff and his young associates remembered him from a similar role in *Dracula Vs. Frankenstein,* a grade-Z 1971 horror film, Al Adamson's wacky tribute to the Universal horror films of the 1940s, and sadly, one containing the final performances of J. Carroll Nash and Lon Chaney, Jr.

Angelo was rarely out of work in the nearly seven decades he was a fixture in films. He was also a landmark on the corner of Hollywood and Vine, usually seated on a high chair behind the counter of his little newsstand that became an institution for show-biz folk to pick up the trades and hear the latest exploits of one of Hollywood's smallest thespians. Legend has it that if a producer wanted to hire Angelo, they simply dropped a script or contract off at Hollywood and Vine.

When I began assembling the press material for *The Offspring,* Angelo came by my apartment one afternoon to go over his publicity and see what photos he would like, if any, from the production. Angelo called in advance and explained he would be dropped off at my place and asked if I could take him back home when we were finished. That was no problem, since I was completely fascinated with his career and the legendary actors he knew from a lifetime in front of the camera.

Angelo arrived at the front of my building aided by two very small walking sticks that allowed him to move slowly but secure that he would not lose his balance. I quickly learned that he was strongly independent, not to mention proud, a man who made it his business to hold his own in a world that must have been overwhelming at best.

The only aspect of meeting him that was a bit of a trial was treating him as any guest, but his size made that almost impossible. For example, when he came through the door and was offered a seat, it was obvious that he could not seat himself on my sofa without a lift, or better yet, a footstool. Fortunately, I had in my kitchen a small stepladder that served admirably. Once I got him comfortably seated, he began looking through the stills and press materials as he had done countess times over the years.

Noticing a large framed portrait I had of John Barrymore in *Svengali* (1931) that was on my living room wall, Angelo said to me, "You know, Jack Barrymore was the finest actor of them all and a great guy to hang out with." He then recalled that in the 1920s, Barrymore sent a car down to Hollywood and Vine to collect Angelo and bring him up to Tower Road for drinks and lengthy conversations. "Barrymore could spin tales for hours and never bore you once, and much of what he talked about was 'man's talk,' you know, about women. He had lived a lifetime before he ever came to Hollywood. Barrymore could out-drink most men, and I tried to keep up with him, but liquor affects people my size a lot faster and I would usually pass out before dawn. He would then just cover me up with a blanket; he always looked after me. I really loved Jack Barrymore. I cried like a baby when he died."

Angelo appeared with the great profile in *The Beloved Rogue*

(1927), which also starred the legendary Conrad Veidt. Angelo revealed that when the two great actors met on the set for the first time, Barrymore said to the German star of *The Cabinet of Dr. Caligari* (1919), "I find I can usually seduce most women using only the hypnotic quality of my voice, but in these silent films, they are drawn to my profile."

Conrad Veidt looked at Barrymore for a moment and replied, "Well, I just fuck them with my face."

The two actors became great friends from that moment on and made a remarkable film together. Angelo was also very proud of the fact that Barrymore himself wrote a scene into the film where his character, "Beppo," demands that one of the guards bring Barrymore "all the wine he wants" during the imprisonment scene towards the end of the film. "That was our little private jest."

The subject of *Freaks* was very much on my mind as we sat and talked about his early career in films. I asked him what sort of impact that film has had on his life, and he responded by telling me the later impact was far greater than when the film was made in 1932.

"When the film came out, it was like a serious crime had been committed by Tod Browning, and MGM instantly regretted the whole thing. Mr. Browning was a fine man and kind of a genius as a picture maker. Some felt he was overshadowed by the legend of Lon Chaney and could not be successful without having him in his corner. Chaney had died just a year or so before we did *Freaks*. The whole experience was unforgettable and very sad at the same time because many of the cast would only make that one film, and sometimes to have all that attention, being in the spotlight for weeks, and then have it taken away all at once, especially when we are told audiences ran screaming out of the theater and threw up!"

Angelo especially remembered the leading lady of *Freaks*, the Russian *prima donna*, Olga Baclanova. "She was introduced to us by Mr. Browning before the film started shooting, and you could see the fear in her eyes at first, and then something changed in her, because during the filming, she became like a protector to all of us, and the fear was changed into a kind of love. She really became fond of Prince Randian. She thought he had a beautiful face and never regarded him as a man with no arms or legs. He could do almost anything by using his mouth, like roll cigarettes or make small gifts out of matches. We all fell in love with her by the time filming was over. All this media attention I have been getting recently as the 'Master Blaster' [in *Mad Max: Beyond Thunderdome*] kind of reminded me of those days way back then, and in almost every interview I give nowadays, the subject of *Freaks* comes up, as it is now some kind of cinema masterpiece. I am just glad I've lived long enough to see it happen. All this praise would have made Mr. Browning so proud. Maybe somehow, in the great beyond, he knows."

I asked him about working with Cecil B. DeMille on *Sign of the Cross*. His response was one of genuine admiration. "DeMille was a no-nonsense director; he never treated anyone better than anyone else. He demanded respect on his sets at all times. DeMille loved to give speeches at the beginning of takes and sometimes played music to get the action going."

Angelo also recalled the most famous sequence where the Christians were thrown to the lions. "I was made up to look like a pygmy.

The whole set was wild with real lions and tigers. DeMille was always good to little people. We admired him, and he never talked down to any of us." The bigwigs at Paramount treated DeMille like a God; his word was law."

There was an abundance of memorabilia featuring both Karloff and Lugosi on display in my apartment, so it didn't take much effort to steer Angelo onto the subject of his relationship with those two icons of horror film.

"Lugosi was my mentor, you know. We worked at Monogram several times and I kind of became his mascot. I even did a magic show with him as his assistant. Bela always called me his 'lucky charm.' He told me in his early days as an actor in Hungary, it was a sign of the mystic for an actor to have a dwarf for a valet; it was supposed to bring luck. During our days at Monogram, Bela would always have a bottle or two of red wine imported from his native land at his disposal after a day's work, and we would toast each other as comrades. Bela was a very generous, thoughtful, and kind man. Karloff, on the other hand, was a cold fish and a real snob. I never felt anything from him other than he was a *star* and never let anyone forget it. Karloff would do a take and then disappear into his dressing room as if he was just too grand to be over there at Monogram. I would take Bela Lugosi any day over Karloff, a very overrated performer in my opinion."

At the time we were working on *The Offspring*, Angelo was enjoying his new-found celebrity from a recent appearance in the Mel Gibson blockbuster Mad Max film, *Beyond Thunderdome*, which he told me was a rough, grueling shoot, working in almost unbearable heat, especially for a little person over seventy-five years old and nearly blind. Angelo loved working with Tina Turner, "a great lady with more talent than she knows what to do with," and got on well with cast and crew, including *Thunderdome* star Mel Gibson.

It is interesting to recall in lieu of later events the way Angelo discussed Mel's alcohol intake on that picture. He told me, "Mel liked his booze perhaps a little too much for his own good, and the beer down there was very strong. I tried a couple of bottles of the stuff and it put me out cold. Mel drank all night and it began to show the next day. That stuff gave me such a hangover, and to spend the next day in that helmet on top of a giant's shoulders was so painful I never touched the stuff again the whole time I was down there. After a time, I had to call my agent to get out of there because the heat was killing me and I knew I would die on that picture if I had to remain any longer."

I could have spent hours more talking to Angelo about his life and especially the people he knew, but it was getting obvious that he had an appointment to keep, so I offered to drive him home. I had been told by people that knew him well that his apartment off Sixth Street near the County Museum was "scaled down" to accommodate his two-foot, nine-inch frame, and I became obsessed with the prospect of actually seeing it for myself. When I asked Angelo if I could see his place, he was very clear that that was not going to happen because he could not be sure if I wanted to make light of his living situation or not. His experience with outsiders had not been positive, so I had to respect his decision to keep his privacy. The drive over was a hoot because we talked all the way across town and I guess it seemed to anyone driving along side my car that I was quite mad talking to myself as no one could imagine I had "little Angie" seated across from me.

Once our film had come and gone, I saw Angelo from time to time at Junior's Deli in Westwood. He loved potato pancakes and Deli food in general. Angelo was also one of the co-founders of "Little People of America," along with Billy Barty, whom Angie could not stand and made no bones about it. "Billy Barty is so full of himself and thinks he is the greatest of all little people working in films. Well, is he in for a surprise."

Angelo was a real trouper, and it was sad to see him lose more and more freedom as his eyesight failed, and going out in public became less and less an option for him. Angelo spent his last days off Fairfax Avenue in the Shalom Nursing Home, and it was there in 1991 that he passed away. He was survived by two children that I know of, both daughters, one normal in size. The other worked as a stand–in for Herve Villichaize on *Fantasy Island*. As for me, I would like to think he died with the knowledge that he lived a remarkable life and would be remembered by a new generation of admiring fans, thanks to a film whose legend will not die: Tod Browning's masterpiece, *Freaks*.

Chapter 27
The Broken Doll

Johnny Eck

One of my most valued contacts for interviews during the 1980s in Hollywood was my friend and fellow author, Richard Lamparski, whose popular series of *Whatever Became Of?* books gave him almost unlimited access to a famous but forgotten collection of celebrities. I was privileged to contribute little bits of information, and he quoted me from time to time in the last three volumes.

It was Richard who first put me in touch with the unforgettable Johnny Eck, the second person from the amazing cast of *Freaks* that I would come to know on a more personal level.

John and Robert Eckhardt were twins who hailed from Baltimore, Maryland, the city best-known as the place where Edgar Allan Poe stepped off a train in a state of advanced delirium and collapsed right on the street, ultimately dying there, as well. Baltimore is also the home of one of my heroes, filmmaker John Waters, another "fan" of both *Freaks* and especially Johnny Eck.

Although the Eckhardt brothers were twins, Robert was a normal baby, but John was born without a bottom half to his torso. Legend has it that when the attending nurse saw the baby she exclaimed, "He looks like a broken doll," and with that rather poetic pronouncement, Johnny would spend the rest of his life being referred to off-and-on as "The only living half-boy" or "Nature's greatest mistake." John proved to be anything but those rude monikers, and in time, he became one of the most inspiring case studies of what a man can do if he puts his heart and soul into living and leaving little or no room for self-pity.

John Eckhardt became the character "Johnny Eck," as he discovered a talent for barnstorming and attracting a crowd through the circuit of sideshows with such showmen as Harry Blackstone, Sr. Johnny's brother, Robert, became his lifelong companion and protector until his death in 1991.

From all accounts, Johnny was very out-going and could do just about anything he set his mind to. He was a very handsome man in his youth, with great agility when it came to walking on his hands. Johnny was also a gifted painter and perfected the art of painting on window screens in his own home and for special friends. His staggering disability was never an obstacle in his mind. Just look at his accomplishments: he traveled and learned so much from the world around him and was able to do more than most regular people could ever hope to achieve with all the advantages they take for granted.

Richard Lamparski had given me Johnny's home address, and I sent him a photograph from *Freaks*, which he sent back with a letter on his personal stationary that was designed by none other than the great Robert Crumb. After a bit of correspondence, he gave me his phone number, and we had at least two long conversations that seemed to give him the pleasure of having someone to talk to who admired his work.

The first thing he told me about the filming of *Freaks* was his lifelong admiration for director Tod Browning, who he felt really understood the sideshow performer and his lifestyle from firsthand experience. Johnny said that if the film had become a success, Browning had plans to star Johnny in his own feature, perhaps even his own life story, but in 1932, public reaction to the film was a real blow. He said, "It made us all feel like we had disgraced our own kind in the eyes of the world."

His memories of working on the film were almost all happy ones, and it seemed to me like that film was the number one highlight of his life. I was glad that he had survived to see the reversal of opinion regarding *Freaks* and enjoy some measure of fame because of it. Johnny was thrilled that people wanted his autograph and collected his pictures. He was introduced by mail to dozens of fans, some of whom even made sculptures of him from his sideshow days, as well as from the film.

Johnny confirmed what Angelo Rossitto had told me regarding Olga Baclanova. He was indeed in love with her. "She was a goddess," Johnny said, "and seemed to become more relaxed with our 'little company' as the shooting went on until we all felt like we were living in a separate reality from life as it was before the film. We were like a family: we ate together and studied our parts as a unit on the MGM lot, and Tod Browning was our protector and advisor. When the filming was over and the negative fallout hit, it was like the rug being pulled out from under us."

I was pleased to hear that Johnny and his brother had opened their house in Baltimore for friends and fans to come over and see his artwork first-hand. He was very proud of the window screens that decorated his home. Johnny also had his own darkroom for developing his pictures. There seemed no end to his talents. However, all that was about to change, when Johnny, then elderly, and his brother were victims of a violent home invasion/burglary that left him traumatized because one of the attackers used him as a "pillow" by sitting on him, during which time they vandalized and stole anything of value in the house and destroyed anything they thought was unsuitable to resell. They even played "catch," using the terrified Johnny as a ball! Later, he would say he was lucky to still be alive, for he thought it was his last day on earth.

That incident left them forever housebound and fearful; never again would they allow strangers into their home, and the socializing that made them so happy came to an abrupt end.

A close friend, Zan Turner, sent flyers all around the country asking for donations to help the brothers, since the robbery left them with very little in the way of assets, and work was no longer possible for them because of age and illnesses.

Johnny Eck never fully recovered from that experience and died in 1991. His brother, Robert, passed away in 1995. Like Angelo Rossitto, Johnny died knowing that he had been a part of something special, achieving the kind of immortality only the cinema can bestow, thanks to Tod Browning and the legacy of the phenomenon known as *Freaks*.

Chapter 28
Herve Sheds His tattoo
Herve Villechaize

My last encounter with the "little people" in show-biz involved a day trip up in the Goodyear Blimp, a very ill-advised photo session with Herve Villechaize and his then-wife, Donna, both of whom were aboard the blimp for the duration. Herve was still working on *Fantasy Island,* earning a cool $25,000 per episode, and he had recently purchased a comfortable ranch in the valley, complete with horses. At just under four feet in height, he had married a tall, lanky lady who was almost six-feet without heels, and who, until recently, had worked as a stand-in on the aforementioned TV show, where she met and won the heart of "Tattoo."

Christopher Lee had worked with Herve in his first breakthrough role in *The Man with the Golden Gun,* a James Bond film with Roger Moore, and he found the diminutive actor to be "surprisingly worldly and sophisticated with great taste in brandy and women, the perfect combination for a James Bond character." Christopher found himself, much like Bela Lugosi, working on occasion with "little people" in some of his horror films, and he knew that the best approach was, of course, to treat them as any other actor in the company; any other way was out of the question.

When Herve and I first met face to face, we had two mutual friends in common that he had worked with in a film years before called *Seizure* (1974), which introduced Oliver Stone to the world of feature films. That film was made in Canada and starred Jonathan Frid, right after his *Dark Shadows* success that ever-so-briefly put him on the cover of *Tiger Beat* as a teen heartthrob right along with Bobby Sherman and The Monkees. The original title of the film was *Queen of Evil,* however both Oliver and Jonathan agreed that the marquee value of "Jonathan Frid in *Queen of Evil*" just might send out the wrong message. They finally settled on *Seizure,* with Martine Beswicke as the Queen, and future cult queen Mary Woronov had a small but showy role playing her usual tough broad routine against a bomber cast of veteran stage and film actors. There were a lot of queens in that film, believe you me.

Seizure would have been a sleeper hit if they had just left the cameras on the cast and crew at night, rather than to even attempt to make sense out of the contrived screenplay about a horror writer at odds with figments from his imagination that came to life on a country estate. Herve played the role of Spider, the nightmarish servant of the Queen of Evil, and he had a field day with those two camp ladies, who allowed him to play the stud, if only in fantasy terms. Herve was very attracted to both Mary and Martine. Both women, besides being friends, knew exactly how to handle Herve and would take turns allowing him to sit on their laps while he made his advances clear. They never said no; they just waited to see how far he thought he would get with two Amazon women experienced in martial arts. Mary knew how to listen, and Herve opened his heart to her. They became soul mates from that time until his death. She also allowed Herve to take some really wild photos of her in the nude, which Mary and I used at one of the autograph shows in 1995.

The problems during the filming of *Seizure* are legendary, since Oliver Stone was working on location in a run down mansion that also acted as a hotel for cast and crew. Martine arrived on set directly from Europe and acted as den mother, while juggling affairs with both director Oliver Stone and the sound man, who was an alcoholic with an addiction that was ruining the film. Martine became his lady for the duration, and her passion kept him off the bottle until the film wrapped. Mary's character is killed off midway into the shoot, but the bond she bridged with Herve remained strong long after the film wrapped, even though the film quickly disappeared after a short run in theaters. *Seizure* is now available on DVD and has established itself as a cult film of sorts, not only as one of Stone's first directorial attempts, but also for its amazing cast of characters. Troy Donahue had a small part in the film, as well, and both Mary and Martine could barely make out what the former heartthrob had to say both on and off-screen.

Martine and Mary both realized at once that Herve was a real man in every way, and in his younger days, had been quite a womanizer in the European tradition. The worst thing you could do with him was to threat him like a doll or anything less than what he was: a man. One of the nightmarish situations Herve found himself in while doing the *Fantasy Island* series were the set visits from guests with children, some of whom were teenagers. They thought nothing of picking up the pint-size actor like a football, and security had to always be on the lookout for any roughhouse antics of that sort. His ego was so fragile that even with a paycheck of $25,000 an episode, he began a long and painful decline into the bottle.

Back on the Goodyear Blimp: we all prepared to board the small cabin under the blimp in order to fly over Los Angeles and shoot photos for *Playboy*. There were about three other models with us for atmosphere, and there was a full bar. At first, that looked like it was going to be fun, but once we were up among the clouds, Herve began to drink. He got upset with me because I accidentally brushed his head with my hand while reaching for a cocktail, so he went off about me trying to pat him on the head like a child. As if things could not get any worse, fuelled by booze, he and Donna went at it for all to see and hear.

It was painful to see that fragile little man so blinded by love that he just let her destroy his peace of mind. She behaved like a woman bored with her current situation. For the duration of the flight, she stared out the window and ignored Herve's attempts at conversation. It was painful to observe. Donna stayed married to Herve for exactly one year to the day before filing for divorce so she would receive the maximum in California for community property. Herve did not even fight back, so he lost most of his savings and his beloved ranch to that "witch from Hell," as one of Herve's friends described her after his death.

That afternoon mercifully ended as soon as we landed back on *terra-firma*, and I never saw him again. It took only a few more years before he had had enough and propped a shotgun up against his chest, blowing his brains out in his truck in 1993. Mary had spoken with Herve a few days before his death and knew something was not right with him. "His attitude was negative and he was now in pain every day, as his organs grew in a body too small to accommodate them, so he was on a lot of painkillers, which the drinking only made worse."

Herve Villechaize was a unique performer with a sense of style and humor that entertained millions of fans on television with the iconic *Fantasy Island*. He would have gone on to more work in films and television had he not been in such physical and mental pain. Herve began his career as a painter and displayed real promise. However, if art had been his muse rather than acting, he would have suffered in any case, because he had an artist's disposition and was too much in awe of beauty not to have it in his life. For one so disabled, that meant rejection and heartache were ever-present.

I always think of the John Huston film, *Moulin Rouge,* when I remember Herve. The similarities are obvious, in particular the death scene, when Henri de Toulouse-Lautrec is brought back to his family estate to die. The moment arrives when he sees the best parts of a life lived in rejection and despair, because he touched so many with his art. So it was with Herve Villechaize.

Chapter 29

In the Name of Hellfire and Blood

Ferdy Mayne

Whenever I am pressed to make a choice as to which actor in the history of movies gave the best performance playing a vampire, my answer is simple: Bela Lugosi. Lugosi *is* Dracula in thought, word, and deed. He gave the Devil his soul the moment he stepped before the cameras over at Universal in 1930, and he is quite beyond criticism because he *owns* the role of Count Dracula and always will, regardless of whoever assumes the mantle as time goes by.

Having said that, I will also say that of all the actors who ever played a vampire after Lugosi, the greatest performance definitely belongs to Ferdy Mayne for his magnificent turn as Count Von Krolock in Roman Polanski's *Dance of the Vampires*. That masterpiece is overdue for recognition by film critics, yet fans always knew that was a very special film in the history of the genre.

I first saw the film at a drive-in under the title *The Fearless Vampire Killers, or Pardon Me, but Your Teeth Are In My Neck*. That version was cut and re-dubbed, however that was all yet to be discovered. Even in the bastardized form, the magic was still there in Douglas Slocome's superb compositions, the enchanting score from longtime Polanski composer Krzysztof Komeda, (which was unforgettable), and, of course, the performances that were hand-picked to perfection under the direction of Polanski. That film is now restored on DVD to the version Polanski meant for people to see, and the film is now rightfully regarded as a classic.

I loved this film for years before finally meeting the actor who played the master vampire, Count Von Krolock. The timing could never have been better, since I was at the time living in Beverly Hills and working in the business. I was still very much a monster kid at heart, when Ferdy Mayne was horror royalty, and attention was going to be paid if I had anything to do with it. I had been at a dinner party at the home of Marion Rosenberg, a powerful producer, who had already done dozens of films including *X, Y and Zee* with Elizabeth Taylor and Michael Caine, *Where Eagles Dare* with Richard Burton and Clint Eastwood, along with *The Walking Stick* starring Samantha Eggar, one of those little British sleepers that very few ever see (unless say you are reviewing films for *Films and Filming,* as I was at the time). The last two films also had the distinction of having Ferdy Mayne in small but showy parts, none of which gave him the majesty Polanski did for that one and only moment of time in the actor's life, when personality and performance became one.

Marion knew just about everybody worth knowing in show business, so try and imagine just how funny it was for her to be asked if she knew Ferdy Mayne, and would an introduction be at all possible.

Marion laughed and laughed, saying to me, "My dear boy, Ferdy will be over the moon to meet someone like you that knows his film and has such respect. You must know, of course, that he feels exactly the same about that film, so you two have to meet—that is all there is to it."

Within twenty-four hours, my phone rang, and when I picked up the receiver, I heard this unmistakable voice on the other end say, "Mr. Del Valle? This is Ferdinand Mayne. I believe you wanted to speak with me."

Did I ever! With that, we arranged a time and, of course, the place was mine. I invited him for cocktails at seven o'clock that evening. Then, he asked if I would mind if he brought someone. I told him that as far as I was concerned he could bring as many people as he liked. He laughed that deep wonderful laugh I would come to know so well and replied, "Oh, one will do. I would like to bring my lady if that is alright," and so we were on for drinks at seven at my place.

Ferdinand Philip Mayer-Horckel arrived at my front door on time and with a striking blond about half his age named Jan. She was, he told me, a make-up artist, and they were a couple. Ferdy wore a tailored, dark blue jacket with a hand-made yellow silk shirt, and a red ascot finished the picture. Ferdy wore a monocle around his neck and knew just when to put it in his eye for the right effect. That was just great, and he was everything I knew he would be: a class act and a gentleman of the old school, as well.

I had iced some Champagne to mark the occasion, and his lady had rolled some joints for us to smoke. Before she could say a word, Ferdy looked over in my direction and said, "Sometimes I will have a puff or two for color." Oh my God, I was not only meeting my idol for the first time, but I was about to get high with him, as well—something that never happened with Christopher Lee!

I had also invited my best friend, Peter, from my days in Sacramento, who also loved the film and Ferdy just as much as I did. In fact, he managed to get a 16mm print of *Fearless* in scope six months after it played in theaters. We knew that film backwards and forwards, so much so that after a few glasses of bubbly, we stood in front of him and did his dialogue from the film verbatim. Ferdy was genuinely moved so much so that he asked us to do it once more. As Ferdy said later, "It was like hearing poetry, and what an honor to be so remembered." In other words, it was love at first sight.

At that time, Ferdy was going back and forth from the flat in London that had been his for decades, off the old Brompton Road and a series of houses and apartments in and around Beverly Hills. Ferdy lived off Mullholland Drive in a leased flat belonging to his long time friend, director Gabrelle Beaumont, whom he always referred to as "Gay Beaumont." That was a very comfortable place except for the parking, which was wicked. One late afternoon, he went for a stroll down the lane, where he ran into a neighbor who, without knowing who he was, told him that way back in 1969 the killers of Sharon Tate washed the blood off their hands in the pond by the fence. That, of course, just creeped him out, since Ferdy had been in living Europe when the Manson killings took place. To discover that he was living so close to it all was nightmarish to say the least. Ferdy never liked to discuss his relationship with Sharon, since he had grown quite fond of her, as had most of the cast and crew during the filming of *Vampires*. "Sharon was a very kind and sweet person in life and, of course, Roman adored her, and that was obvious from the first day of filming."

Not too long after the Polanski film, Ferdy had made another vampire film for cameraman-turned-director Freddie Francis. It was shot in Germany under the title *The Vampire Happening*. That film tried to capture the same spark that made Polanski's film a classic, but it missed the mark entirely.

That film had no humor or charm and very little sex, so there would have been no reason to bother seeing it except for Ferdy's star turn, that time as Count Dracula (or rather, a parody of the master vampire). His part was played for broad laughs including the unlikely sight of seeing Dracula with his pants down after a night of bawdy bloodsucking. He tells a young girl "something has come up" as he unpeels a banana. I mean, really! He does get to fly away in a helicopter made especially for Dracula. If you must watch the film "for color," as Ferdy said, just watch the last half and catch Ferdy's remark about Christopher Lee. No one will stop you.

The leading lady in the film, Pia Degermark, had been quite the star and jet-setter before and after filming, since she had once played the title role in the classic *Elvira Madigan,* and then married a millionaire playboy only to lose everything in the end to drugs and drink. Pia actually wound up going to prison for awhile, but then she became clean and sober, a sadder but wiser girl, no doubt. Ferdy always wondered what it was about his vampire films that seem to curse the leading ladies.

I had been following his career ever since the Polanski film, as well as after we had become friends. At the time we met, I was doing a column for John Russell Taylor's *Films and Filming* magazine out of the UK, so I was able to be in London at least twice a year. I got to know not only Ferdy but his two beautiful daughters, Belinda, who was following her dad's lead into acting, while his other daughter, Fernanda, chose to raise a family. Good choice, since it turned out that she seemed happy and content with her life.

There are not many actors that one could forge such a friendship with, and Ferdy certainly did not suffer fools gladly, so I counted myself blessed to have him in my corner. I was still trying to act as an actor's agent when I first met him, and had just lost my own agency in a year-long commercial strike. Ferdy being Ferdy was always arranging meetings with other agents and businessmen in hopes of helping me get back in the game. However, I was writing more and more, and in time, I decided to work as a journalist and leave artist representation to Sue Mengers and her kind.

Ferdy loved shirts and collected them as kind of a hobby. He had dozens of beautiful handmade shirts, and just needed more hours in the day to wear them all. After awhile, he moved out of Gay Beaumont's flat and bought a condo right around the corner from the place where I lived for twenty-five years, at the corner of Oakhurst and Beverly. Ferdy bought a condo, which was about eight floors up in a high rise building on Doheny Drive. At that time in his life, he was working more than ever in both television and movies. I am so pleased to have known him during that stage of his life because he loved what he was doing so much. Belinda was also working at that same time and getting bigger and bigger parts in films such as *Krull* and *Lassiter* with Tom Selleck. Ferdy took out wonderful full-page ads when he was in such demand. One that I still have from *The Hollywood Reporter* has two handsome portraits, one of him, and the other as Ben Ishak in Francis Ford Coppola's *Return of the Black Stallion*. That film was special for Ferdy, since he went on location for it and sent me postcards that described him as "feeling ten feet tall walking around this ancient city as the star of a Coppola production."

Ferdy had such elegance in his appearance in private life. I can still see him, always natty in bright colors and wearing his beloved monocle around his neck, enjoying the attention he seemed to create wherever he went. Ferdy loved women and was always in pursuit when opportunity presented itself.

He was gone quite a bit during the 1980s doing the Dan Curtis miniseries, *Winds of War,* playing Herr Rosenthal, a part my friend, Barbara Steele, suggested him for after meeting Ferdy during a casting call. Ferdy always referred to Barbara as "Miss Cheekbones." He was always grateful to be employed and especially in such a project as that one with almost every working actor in Britain playing one part or another.

I have one very special memory with Ferdy and that was our time together on the film, *The Horror Star,* also known as *Frightmare.* That could have been a classic little sleeper of a horror film if the script had paid more attention to details and actually tried to be a black comedy about the picture business—especially the horror film picture business—since it was being done in Hollywood at the very moment we were shooting our epic of terror. The director, Norman Thaddeus Vane, was a real piece of work in his own right. He had worked in England for years trying to get projects off and running, and sometimes he actually did succeed. Norman wrote the occult Indian thriller, *Shadow of the Hawk,* with Jan Michael Vincent and Chief Dan George. *The Horror Star* seemed to be written for Ferdy because he was a veteran of the genre, having even done a Hammer film (*The Vampire Lovers*), so he had the right persona to play Conrad Ratzoff, horror star. Norman could never raise the bar beyond luring a bunch of teenagers into a haunted house and then killing them off one by one, which is a formula we just don't need to see anymore of, and that was 1985 already.

One of the things Ferdy liked about the film was the food. Norman had a Thai cook for the first week or so of the shoot, and that made up for the dry ice and fog that smelled just like Black Flag insect spray. One night, we were filming in a Chinese cemetery, when one of the owners offered to let Norman film a real cremation the next morning, which, of course, was illegal. If you ever find yourself watching that little epic, do check out the cremation scene and wonder just which poor Chinese soul was going up the chimney at the time! Nita Talbot, who was a real pro at playing Ferdy's wife in the picture, really went off on Norman one day after her death scene that involved Ferdy killing her by stuffing a wad of real money in her mouth until she choked to death. What Norman did not take into account was the fact that money—real money—is filled with germs and you must never put paper money into your mouth. Nita was going to see her doctor about getting a shot for tetanus, and then she was going to see her lawyer after that. Norman had to really put on the charm to get out of that one, but he finally calmed the lady back into his good graces, if only for a moment.

Jeffery Combs was in the film, which might just have been his first picture, and he was already showing signs of playing in horror films. I told him he reminded me of Colin Clive, who played Dr. Frankenstein in the Boris Karloff 1931 classic. A few years down the road, Jeff became world-famous as the *Re-Animator* for Stuart Gordon. *The*

Horror Star was great fun to make, but nobody really expected too much out of it. Today, the film enjoys an afterlife as a video rental with a bit of a cult following, perhaps thanks to Ferdy's presence in it. I actually made it into a scene as a mourner at the funeral of Conrad Ratzoff. Norman was a real hoot and definitely worthy of a "Lost Horizon" of his own one day, since he went on to make the truly awful film, *Club Life,* based (although you would never know it) on Studio One in West Hollywood, and written from a treatment by Bleu McKensey, the bouncer at the club, but that is another story.

A must-do with personalities like Ferdy was, when the opportunity presented itself, to take him up to Griffith Park to meet the greatest fan of them all—Forrest J Ackerman—and that is just what I did one fine Friday evening. Ferdy and Belinda went with me to meet the most famous monster in his Ackermansion (as he liked to call it) on Glendower below the Frank Lloyd Wright house near Griffith Observatory. Forry met Count Von Krolock on his own terms: dressed in one of Bela Lugosi's own capes. After a few photos, Forry had Ferdy sign his special first edition of Bram Stoker's *Dracula,* which had been signed previously by every Vampire actor on earth. (That edition was auctioned off in Hollywood following the death of Forry in late 2008.) Belinda wore a monster mask and had no clue why we would do that ritual, and yet she gave it her all regardless, trooper that she was and is.

Ferdy was always such a good sport at things like that. He also showed grace under pressure, when he received an award from Dr. Donald A. Reed from the Academy of Science Fiction, which, like most awards in town, meant absolutely nothing in the grand scheme of things, yet it was always nice to be honored for your work regardless of the idiot giving out the statue (in this case, the presenter was dressed as Count Dracula). Ferdy wore his tux and used his monocle to great effect. The next day, he ran a full-page ad in *Variety* thanking the good doctor for the award.

Ferdy was doing a series of appearances on the award-winning show, *Cagney and Lacy,* playing a charming rogue named Albert Grand. We all felt that was spin-off material, so my Partner Chris, who worked for a law firm, and I decided to send the network an avalanche of fan mail requesting the return of Albert Grand. It worked at least for a season; Ferdy was brought back for three appearances that year. Our gesture moved Ferdy once again, and I must tell you that he was worth it. There aren't many actors I would do that for, but Ferdy was always tops in his field.

In my opinion, Ferdy should have had the career that Christopher Lee or Peter Cushing had for a time at Hammer Films. His range was similar, and he certainly had the look for those costume horrors like his fellow actor and mate, Michael Gough, who made his own share of mad doctors and maniacs on both sides of the pond. During the filming of the sequel to *The Howling,* Ferdy was cast as a werewolf, while Christopher Lee played the monster slayer. At the time, Lee was ill, so he basically walked though the cheesy special-effects in a daze. That was the only moment I can recall where Ferdy wished he had played that part himself. "I could really have made that part shine if they had given me a chance." Well, as much as I would have given it to him were it my place to do so, having seen almost every aspect of that production, not even Ferdinand Mayne could have made much of a difference one way or another.

It was very rewarding for me to meet some of Ferdy's friends, especially his fellow actors. Some had already passed away, and so Ferdy told me about the ones that left their mark on his life and career.

John Le Mesurier may not be a household word, but one look at his face and, if you ever watched British cinema, you would know him straight away. John usually played butlers or shady lawyers and he possessed a canny sense of humor. When he knew he was about to die, for example, he had his wife, Joan, place a notice in the press saying, "John Le Mesurier has finally conked off, missing his loved ones very much." Ferdy and John went way back as mates in show business. They even perfected little bits of business while on camera that stayed with them throughout their careers. In the film, *The Baby and the Battleship* (1956), Ferdy played a character that places a medal on John's jacket during a shipboard drill. Every time John did something or spoke, Ferdy would pin another medal on him. That caught on, and they used the bit over and over in different films. Ferdy even did it in *The Vampire Happening* when Dracula gives medals to his followers.

Once when I was visiting London and Ferdy was away filming, he left word for me to have lunch with another character actor that worked for years in British films, yet you could never remember his name: Brian Coleman. Brian and his lovely wife had me over to their flat for lunch, and we spent the whole afternoon looking through his scrapbook at the films he made with stars like Rex Harrison and Alec Guinness. At one point, Brian showed me a shot of him in armor with Michael Gough, well-known as the butler, Alfred, in the Batman series. I told Brian I was just with him doing an interview over at the Haymarket. As I was about to leave, I mentioned the actor, Dennis

Price, asking if he ever worked with him. Both he and his wife gave me a very odd double-take, and then Brian said, "Dennis used to rent the flat below, and my dear, what tales me and the wife could tell you! But our time is all used up for now. Poor old Dennis. We used to almost fall over the empty Guinness crates he would leave by his doorstep. Dennis could certainly pack it in, couldn't he, dear?"

I was so sorry they did not have more time, since that was a story I would have liked to have heard. I felt like there were just too many gaps in my education regarding British Cinema; so many of the films Brian had worked on were unknown to me. Of course, Ferdy knew them all, since he was there making them right alongside those men.

When I got back to United States, I was at a screening of the Bob Hoskins film, *Mona Lisa,* which was about the London underworld of prostitution. There in a seedy peep show, stark naked with a black hooker, was Brian Coleman as dirty an old geezer as you were ever likely to meet, and all I could do was turn to my guest and say, "You know, I just had lunch with him the other day in London."

One actor that went back a ways with Ferdy and was not so well-remembered was David Tomlinson, who is known in the United States for playing in the Disney films, *Mary Poppins* and *Bedknobs and Broomsticks.* It seemed that David was working with Ferdy in a play years ago, when they both heard a joke that was so funny it nearly killed them with laughter. David never forgot the experience, and one day when both of them went up for the same part, David told that joke to Ferdy and the result was that Ferdy got such a case of the giggles that he lost the job. David, according to Ferdy, was a terrible man with few friends in the theater, because all he seemed to care about was his own career and did whatever it took to further it. Ferdy was what his mates in the profession called a "jobbing actor," which meant that he looked for parts, and when he got them, did his best and then moved on to the next one with little or no fanfare. Ferdy was much-loved by his peers, and after fifteen years of friendship, I knew why.

Since it was Roman Polanski that brought us together in the first place, I wondered if Ferdy would ever be asked to work with Polanski again after the Manson murders and his exile from the United States after his rape trial in Los Angeles. My question was answered one afternoon at Ferdy's flat. A telegram arrived from Paris asking if Ferdy was free to work the following summer on location in Tunisia on a project to be called *Pirates*. Excitement was at a maximum level, when Ferdy realized he would be reunited with his favorite director in a film with ten times the budget of the 1968 vampire film.

Ferdy, of course, knew what had passed over the years with Roman, but remained confidant that he was still the director he remembered him to be. Off he went to the location, far off from the mainland, where the studio had built Roman a gigantic set with a full-scale, carefully detailed ship. Ferdy was to play the captain of a ship about to be hijacked by Walter Matthau and his pirates.

The first thing to go south apparently was the rapport between Roman and Walter, who was a bit too old to be hanging from the rafters at that point in his long career. I had given Ferdy a couple of vampire stills to have Roman sign as a keepsake from our bonding film of yore. I received several postcards while Ferdy was on the film and almost all of them were dire in describing what daily life was like on a pirate flick of that scale.

Apparently, Roman was not even remotely the same man Ferdy remembered working with years before. Polanski was out to prove just how constantly virile he was. Girls were flown in by the dozen, and Roman was so fogged out by the time daylight arrived that he was a total monster on the set. At one point, it looked like he was going to explode from pressure during a morning workout with his personal trainer. He had dislocated his back to the point of walking sideways like a limbo dancer. According to Ferdy, that was the only time that Roman was civil to people and behaved a bit more like his old self. During that period, Ferdy made Roman sign my photos, but even that was a nightmare since Ferdy had to explain, "Look Roman, this is a dear friend who worships this film. You must sign these as a personal favor for me." I will always love Ferdy for the lengths he went out of friendship to acquire those for me.

When the film was about to come out, Ferdy arranged for me to see a sneak preview in Long Beach with no press allowed. I was able to see, perhaps for the only time, the nearly three-hour cut of Roman's film. Ferdy had a nice cameo with some inspired bits of business as the captain of a doomed ship at sea. The film was so disappointing because broad comedy was just not Roman's forte, and the critics thought so, as well. I was parked a car away from Walter Matthau's limo and could hear him yelling at one of his people to "get that goddamn Polack on the phone!" Hollywood babbles on . . . .

Ferdy would work throughout Europe for the better part of the next two decades until near the end of the 1990s. Ferdy began to slow down a bit, and he was in residence in his Doheny condo more and more. I went up for tea or just to visit and have a gossip, but by then,

Belinda was staying there off and on, so he was never really alone, and I lived just around the corner. One of Ferdy's lifelong friends was actor Herbert Lom, a character star of long standing and one of the nicest in the business. One evening, I took the two of them for a screening at the Academy of Motion Pictures over on Wilshire to see—of all things—*Broadway Danny Rose*, the new Woody Allen film. There is nothing to compare with two fussy character actors out on the town. Both men having seen it all, not to mention a lot of it together, walking arm and arm down the street saying things like, "Oh, Ferdy, put your coat on, not around you, it makes you look like a *haus frau.*" After the screening, we all returned to my place, whereupon Herbert went in my bathroom only to emerge asking, "David, I take it we have met somewhere before?" He had seen a photo in my bathroom that was autographed to me from him in Helmut Berger's *Dorian Gray*. I quickly explained that he sent me that through a writer friend of mine long before we met. Herbert seemed amused by my fan-like ways, and we said no more about it. One month later, I received a package in the mail from Herbert: in it was a beautiful, original poster of him as *The Phantom of the Opera,* and it was signed to me. I still have it to this day.

The last couple of years prior to 1997 were difficult for Ferdy. His health began taking a turn for the worse, yet he still was able to get around, though not enough to act in anything, which was driving him up the wall. One afternoon, he came by with the news that the Goethe-Institute of Los Angeles was planning to honor him with a special evening on September 26, 1996, just two days after my own birthday,)which Ferdy honored by singing Happy Birthday to me over the phone). I received a formal invitation from the Institute a few days later. They were giving him a reception followed by a screening of—what else?—*The Fearless Vampire Killers*. He called to make sure I would be there, or as he put it, "Let's celebrate the film that brought us together in friendship."

I received another letter canceling the event about five days before the tribute due to the sudden illness of the guest of honor. My heart went out to him, since I knew how much he was looking forward to it. I was also honored that they ran a quote from me on the tribute page from my review of the DVD of *The Fearless Vampire Killers* in which Ferdy had said it was the greatest review of his life. I stayed in touch, but was not allowed to see him since he was bedridden and had no energy to see anyone but his doctor and Belinda.

The next thing I was told was that he was being moved to a hospital for observation, and then he was flown back to London, where his family placed him in a private sanitarium in the country, one of those stately homes that had been renovated into a nursing facility. Ferdy remained there for six months. One morning in early 1997, I received a call from his daughter, Fernanda, telling me what I did not want to hear: that our beloved Ferdy had died.

She went on to tell me that he simply gave up and chose to die rather than live his life sitting on a lawn with no pretty girls to look at and no particular place to wear his fancy shirts. Ferdy Mayne lived a wonderful life with many people that were touched by his spirit and talent to entertain, yet in his own mind, Ferdy never reached the heights he knew he was capable of reaching, and that, of course, was his Lost Horizon. Yet for those of us who were privileged to know him, his vistas were glorious to behold, and I, for one, shall never forget him.

In *Richard II,* Shakespeare had an actor ask, "Is not the king's name twenty thousand names?" And yet that player knew, as every actor that came after him knew, it was the actor—not the monarch—who enjoyed twenty thousand names. Few men can have enjoyed more roles than the man we honor, Ferdy Mayne. His career glimmers with performances that will be recalled as long as movies are screened and beyond.

Chapter 30
I'm Wild Again

Francis Faye

I thought it was about time I exposed my readers to the wildly intoxicating talent of Frances Faye. Her legend is ever-growing among devotees of the lost era of nightclubs, especially the jazz showcases of New Orleans. In 1977, I was one of those fans, and I was privileged to see her perform in person at the Studio One Backlot Theatre, the hottest nightspot in Los Angeles. I also saw legends such as Eartha Kitt and Barbara Cook perform their nightclub acts that only devotees on the east coast usually got to savor and enjoy. At some defining point that year, a TV movie-of-the-week entitled *Alexander: The Other Side of Dawn* was filming in and around West Hollywood using the infamous gay cabaret in their story line, and I, for one, will always be grateful that they included the then-current act featuring the staggering Frances Faye and the "Live If You Can Take It" revue. It is worth renting that rather tired soap opera involving a small town hunk arriving in Hollywood on a Greyhound bus and— guess what?—selling his ass on Hollywood Boulevard before finding true love with a small town girl who also happens to be a hooker (the "Dawn" character we are on the other side of . . . I told you it was a movie-of-the-week).

Director John Erman allowed me to be part of the working audience while they were filming, and Francis was up there banging madly away on her piano, when it was brought to her attention that Tab Hunter was in the audience. Without missing a beat, she launched into her version of "Red Sails in the Sunset," a tune once recorded by Tab in his teen idol period.

Frances was held in a state of awe by the waiters and busboys of the club for an incident that occurred during that run when, overcome with way too many hits of coke, she passed out over the keyboards. Before paramedics could be summoned, she came out of it and started singing right where she left off . . . talk about being professional! She was one of a kind. Frances had been a world-famous, best-kept-secret for the last half of the twentieth century, but I was quite a late bloomer to being hip to her wild scene. That woman, who inspired Peter Allen to be a performer, was an influence on most of the musical talent of the last five decades, including The Beatles, Judy Garland, and Sammy Davis Jr., not to mention Bette Midler. They all saw Frances perform, and she blew their minds.

Frances was pro-gay before anyone knew or cared to know what gay meant. All the jazz greats lined up to work with her, such was her reputation. After I saw her act there at the Studio One Backlot Theatre (and I mean I saw *every* performance), the great French director, Louis Malle, and his designer, Polly Platt (the former Mrs. Peter Bogdonovich), came to see Francis, and soon after cast her in his film, *Pretty Baby* (1978) in a pivotal role as the coke-snorting madam who first places child prostitute Brooke Shields up for sale.

My old friend and former client, Barbara Steele, had given the *Storyville* novel, on which the film is based, to Malle as a possible film project years before when she was involved with Louis romantically. Barbara was rewarded with a small role in the film. Barbara first told me of the wild nights at the old St. Charles Hotel in New Orleans where the film company was quartered. She was well into her seventies, and with her girlfriend in tow, held court in her hotel suite that was filled to the rafters with musicians and crew doing bags of coke. She yelled "Eat my pussy!" at the top of her lungs, and the divine Faye could not have care less what other people thought of her.

Barbara fondly remembered her first encounter with the diva. "I can't tell you how many times I had to remove Francis's hand from my leg, as she always made a passes at me, and listen, I was flattered, but still, she was older than my grandmother."

When the film was done and Barbara returned to Los Angeles, we all went back to the Studio One Backlot Theatre to see her again.

There is just no way to capture the party-like atmosphere she could create. She took a lifetime of songs and broke them down into cues for her own amusement. For example, Francis would begin "Up the Lazy River" and then go into "Besume Mucho," while making cracks like, "This song is dedicated to Johnny Mathis, wherever *she* is." She began Nat King Cole's "Mona Lisa" saying, "Mona Lisa, Mona Lisa, men have laid you." Then there was "Bewitched, Bothered, and Bea Arthur," or changing a tune from Lionel Barts' *Oliver* to "As Long as *She* Needs Me," a decidedly lesbian take on the familiar melody. It seemed that Francis was also a groundbreaker for never backing away from her bisexuality, even in the 1940s. Her candor may have cost her mainstream immortality, but she deserves her place in the sun as a truly one-of-a-kind entertainer.

It pains me to think she might be forgotten. We still remember Mae West and Sophie Tucker, and believe me when I say that Francis was every bit as great as those ladies. A number of her recordings have made it to CD, so please check out this fabulous entertainer for your own edification. Also you must go, go, go to the fabulous new website dedicated to her at www.tyleralpern.com/francisfaye.html. This is one of the most comprehensive websites I have seen so far and, as Frances would say, "It's *wild*! Log on ASAP."

I will close by quoting the lady: "When you're pretty, it doesn't matter how you fix your hair." Remember, if you ever watch the infamous Ed Wood's *Plan Nine From Outer Space* again, watch for the saucer flying by a nightclub in Hollywood and check out who is headlining the joint: Frances Faye. She's gay, gay, gay. Is there any other way?

Photographs

Vincent Price creeps up on an unsuspecting
Elisabeth Shepherd in character as "the Lady Ligeia."

John LaZar as "Superwoman/Z-Man Barzell examining his "breasts"
designed by John Chambers for Beyond the Valley of the Dolls.

Hiram Keller as seen by Fellini in 1969.

Hiram Keller as Anne Rice's vampire, Lestat, photographed
by Steven Arnold for a Paramount screen test.

Helmut Berger as "Martin" in Visconti's The Damned,
performing homage to Marlene Dietrich.

Helmut Berger out of drag and into drugs in The Damned.

Terry Southern in shades with David Del Valle
in his Beverly Hills Apartment.

Timothy Leary with his inscription to David Del Valle,
"We sure got high, Honey!"

Calvin Lockhart with Rex Reed in Mike Sarne's *Myra Breckenridge,*
the other side of midnight, for real.

Russ Meyer directs John LaZar and Michael Blodgett in the infamous
beheading scene from *Beyond the Valley of the Dolls*.

Florence Marley at dinner in Hollywood in 1946.
Her date for the evening is Vincent Price.

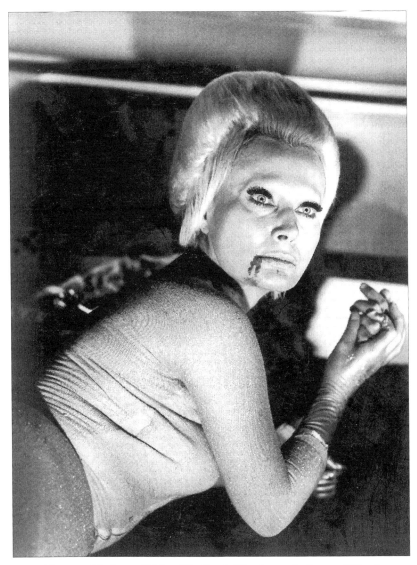

Florence Marley as "Velena" in Curtis Harrington's *Queen of Blood*.

Hermione Baddeley and David Del Valle
photographed in her Hollywood Hills Home in 1980.

Hermione Baddeley at David Del Valle's Christmas party in 1978.

Composer Les Baxter drops in on Roderick Usher (Vincent Price) relaxing
between takes on House of Usher, a film he just scored for AIP.

Vincent Price enjoys a glass of wine as
Julien White in *From a Whisper to a Scream*.

A Whisper to a Scream's Unit Publicist, David Del Valle,
stands in for Vincent Price.

Vincent Price receives an impromptu set visit from scream queen Hazel Court
(a frequent co-star), and she is joined by David Del Valle.

Two behind-the-scenes photos of Vincent Price during the making of *From a Whisper to a Scream*. (Top) Vincent rehearses before a take with clapboard in foreground. (Below, left to right) screenwriter Courtney Joyner and impressionist Tony Clay stand, as Vincent holds a rubber knife in place until it dries, while publicist David Del Valle attends to him.

Director Jeff Burr and David Del Valle at the
From a Whisper to a Scream wrap party

John Carradine and David Del Valle, as photographed by Dan Golden.

Vincent Price and his director, John Brahm,
look at one of the masks used in *The Mad Magician*.

Two candid poses of director John Brahm taken at his Malibu home on his
80th birthday, with David Del Valle helping him with autographs.

Monique Van Vooren at the time of signing with David Del Valle for
representation for her new cook book, *The Happy Cooker.*
Warhol gave her fifteen minutes of fame, but she took a whole lot more.

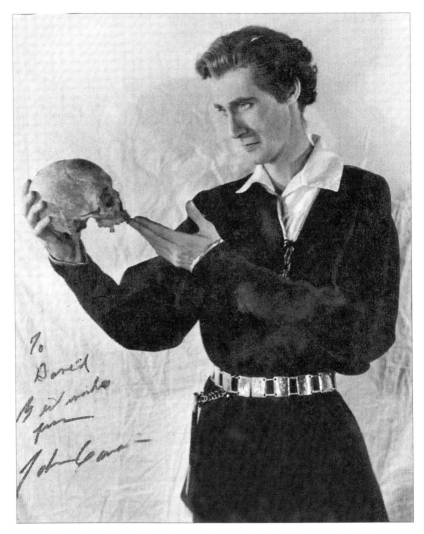

John Carradine as Hamlet in a photo taken in Hollywood in 1941,
where John had his own Shakespearian touring company at the time.

Elisabeth Brooks as "Marsha," werewolf
queen in Joe Dante's cult film, *The Howling*.

Sybil Danning and David Del Valle at his Christmas party and
before the fireworks set off by one Scott Dacy.

Sybil Danning wardrobe test for *The Howling Part II.*

Gale Sondergaard selects a hypo from servant
Rondo Hatton in *The Spider Woman Strikes Back*.

Gale Sondergaard having cocktails with David Del Valle.

Gloria Stuart poses by a French poster for *The Invisible Man*
at David Del Valle's party in her honor.

2075   Photo by: Merie W. Wallace

Gloria Stuart stars as Rose Dawson Calvert in "Titanic," an epic, action-packed romance set against the ill-fated voyage of the R.M.S. Titanic. Paramount Pictures and Twentieth Century Fox present a Lightstorm Entertainment Production, a James Cameron film, "Titanic," starring Leonardo DiCaprio, Kate Winslet, Billy Zane, Kathy Bates, Frances Fisher, Bernard Hill, Jonathan Hyde, Danny Nucci, David Warner and Bill Paxton. Written and directed by James Cameron, the film is produced by Cameron and Jim Landau. Rae Sanchini is executive producer.

Gloria Stuart as "Rose" the 101-year-old survivor in *Titanic.*

"Little"Angelo Rossitto offering John Barrymore a drink in a scene
from *The Beloved Rogue*, a part that was written especially
for Angelo by John as a token of their friendship.

In 1983, Martine Beswicke and David Del Valle were under the spell of
Count Yorga, who was better known to genre buffs as Robert Quarry.

Joyce Jameson cuddling up to co-star Lou Costello for a TV pilot they had hoped would make it into prime time, but this was not to be.

(Left to right) Hurd Hatfield, David Del Valle, Elisabeth Shepherd, and Curtis Harrington having cocktails for four.

(Left to right) Elisabeth Shepherd, Reggie Nalder, Forry Ackerman, Joyce Jameson, Angus Scrimm, and Barbara Steele standing in front of the Robert Florey Frankenstein billboard. This is a historic photo because it was the first and only time all three actress who had played the wives of Vincent Price in his Roger Corman / Poe films were together in one room. Joyce had appeared in Tales of Terror, Barbara had appeared in Pit and the Pendulum, and Elisabeth had appeared in *Tomb of Legeia*.

The legendary Samson De Brier, a fixture in Hollywood for decades, appeared in films including one for Kenneth Anger.

Zita Johann in The Mummy. Her performance assured her cinema immortality as the Princess that Boris Karloff came back from the dead to possess.

Director Robert Florey with two priceless French posters from
Frankenstein that were given to him by Universal as proof of his
writing credit on a film he nearly directed.

Ferdy Mayne gave me this rare candid photo of himself looking through
the Panavsion lens between takes on *Dance of the Vampires*. His
performance ranks with the very best screen vampires in cinema history.

Christopher Lee poses for the first and only time with memorabilia from the Lugosi Dracula since assuming the mantle of Count Dracula in 1958.

Christopher Lee and I standing in front of a poster for the Robert Florey
Frankenstein. This photo was sent to Mrs. Karloff as a tribute to Boris,
who was a close personal friend of Lee's for many years.
He appeared in Boris' final film, *The Crimson Altar*.

(Left to right) David Del Valle, Gloria Stuart, Curtis Harrington, and Reggie
Nalder at the going away party that David gave for her.

Martin Kosleck on a night out visiting the home of his co-star,
John Abbott, from the Sherlock Holmes film, *Pursuit to Algiers*.
The reunion was about to go south, as Martin was getting stiff.
They are holding a still of themselves from that film in the photo.

Vladek Sheybal as Herod and Lindsey Kemp as John in the London stage
production of Oscar Wilde's *Salome at the Roundhouse.*

Kenneth Anger in a rare moment of jest allowed me to play a vampire
about to drain him of his blood . . . what was I thinking?

Herve Villechaize sits on the lap of a nude Mary Woronov. They worked together on Oliver Stone's *Seizure*, and they were soul mates ever since.

Chapter 31

Too Long at the Fair

Joyce Jameson

One of the brightest and most talented comediennes of the late 1950s and 1960s was without a doubt the blond and buxom Joyce Jameson. Joyce appeared to great effect alongside such comic icons as Red Skelton, Danny Kaye, and especially Steve Allen, who really understood her gift for impersonation, not to mention her genius for comic timing, making her the perfect partner for those master clowns of television.

Joyce achieved her first real taste of success with the *Billy Barnes Review*, which was the toast of Hollywood and New York during the 1950s and 1960s. Such stars as Lucille Ball and Bette Davis attended whatever Billy Barnes cared to showcase. Billy was celebrated for his uncanny ability to write tailor-made material for individual stars such as Angela Lansbury, and he was in great demand writing material for not only the Academy Award telecasts, but also for *The Carol Burnett Show* and *The Cher* Show, her TV variety show that followed *The Sonny and Cher Comedy Hour* after she went solo. Billy Barnes almost single-handedly created "the revue" as we would come to know it, creating yet another important element of American musical comedy.

Joyce became at once Billy's muse and then his wife, introducing many classic comedy routines and songs to both coasts. Joyce did spot-on impersonations of Jayne Mansfield and Marilyn Monroe to such an extent that most of her film roles exploited those sketches she created with Billy. The great director, Billy Wilder, and Jack Lemmon worked with the real Marilyn in *Some Like it Hot* (1959). The following year, Joyce's most famous Marilyn impersonation on film was for Wilder, who cast her as the dizzy blond led up to Jack Lemmon's apartment for a tryst in his classic, *The Apartment* (1960). Jack became an instant fan of Joyce's comic talents, and he performed with her again in *Good Neighbor Sam* (1963). He remained a lifelong admirer of her work.

Joyce entered my life as a result of the lasting impression her classic performances made in two horror-comedies, holding her own alongside Vincent Price and Peter Lorre in a film produced by the legendary American International Pictures (AIP) during the "horror boom" of the 1960s. Her first film for AIP, *Tales of Terror* (1962), broke new ground by displaying the newly-discovered comic timing of Price and Lorre in the popular *Black Cat* segment of the portmanteau film. Joyce shines with a performance that brings both humor and pathos as Annabelle, the neglected wife of a very inebriated Peter Lorre, who has the misfortune to bring home his newfound drinking companion, wine connoisseur Vincent Price. The two become lovers and suffer a fate worthy of . . . well, Edgar Allen Poe. That sequence was so popular that AIP made their next Poe film, *The Raven* (1963), an all-out comedy, and it was again with Price and Lorre. Soon, they reunited their *Tales of Terror* stars for yet another romp in the cemetery, originally entitled *The Graveside Story*, which boasted an all-star cast of "ghouls" including Boris Karloff, Basil Rathbone, and that newly formed comedy team the critics dubbed "an unholy Laurel and Hardy," Vincent Price and Peter Lorre. In a clever change of pace, Joyce played the neglected wife of undertaker Vincent Price who prefers the bottle to his (very off-key) opera-singing diva of a wife, who finds comfort and then true love with her husband's partner, fellow undertaker Peter Lorre. *The Comedy of Terrors* (1964), as it came to be known, was not a commercial success. Instead of being a turning point in the studio's output of horror comedies, it signaled the demise of such projects, and the following year, Vincent was resigned to keeping his tongue even more firmly in his cheek and had to make due without Peter, who died suddenly during the release of what would prove to be their last film together. That was also be the last time Joyce played a leading role in a motion picture.

Fortunately, time has been rather kind to both films, and today, thanks to the advent of home video and the DVD format, a whole new generation of fans has created a substantial cult following for the films, including a renewed appreciation of Joyce's considerable comedic talents.

In 1980, I began working on my Corman/Poe book in earnest, and to that end, started interviewing as many of the principals as I could locate. I had already interviewed Roger Corman and several others, when Dick Miller told me where to find Joyce. She was represented by an old-time Hollywood agent named Lew Deuser, whose most successful client at that time was Vic Tayback. Vic had a recurring role on *Alice*, a then-popular sitcom starring Linda Lavin that was based on the Oscar-winning film, *Alice Doesn't Live Here Anymore.*

After a couple of phone calls to Lew's office, I received word that Joyce would be pleased to meet with me and left her number. Within a week after my call, on a warm summer afternoon, there came a knock at my front door, and from my kitchen window I could see this small, rather top-heavy woman wearing an orange parka and clutching a large scrapbook to her ample bosom. From the moment I opened the door, the woman's beautiful face still reflected her on-screen persona, with delicate features possessing bright joyful eyes that exuded warmth and humor, and made her instantly familiar and loving. Joyce made friends easily, and I quickly came under her spell.

"My goodness, you're a handsome young man, and just my type," she said, as she entered my apartment for the first time. "I have a son, Tyler Barnes. He's very good looking too, and just a little bit younger than you are. Now where do you want me to begin, as I have a lot to share with you since my career goes way back, honey . . . all the way to *Showboat*, and you have to guess which version." With that she broke out in that dizzy laughter I remembered so fondly from watching her countless television appearances during my ill-spent youth. I mean, that lady taught Herman Munster how to rumba, for God's sake!

Joyce was, from her own accounts, a woman who found her niche in comedy and was blessed with finding powerful men in show business that recognized her abilities early on, especially Billy Barnes, Sid Caesar, and Steve Allen. The one comedy genius she could have done without knowing was Jerry Lewis. Joyce was a regular (if you can call it that) on Jerry's 1963 mammoth two-and-one-half-hour talk show that supposedly cost a million dollars, but flopped after just thirteen weeks of broadcasts. Joyce recalled how Jerry came on to her sexually before and after the tapings. He made it clear that what Jerry Lewis wanted Jerry Lewis got—end of story. Joyce said she had never encountered anyone before or since with an ego like his.

The two horror comedies were a lark for Joyce, since she recalled working with Vincent and Peter, veteran actors in decline from their glory days at Warner Bros. and 20th Century Fox, when fate forced them to appear in low-budget films at a makeshift studio. She remembered Peter as a sad little man, whose weight problem made it impossible for the black cat of the title to sit on his lap. "Peter didn't have a lap for the cat to sit on and it would just slide right off onto the floor!" Joyce made a point of saying that both films were shot very quickly and cheaply. "Especially with Roger on *Tales of Terror*; that one was like twelve days shooting and hurry-up-already."

It was becoming obvious that our interview was turning into an all-day social visit and we were becoming fast friends. Joyce really needed a friend at that point in her life, and aside from another writer/confidante she trusted named Patrick Agan, who also wrote about the movies (*The Rise and Fall of the Love Goddesses*), I was about to become her new best friend and escort on short notice.

Joyce had a son, Tyler, by her marriage to Billy Barnes. At that time, Tyler was in his early twenties, living in the Bay Area. She was very close to him (he virtually grew up on her film locations and television shoots), yet to her credit, she let him live his own life and chose to live alone in a modest home her mother had left her in the Wilshire district. She kept two telephones in operation in her house, one for all business and most of her social calls, and the other phone in her bedroom with a different number. It was two years before I knew that number and then it still was too late to really be of any help, as I will explain further on.

One of the most tragic aspects of Joyce's life was her decade-plus relationship with actor Robert Vaughn. She was already well into dating him at the time *The Man from U.N.C.L.E.* craze was in full swing, and she was at his side right up through the filming of the classic Steve McQueen film, *Bullet.*

Robert was to be the love of her life, and being a Catholic, he could never seriously envision marriage to Joyce, yet they were engaged at various points in their long relationship. The biggest fly in the ointment however was not the question of religion, but the question of politics. It seemed our man from U.N.C.L.E. aspired to a position in a higher office, like perhaps Senator Vaughn, or even Governor Vaughn, and one must remember that in the "Camelot" atmosphere of Washington D.C. that marked the Kennedy years, a certain image was required with a socially appropriate wife to stand by your side as you placed yourself in the forum of public opinion. It certainly could not include a divorcee with a child, not in the 1960s.

Yet Robert could not bring himself to break the bond between them, so time and convenience led her to believe there was still hope right up until the end, when it looked like he might actually run for office. Joyce told me that he actually recreated the Oval office in his home like it was a film set, right down to the flag on the rug. "Bobby was obsessed with the Kennedy family and especially RFK, who was a close personal friend." She always referred to them as "The two Bobbies." At that point, I refrained from connecting yet another parallel with Marilyn Monroe and Joyce's uncanny connection with her persona. Joyce went along with all of Robert's eccentricities because she knew she had found her soul mate and that was that. Joyce tried keeping in touch with Robert, but his newfound freedom from their relationship doubled his fondness for drinking and womanizing, which were already the stuff of legend. Joyce loved to tell the story of Robert picking up a willing starlet and bringing her back to his house very late one night and then forgetting the whole evening thanks to a load of cocktails. Somehow, he locked the woman out of the house and turned the lawn sprinklers full blast hoping she would just float away before passing out. He was awakened by the Beverly Hills Fire Department and one wet, screaming starlet, not to mention all the elite neighbors awakened from a sound sleep to witness the front lawn floorshow.

The long-term impact of Joyce and Robert's break-up resulted in Joyce taking less interest in her career and spending more time by herself. Joyce was always in demand for voice-over work in commercials and cartoons and could have easily made the transition to character parts like Kathleen Freeman and Carole Cook, both of whom were protégés of Billy Barnes, as well.

However, with her solitude and loneliness came the inevitable weight gain, and Joyce, being a proud woman, had real tunnel-vision when it came to her looks. She could behave like a diva, and only Clint Eastwood could convince her to appear overweight on screen. For him, she made her last major motion picture appearances in *The Outlaw Josie Wales* and *Any Which Way but Loose*. Joyce loved Clint and felt embraced in his company and especially around his crew. Joyce remembered how Clint practiced spitting his tobacco into a spittoon. "Clint just became that character in *Josie Wales* and spitting was his motivation." If only Joyce could have found a few more like Clint, she might have chosen to stay with us a bit longer.

The greatest moment during the time I had with Joyce (and believe me, there were many wonderful moments in the five years we knew each other) had to be the night of the televised tribute CBS gave for Jack Lemmon in honor of his new film, *Tribute*. Joyce received a beautiful engraved invitation to the event, which was black tie, and yes, we all had to sign releases because it was to be aired on national television the following month.

Joyce called in a complete panic, embarrassed about her weight. What, if anything, could she wear, and would I take her to the event? In other words, would I be her escort for her "Cinderella" night of nights? Of course, I was honored to take the fabulous Joyce Jameson to any event and I told her so. She was also a bit nervous about what Jack Lemmon might think, seeing his former co-star looking less than her old self.

The big night finally arrived, and Joyce drove over to my place looking elegant in a black cocktail dress. Draped around her shoulders was a white fur stole. I was in black tie and ready for whatever Jack Lemmon and company had to offer. I drove her car that night to the CBS studio that had been turned into a fabulous nightclub set for the party and taping that was to follow after dinner. As we merged onto the freeway, Joyce produced a small bottle of vodka from her purse and fortified herself. She really was a nervous wreck about what people would think about her weight, and if anyone would even remember her work.

We made it through the main gate and advanced to valet parking.

I took her arm and she held onto me like a life jacket, as we made our way through the crowd of celebrities into the amazing makeshift set that looked like a nightclub in a Fred Astaire film, complete with cameras and cable lights everywhere. The white fur stole that Joyce chose to wear had one serious drawback and that was that it shed. There was white hair all over my black jacket, and it was especially apparent on my arm, which steadied Joyce up the ramp into the studio.

As soon as we were shown to our table, I made a dash for the men's room for damage control. It was there that I ran into the ever dapper Cesar Romero and Dana Andrews, who found my situation very funny and, to their credit, those two gave me the benefit of years of experience. With a brush and some hot water, we managed to remove the fur from my jacket. I knew Dana from the PBS documentary we did earlier that year, and Cesar was always out socializing, a habit from a lifetime of being part of the Hollywood scene. He remained until his death one of the nicest men in show business.

The well-worn phrase "star-studded" took on new meaning for me that evening, as I was, for one night only, part of the Hollywood you only read about in fan magazines or see on television during the Academy Awards. The caliber of celebrities coming out that night to honor Jack Lemmon was literally the *crème de la crème* of show business. The tables were all terraced in a circular fashion allowing the cameras to roam at will from one grouping to another. Joyce and I were seated with Jack's son, Chris Lemmon, (who was scheduled to play the piano), and his date, Robert Picado (who had appeared with Lemmon in the Broadway production of *Tribute*), and the great comic actor, Jack Gilford, and his wife.

There were at least 500 people in attendance that evening and nearly all of them were famous. Billy Wilder and wife Audrey were seated with Lew Wasserman and his wife, and completing their table was Fred Mac Murray and wife June. Cary Grant was seated with Blake Edwards and Julie Andrews. Those random groupings of people you just never imagine being so close and real were all part of this fantastic night of honoring one of their own. In honoring Jack Lemmon, their tributes were indeed heartfelt.

Whatever fears or anxiety Joyce may have had prior to our arrival were beautifully put to rest, when the guest of honor came up to our table and said to Joyce, "I wanted to take a moment and thank you so much for being part of this evening. You are without a doubt one of the finest comediennes in our business and it was my pleasure to work with you." Joyce could not speak, for the tears had welled up in her eyes, and she barely could say thank you when Jack knelt down and kissed her cheek. It was so moving to watch and I thank God for what Jack did for Joyce that night because it proved to her once and for all that she was who she was and more than worthy of praise from her peers.

As much as we might have wished the party would just go on forever, the evening finally came to a glamorous end with countless friends and colleagues approaching Joyce and making her feel like she must have felt twenty years earlier out on the town with her beloved "Bobby Vaughn." As we were driving home, she kept wishing every night could be like that and said how happy she was at that moment. It was a moment I have kept close to my heart all these years later.

It took about a month for the glow to wear off from the *Tribute* party, and then Joyce was back to her old insecurities of not answering her phones and staying in that old house of hers for days on end. Her mother's house was in a nice part of Los Angeles in a rather upscale neighborhood, but she had no gardener to keep the lawn up, so it died and turned a bright yellow. She never used the front door and always exited from the back of the house through the kitchen, thus the junk mail piled up on the front porch until it looked pretty much like a deserted house. I started having surreal dreams of Joyce as Miss Havisham in *Great Expectations*, yet I could never dream a part for "Bobby Vaughn," thank God.

Joyce started 1986 off with few attempts to come by and say hello to me, and we kept in touch almost entirely by phone. She had been given a little toy poodle and lavished all her affection on it for a while, until one morning when I got a call from Joyce, who was almost hysterical with sobbing. It seems that during the night, she rolled over in bed and accidentally broke the poor little thing's neck in her sleep. Joyce said she was going to quit eating altogether. Her weight was just not acceptable anymore, and she was no longer interested in work of any kind, and that included voice-overs, which had paid a lot of her bills in the past. Joyce was going into a shutdown mode and there was very little I could do about it.

By the middle of 1986, she quit calling me altogether, and with Tyler miles away, there was really no one left to check up on her. I drove over to her house from time to time and rang the bell and walked around to the windows begging her to answer her phone, all to no avail.

Finally, the inevitable happened. On January 16, 1987, Joyce had suffered enough with the pain of living and took her own life using a stockpile of pills that she had saved up for that final curtain on a color-ful life that had taken too many wrong turns on the road to happiness for such a fragile soul.

Among the things that were forgotten was a particular song Billy Barnes wrote, which was first introduced by Joyce: "Have I Stayed too Long at the Fair?" Barbra Streisand's recording of that song quickly overshadowed anyone else's interpretation of it. When I first heard of Joyce's death, the words to that song haunted me for days, as I could just hear Joyce singing Billy Barne's lyrics in that little girl voice of hers:

"I wanted the music to play on forever
Have I stayed too long at the fair?
I wanted the clown to be constantly witty
Have I stayed too long at the fair?
I bought me blue ribbons to tie up my hair
But I couldn't find anybody to care
The merry-go round is beginning to slow now
Have I stayed to long at the fair?
Oh mother dear I know you're very proud
Your little girl and kingdom is so far above the crowd
No, daddy dear
You never could have known that I would be successful
Yet so very much alone.
I wanted to live in a carnival city with laughter and love everywhere
I wanted my friends to be thrilling and witty,
I wanted somebody to love;
I found my blue ribbons all shiny and new,

But now I discover them no longer blue
The merry-go-round is beginning to taunt me
Have I stayed to long at the fair?
'There's nothing to win and I have
No one to want me,
Have I stayed to long at the fair?

Chapter 32
Queen of the Nyack

Zita Johann

Zita Johann, the legendary actress of *The Mummy*, a landmark film made during Universal's Golden Age of horror, left a lifelong impression not only with yours truly, but an entire generation of admirers, who never forgot her exotic performance as the reincarnated princess Anck-es-en-Amon, a remarkable achievement resonating such otherworldly allure that she elevated the standard for all that followed in the genre. Her performance in the original seventy-eight-minute cut included a tour-de-force of three reincarnations reflecting past lives, allowing her scenes to develop into a three-dimensional character steeped in mysticism and spirituality. "The love that outlasted the temples of our Gods" becomes the eternal obsession that condemns Boris Karloff's Im-I Io Tep to a living death in the 1932 classic.

Zita's performance should have catapulted her career towards stardom, yet circumstances during the filming of *The Mummy* led the fiercely independent actress down a very different path. At that time, Zita was a respected actress hailed by Broadway critics as "the white flame of the American Theater." The lady in question was unique by Broadway standards and steadfast in not forsaking her artistic standards to the studio system of the Depression-era Hollywood she came to loathe. "I have more respect for the whores on 42nd Street than I did for the stars in Hollywood."

My initial relationship with Zita began with a telephone interview in the fall of 1981. My ever-reliable source for such encounters, Richard Lamparski, had already profiled her in his latest *Whatever Became Of* books, well aware that I would appreciate an introduction. Boris Karloff's *The Mummy* was one of my favorite horror films made during the era when Universal pictures rocked the film world with the success of *Dracula* and *Frankenstein*, setting into motion a series of films that set the genre standard for horror from 1931 until the end of World War II.

The Mummy was created especially for Karloff after *Frankenstein* had made him a star. In fact, his fame reached such lofty heights that Universal billed him only by his last name, an honor till then afforded only to Garbo over at MGM. Universal, impressed with Zita's work on the film, and with her reputation on Broadway, offered her billing alongside the newly anointed super nova "Karloff."

The casting of the mummy's *amorata* almost went to a very young Katherine Hepburn, however a previous commitment and fate decreed otherwise. Zita made her screen debut in what proved to be D.W. Griffith's last motion picture, *The Struggle*, in 1931. Zita recalled, "Griffith financed the film personally, and we filmed it at his small Biograph studio in the Bronx. I admired him so much; he was a real gentleman, and he always told the press that I was an actress with a brain." Sadly, the film was roasted by the critics, and Zita remembered how "it just broke his heart. He was a target of the envy and resentment of critics over his exalted reputation with *The Birth of a Nation*." Griffith went into a career decline that was further fueled by alcoholism, doomed to wander through Hollywood as a cruel reminder of just how fleeting fame can be. *The Struggle* deserves to be rediscovered, not only to redeem its director's reputation, but to appreciate the performance of the uniquely exotic Zita Johann at the height of her powers.

It was disappointing to discover that she had not seen the film in years, as she explained that the making of *The Mummy* was not a positive experience for her. In fact, the film ultimately ended whatever chance Zita might have had to become a Hollywood star. She possessed talent, beauty, and intelligence— perhaps too much to suffer fools gladly. Zita was infamous at the time for asking MGM's "boy wonder" Irving Thalberg, "Why do you make such rubbish?"

She was still being pursued by Hollywood in spite of the Griffith disaster, resulting in *Tiger Shark* (Warner Bros. 1932), which was a Howard Hawks potboiler starring a totally over-the-top Edward G. Robinson playing a Portuguese fisherman with a hook for a hand. Zita did not enjoy the experience, since her old co-star from the Theater Guild days had, to her horror, "gone Hollywood with his ego." She still managed to steal the film by just underplaying against "Eddie's hammy theatrics," making Robinson angry enough to complain to the main office about her "having too many close-ups." I remember reading about Robinson years later when he was working on Orson Welles' *The Stranger*. Orson always laughed about his vanity. "Eddie Robinson called me up the night before shooting to tell which side of his face was his 'good side,' and to inform the cameraman to favor that side. I mean, looking like Eddie Robinson, I could only laugh and listen to his demands."

Despite the tempest in a teapot with Eddie, the film opened and RKO was impressed enough to offer her a contract and a film entitled *Thirteen Women*. They had, in fact, made the offer while she was still at work on the Hawks film. Another factor in the mix was her marriage at the time to John Houseman. Zita had met the then-young businessman during her first triumph on Broadway, winning rave reviews in a play entitled *Machinal*, which featured a very young Clark Gable. Houseman won her over and they were married in 1929. Zita discovered that her Romeo was still tied to his mother's apron strings, and soon, mother and son were dependent on the income of Zita's acting career. That situation led to Zita accepting all those film offers in the first place. She told me when I got to know her better that "it was humiliating enough having to support the Houseman's, but I soon drew the line when John moved his lover, Eric, a playwright, right into his bedroom. Even then, I still did not grasp the situation. How I endured those days in Malibu I will never know. I had been so naïve."

Zita was still under contract to Universal at that time and was to begin filming *Laughing Boy*, a screenplay by John Huston. The film was cancelled when a leading man could not be found. She suggested a then-unknown Humphrey Bogart, whom they rejected, so Universal offered her *The Mummy*. The director for that project was famed cinematographer Karl Freund, who was making his directorial debut after photographing *Dracula* and *Murders in the Rue Morgue* (which, by coincidence, was a John Huston script).

"The first words the 360-pound Mr. Freund ever spoke to me with his heavy German accent were, 'In one scene, you must be nood from the vaist up!' Knowing the censors would never allow it, I called his bluff and told him, 'It's alright with me if the censors allow it,' thus preventing a confrontation for the moment;" yet Freund was determined to break her will one way or the other.

The shooting of *The Mummy* began in September 1932. According to accounts by Zita and Boris Karloff, they worked twelve-hour days late into the night. Both actors suffered exhaustion and fatigue (the union had yet to be created to prevent that gross injustice to actors while on a set). Boris endured a painful torture with his make-up—he appeared in the beginning as a mummy rotting in a case, and later, his make-up was less confining, but still a torture. Zita suffered much worse under Freund's direction. She told me that "I had nowhere to sit between takes. The reincarnation sequences, all four of them, were cut after the filmed wrapped because I told Junior Laemmle, the son of Universal's founder, not to renew my contract. One of the last scenes, where I played a Christian martyr, involved my death by lions in the arena. It was very dangerous, and Freund and the crew were all placed in steel cages, while I was just thrown to the lions without any protection. Well, by this time I weighed next to nothing, and those lions just looked at me like I wasn't even worth the trouble, and the scene was wrapped and I walked off that set for good."

She remembered Boris Karloff as a marvelous person and a good actor. "Karloff had a dark, hidden sorrow that came from his soul right through his eyes, and yet we never spoke of it." James Whale must have sensed that sorrow, as well, when he cast Boris as the monster in 1931. He even said as much in interviews of the period. There was a moment when Boris shows her some of her past lives in his pool as Zita literally passed out for over an hour. According to her, "I went into a trancelike state where I felt death all around me. I was sure that I was never coming back, and when I finally did come out of it, Karloff was the first thing I saw. He was holding my hand as they waited for the studio doctor to arrive." By then, she said, "Even the crew had turned against Freund for his mistreatment of me. Since this occurred just before midnight, a doctor could not be found, so that crew literally prayed me back from the dead."

For all her suffering, *The Mummy* was a huge success for both Universal and Boris Karloff, yet for her complaining, and especially for walking out on her contract, Zita lost her star billing and all her scenes of reincarnation were removed, thus taking away some of her character's motivation and lessening the impact. The legend of the missing footage from that film is right up there with finding the lost Lon Chaney film, *London After Midnight,* as a "holy grail" for film historians.

After suffering through the film, Zita still had the burden of supporting husband John Houseman, his mother, and John's lover, Eric, all still with their hands out. That led to Zita taking yet another film, this time over at Paramount—1933's *Luxury Liner* with George Brent. It was during the opening of that film that Zita was an eye-witness to one of the more sordid scandals in Hollywood. While driving with John Huston, they had a serious car accident, sending Zita to the hospital and Houston to jail for drunk driving. That incident nearly destroyed Huston's career, and it took several strings being pulled, including sending Huston out of the country, before all was covered up. Later on, Huston came back to Hollywood, luck brought him together with a certain black bird over at Warner Bros, and all was forgiven.

In 1934, Zita finally got a divorce from John Houseman, his

mother, and the boyfriend. "Houseman likes to put it out that I married him when he was rich and I divorced him when he was poor and he got away with that line. He didn't have a dime. He liked to say he was the president of Oceanic Drain Company. He was not the boss; they just used his name. He had a very small income, and then he lost that job and had no income. He went to London to write a play. Well, he couldn't even do that in those days, so I helped him finish the play so he could collect a paycheck. Same thing at Metro, where I helped him get a job for $250 a week that didn't last, as he really couldn't write in those days at all. Houseman always puts me down in print, but remember this: I opened all the doors for him in Hollywood. He had never heard of show business before he married me, yet he still likes to distort the truth in his books about his 'salad days in the business.' What a pompous liar he has become."

She made a couple more films and then said goodbye to Hollywood. A year later, she did tests for both *A Midsummer Night's Dream* and *Dracula's Daughter*, yet she made no more films in Hollywood.

Zita returned to New York, and after two bad marriages, bought a pre-Revolutionary house in the wilds of West Nyack, New York, where she remained for the rest of her life. After my first long phone conversation with her, I had asked the important questions regarding my cherished mummy film and began talking with her on all kinds of subjects. Later, I received a letter inviting me to visit her if ever came to the east coast.

In the fall of 1981, I visited her, and the experience was more than worth the effort. Zita had very wisely purchased her large, rambling house near the Hudson River around 1939. After about three days in New York, I needed to rent a car to make the trek to West Nyack, since her property was way off the beaten track and no taxi could ever hope to find it. I leased a car for the weekend, only to discover that the one the agency could locate the day I needed it was a stretch limousine, which was the usual mode of travel for opening nights or funerals. So, off to the country I went in a long white limousine. Within less than an hour, we were getting near the first exit to reach her abode. The trees were losing their leaves and the sky had turned gray; it was all turning into "horror movie weather" and I loved it. Finally, the last turnoff proved to be a dirt road that curved around to where one began to observe the outline of an old two-story wooden-framed house—definitely the kind George Washington might have slept in, or at least Jack Benny.

I felt somewhat self-conscious about arriving at her home in such an outlandish mode of transportation, but I soon discovered that very little could ever faze the mystical Zita Johann. As I made my way up to her front porch, I noticed a woman's red silk high heel shoe (what happened to its mate?) lying on the ground. I immediately conjured up visions of some terrified debutante running for her life past that haunted dwelling of our founding fathers.

It took some doing to get the lady of the house to answer the door, but soon I was face-to-face with the Princess Anck-es-en-Amon from my youthful days when I was glued in front of late night television waiting until all hours to watch The Mummy for the umpteenth time.

Zita took one look at what I arrived in and said, "You must be very rich or a terrific spendthrift." With that, she allowed me to enter the darkness of her hallway and then into her large living room complete with a fireplace. As my eyes adjusted to the half-light, a youthful Zita stared down at me from a striking oil painting hung on the mantle as a reminder of things past but not yet forgotten.

Once the pleasantries had been exchanged, we sat by a "roaring fireplace," as they say in Gothic novels. Over drinks, Zita began to explain her philosophy of life and her interest in the occult. "I have always been interested in the occult, but during the filming of *The Mummy,* I had to keep such things private, especially in those days. I used the occult auto-suggestively . . . I mean, before I would play a scene, I would get into the spirit, so to speak, with certain prayers. As a child, my father gave me an Ouija board, and soon, I started to get messages, then I moved towards the Tarot. By the time I was in Basil Sidney's company, I was asked to read cards all the time for the other players, and Basil himself depended on what I saw in those cards."

Zita had long ago abandoned acting, yet she had much wisdom to impart to others and that is precisely what she did with her time. She taught acting to students from the village, and devoted much time and energy to working with handicapped children. Her greatest joy was helping a student who was a deaf mute with an I.Q. of 20 learn to hear and speak. "I build a bridge with love and expect you to meet me halfway across."

After what seemed like a suspension in time for me, our visit was at an end, and I asked her if I could take a photo with her. She was very determined that no pictures of her be printed as she looked then, and I could not understand why, although a lady has the right to remain mysterious, so she allowed me to take pictures instead of her portrait over the mantle, which I did, as well as the front of her house. Two years later, when she looked even less like her old self, she went out and made her first film in fifty years! The project she allowed to bear her name and forever be known as her final film, *Raiders of the Living Dead*, was a dreadful student film with a zero budget. That, from the woman who would not let me snap a photo? All I can say is that producer Sam Sherman must have been some kind of genius to coax her into such a shabby affair as that one turned out to be, and now it is out on DVD from Image Entertainment in a "deluxe" director's cut edition.

We kept in touch over the next few years and she had moments of regret over the film that could have launched her career. "I wrote to Junior Laemmle just before we met in 1979, just before his death, and made peace with him about *The Mummy*. I apologized for not getting along with him. I told him he was a fair and just man and I would have been well-advised to have taken his contract and gone with it, but other things were meant to happen in my life."

Zita Johann passed from this life in1993. She believed so strongly in the spirit, we must remember she would say "that all art and beauty comes from the spirit, and that spirit is forever a part of all of us."

I will always remember what Boris Karloff said to her in *The Mummy* over half a century ago: "Our love has outlasted the temples of our Gods." Surely, her legacy will do the same.

Chapter 33

The Road to Yucca Loma

David Manners

Around 1924, while Zita Johann was learning her craft performing in Basil Sidney's theatrical company, she crossed paths for the first time with a handsome young actor named David Manners. By 1932, they were toiling away at Universal as star-crossed lovers in the horror classic, *The Mummy*. Zita recalled nearly half a century later that "David was just the nicest young man you could ever hope to meet." The production was such a nightmare that it was one reason why David closed the door on stardom a few years later, unlike Zita, who had the door slammed shut for her.

I still marvel at the fact that I got to know *two* of the leads from a classic film such as *The Mummy*. David also appeared in *Dracula* (1931), *The Black Cat* (1934), and many other classics from the early 1930s, yet he was not the easiest person to interview. Like Zita, he had no interest whatsoever in Hollywood or his participation in what he liked to call "that old tinsel town." His reluctance to engage in film work is well-documented by a few other accounts published in horror journals and specialty books on horror film history.

In 1991, I made a pilgrimage to the coastal town of Montecito, just twenty miles outside of Santa Barbara. David had lived a very full and rich life after leaving the picture business in the 1930s. When his health was better, he lived in Pacific Palisades with longtime companion William Mercer, who was responsible for the screenplay of *The Velvet Touch* (an enjoyable murder mystery with Sidney Greenstreet). They had a beautiful home filled with art and antiques from a lifetime together. Mercer died in the summer of 1978, and David was devastated. He moved to a smaller apartment in downtown Santa Barbara. In 1990, he no longer wanted to cook for himself or clean his apartment. As he put it, "I'd rather spend my time writing books and living life than being a domestic." That was when David moved into the beautifully landscaped Wood Glen Hall for seniors (also in Santa Barbara), where we met for the first time.

When his health was up to it, David could become full of salt and vinegar. He loved to be the center of attention, as his good looks still made him the "darling of the dayroom." All the old dears wanted him to hold their hands and flirt. It was, however, the rose garden that gave David his real pleasure in living there. He became responsible for suggesting much of the garden. I was warned beforehand that he hated talking about not only his film career but especially the horror films that made him the last link to an era, the only surviving cast member of *Dracula*. Moreover, he was rapidly becoming the last survivor, period, of all his early films in Hollywood.

My first visit was tolerated because I had brought with me a tall, good-looking young man who loved the old horror films but made his living in Hollywood doing soft-core gay films.

David took one look at my companion and you would have thought he was a matinee idol all over again. "Oh Hello, I'm David. You really are a tall one; you must be an actor," he said.

Our visit was pleasant enough, yet when I dared to bring up the unmentionable—such as working on the set of *The Black Cat*—he said very little until it was obvious my "friend" wanted to know, as well. Then, David broke his silence long enough to say, "Karloff was a gentleman, very aloof, but nice enough to work with. He always got on with Lugosi in spite of rumors to the contrary. It was Lugosi that seemed dissatisfied with all the attention and success Karloff was attracting at the time. Lugosi was a great star . . . in his own mind." David went on the say that he was never directed by Tod Browning on *Dracula*; it was Karl Freund that really called the shots. That was very interesting for me because of Zita. Perhaps that was why Universal gave Freund *The Mummy* to direct in the first place.

There was yet another revelation before we left David's room. One of the books I brought to donate to the home's library was one of those "Films of . . . ." books on Joan Crawford. When David caught sight of that book, he looked at my friend and asked if he was a fan of hers. We both said we liked some of her work, and at that point, having our full attention, David began to explain the incident that made him decide to leave Hollywood altogether.

"I never felt at home working in pictures, and more and more, I went back to Yucca Loma to recharge my batteries, never wanting to leave the ranch once I got there. Well, one afternoon, my agent told me to drive over to Metro to take lunch with Miss Joan Crawford and discuss doing a film with her.

"I could really have cared less, but my agent seemed overjoyed that she had asked especially for me, so I went. Metro was Joan Crawford's personal playground, or that is what she was led to believe, so while we were having this lunch in her enormous movie star dressing room, she made a pass at me and in no uncertain terms explained that she liked to have her leading men in her bed as well as on the set, and that sometimes included directors. I was as polite as possible and said no. Within minutes, her demeanor changed into what she really was all along, a whore, a foul-mouthed tramp who called me every name under the sun, following me out of her trailer as I went to my car, and was still cursing as I drove off the MGM lot and right out of town, never to set foot on a movie lot again. So, thank you Miss Joan Crawford for making my decision so easy."

David walked us to the main entrance, arm in arm with his new "friend." As we left, David winked at me and said, "Do come back, and bring some more of your friends if they are anything like him."

My next visit revealed yet another side of David, the Golden Years from 1936 until the mid-1950s, when he lived in magic time at a place in the Mojave Desert by the Sierra Madre Mountains near Victorville called "Rancho Yucca Loma." David was a partner in the thousand-acre guest ranch, with separate housing in which guests could stay, while building a little cabin there just for himself. For a few years, men like Albert Einstein and Horowitz made the ranch a retreat, while movie stars like Greta Garbo journeyed there for privacy.

David was a deeply spiritual man, very much like Zita Johann. He knew that love was the most powerful force in the universe, and nothing else was important but shaking off the layers of pretense to embrace just that concept. David had written books with titles like *Under Running Laughter* and *Convenient Season*. He also edited newsletters on the subject of spiritual growth and well-being. David was also an accomplished painter, a true renaissance man if ever there was one.

There was so much I wanted to ask David, yet his condition—that of just being in his late nineties—made the task almost impossible. David had his good days and then bad days when he could hurt someone's feelings or break a heart. By 1994, David had to be moved from Wood Glen to Marge Mason's senior care home in Montecito, an exceptional facility that allowed seniors as much dignity as possible, while looking after those who just couldn't be left on their own anymore. David was in a wheelchair by that time and, at ninety-seven, he would fall asleep in his chair or, as most do when their life slips away and they spend more time in the next world than in this one. The death of his lover, Bill Mercer, left a void that only work and writing kept at bay. As he reached the time when those tasks were taken from him, he slipped into self-pity and depression. Thankfully, there were several young men who came into his life, taking David out of his loneliness and giving him someone to dream about and love. That experience kept him alive beyond what most people know as a lifetime.

Towards the end, Sir Ian McKellen came to visit David to ask about James Whale, and while David was impossibly rude to him and remained in bed being less than responsive, at some point the ever-patient Sir Ian asked if David found Whale attractive. David screamed at him, "NO!" Then, as Sir Ian was leaving, David rallied enough to take his fingers and twists them around, saying to Sir Ian, "Whale and I were like that . . . ." He ended the conversation with, "You are seeing me on my deathbed." Sir Ian told this story to my friend Curtis Harrington, and Curtis said that it left a profound impression on Sir Ian.

Not too many months later, David was residing at a convalescent home known as Valle Verde. On the afternoon of December 23, 1998, he was brought into the dining room by wheel chair to enjoy his dinner. He managed one helping from his plate before simply smiling and lowering his head as if in meditation. David Manners passed from this earth at that moment after ninety-eight years of intense productivity and spiritual growth. He embraced everlasting bliss as he would have wanted simply by just going to sleep forever.

Chapter 34

Just Be the Bitch, Darling

Vladek Sheybal

The Cinema has on occasion been rather wicked in unleashing upon an unsuspecting public a Pandora's Box of dramatic personalities whose faces light up the silver screen like no other, creating impressions of altered states fraught with subtexts that might confound Freud himself. The Polish character actor, Vladek Sheybal, had just such a face, with a fascinating persona to match, leaving in his wake a gallery of dazzling performances that shall not be forgotten.

The delightfully decadent actor made his entrance into my life thanks to the artistry of that brilliant (if not exceedingly eccentric) English actor/director Lindsey Kemp. Lindsey was a true renaissance man with abilities in all aspects of theater and film, a perverse individual to be sure, but a genius in all things outré and fantastic in the theater.

Lindsey had produced the infamous Ziggy Stardust shows for David Bowie during his glam-rock period, as well as acting in such cult films as *The Wicker Man*. Lindsey had created his own bizarre vision of Oscar Wilde's *Salome*, and staged it at the Roundhouse Theater on the Chalk Farm Road in the outer regions of London.

Vladek was honored with special billing in that production and, not one to disappoint those people out there in the dark, his first entrance as Herod was spectacular. Glittering in gold lame and covered from head to toe in jewels and feathers, he succeeded in channeling both Wilde and Josephine Baker in his performance, with more than a nod to Genet.

The theater was filled with the fragrance of exotic incense. A combination of that with the Beardsley décor, lit in smoky blues and reds, left me feeling like two pipes in an opium den; in others words, Oscar Wilde would have been in his element, appreciating that kind of yellow book ambience, not to mention some of the more attractive members of the cast.

I was visiting London at the time, and the Roundhouse location was a bit out of the way, with the train as the only transportation back into town. When the performance ended, most of the cast, along with Lindsey, had a wine bar reception in the dressing rooms behind the stage area, and I was invited to join them for a drink and to meet the cast. Vladek was in his element as both teacher and star of the company. I made a point of telling him that I came all the way from Los Angeles to see his performance, as well as to meet with John Russell Taylor, my then-editor at *Films and Filming* in London. Vladek was genuinely moved and flattered with my sincerity, so we then went through more than one bottle of Champagne, chatting and laughing away for well over two hours. As the party was breaking up, I realized that I had missed the last train to London for the night and the possibility of finding a taxi was almost non-existent at that hour. Vladek and one of the actors in the show named David Haughton offered to drive me back into town.

Later the next day, I received a call from Vladek inviting me out for dinner. We agreed on a time and place, and Vladek suggested coming by the hotel to collect me. During our conversation, he asked how the hotel was treating me, and I said considering I arrived without notice I was just happy to get a room, even if the bath was down the hall. I thought nothing more about confiding to Vladek about my tiny accommodation without a bath until I was on my way down to the lobby. As the elevator door opened, I could hear the unmistakable voice of Vladek Sheybal yelling at the desk clerk as he hit the counter with a very ornate cane with a Dragon's head made of gold. "How dare you give my friend a room without a bath! What do you expect him to do, urinate in the sink?? Do you know who he is?? This is David Del Valle the famous columnist from America!"

Within minutes, I was back in my room packing my things for the move up to the seventh floor and my very own bathroom. David Del Valle was not be urinating in the sink that night, thanks to that fabulous madman who decided to be my protector and confidant. His parting advice was always, "If you act like a star, then people will treat you like a star." Vladek lived by those words, and most of the time it seemed to work for him, although for others, I think it helps enormously if you look and sound like Vladek Sheybal.

Thus was the beginning of our friendship, which would include more than one trip across the pond for both of us in the years that followed.

Vladek achieved worldwide attention playing "Kronsteen," the chess master with ties to S.P.E.C.T.E.R. in Ian Flemings *From Russia With Love*. Vladek was always grateful for the support he received from Sean Connery, who suggested Vladek to director Terence Young.

Vladek also loved working with Lotte Lenya: "She was a fantastic lady that I adored. You know, of course, I nearly said no altogether to James Bond. It was Sean calling me personally at home telling me, 'Look Vladek, Listen to me, this is going to change the world. It's a new series, James Bond, and if you take part in it you are in a cult thing.' So I agreed to play the three scenes, including getting killed by Lotte's lethal shoe. My first day of work, Sean Connery was standing by the doorstep of soundstage door and said, 'Welcome to *From Russia With Love.*' What a sublime gesture and it made me feel like a star.

"The only sour note during the filming was producer Harry Saltzman standing on-set trying to explain my part to me and how it should be played. This went on for the better part of two days until I had just taken all I was prepared to take from someone who knew nothing about acting on screen or in the theater.

"At that time, I felt confident enough to behave like a star, so I told Harry, of his 'suggestions' regarding my acting, to allow Terence Young to do his job. Well, Saltzman reminded me that he was the producer of the film, and I said to him, 'Well, you provided the money, but not the acting,' and with that, I walked off the set. Now Lotte backed me up totally, but still I went to my dressing room and took off my make-up and went home. Later that night, Terence Young called and asked me to return to the film and swore that I would not see Harry Saltzman on-set again while I was working on *From Russia With Love.*"

One of Vladek's greatest mentors in films was Ken Russell, who first worked with him on his feature-length television play, *The Debussy Film* (1965). "Ken had seen me in my breakthrough role in Andrzej Wajda's *Kanal* (1957) and approached me in the BBC canteen one day and asked if I would appear in his *Debussy* as a film director. I suggested that I might accept if I could also play another role, as well. At first, Ken thought me very greedy and said no, and then later let me have my way, and so Ollie Reed and I worked for six weeks day and night on that film. After that, Ken and I were connected in some magical way because I worked for him several times afterwards on *Billion Dollar Brain* (1967), *Women In Love* (1969), *Dance of the Seven Veils* (1970), and *The Boy Friend* (1971), not to mention the unfinished *Moll Flanders* (1989).

(Vladek was not in *The Music Lovers*, as many filmographies state.) Years later, an elderly Ken Russell told me about the last days of our friend, in the back lawn of the British Counsel General's house in Hancock Park. By then, with his glory days well behind him, Ken looked like a tired strawberry in a white wig.

Around 1984, I had made a few trips to London, always finding the time to visit Vladek at his comfortable digs on Farm House Road (which had a pub conveniently on the corner), when he confided to me that he was planning to teach acting classes in Stanislavski in California. A few months later, Vladek turned up at my flat in Beverly Hills to watch *Women In Love* on tape, as he had not seen it in years. He was more than pleased to see that I had in my archive several photos from his films with Ken Russell, and he made a point of sending me many others from his then-busy career as a working actor.

One of my favorite things to do with movie actors was to watch their performances on tape with them. I hoped they would remember, perhaps for the first time, little tidbits from the shooting, etc. Vladek recalled Glenda Jackson worrying endlessly about her weight since she was seven months pregnant, and how it would photograph. He indicated how much he was responsible for the subtext he brought out of his character—Loerke's homosexuality—including his retelling of Tchaikovsky's horrific wedding night on the train that literally foreshadowed an infamous sequence from Russell's yet-to-be- filmed production of *The Music Lovers.*

Vladek was good friends with Isabella Telezynska, who I have already profiled in another chapter about her life in Hollywood. He also acted in Rome with Martine Beswicke in a very decadent film, *Il Bacio* (1973). "I play her slave and Martine gives a very wicked turn as a Devil-worshiping, drug-taking witch. Martine and I would wear outrageous costumes to orgies, and we were invited to all of them at the time, during the shooting of that film."

After we finished watching the film, the subject turned once again to Vladek's future and if he should move to Hollywood for a while. I suggested that he wait, since most of his work came from Europe, and if he wanted to work in Hollywood it would most likely be in television, and he was just too exotic for his own good in a place like Hollywood. He weighed the prospects and wisely chose to remain in England.

Once Vladek was back in London, he wrote, "I feel so happy at home, alone or not, with my scripts, songs, painting, and in my apartment in Paris, that *why* the hell should I bother to stay *again* in front of the camera and die of boredom? I had hope of Hollywood and being near you, but the thought that I had to organize everything myself and start (again) from scratch put me off that idea this year (1985). I have no 'American spirit of adventure.' I have not an American *push.* Voila."

Vladek tried on several occasions on my behalf to locate film personalities for me to interview for *Films and Filming*, which was still a prestige venue even as late as 1985. He tried to set up Jerzy Skolimowski and his wife, Joanna, who were great friends of his at the time. However, our schedules never mixed and we just never connected. As much as I adored *Deep End*, we still have not done our interview.

By the time I was back in London again, Vladek had organized a little dinner party for me and kept the guest of honor as a big surprise. However, the biggest surprise was yet to come. Vladek loved to cook and entertain for his friends, and especially his mother, who always cooked for him when she came to visit. That was to be a special night, and for starters he prepared baked potatoes filled with caviar and sour crème, with the rest of the menu to be Polish delights.

I arrived still not knowing what celebrity was to be offered up for the evening's surprise. Vladek answered the door dressed all in white with a red silk belt around his waist looking very *Oh, Calcutta!*. As I walked through the door, he said, "You are in for a real treat and our guest is already here." Our guest turned out to be the Indian producer Ismail Merchant who, with his life-partner, James Ivory, created films the entire world has applauded for decades. Mr. Merchant was a modest and charming man, who put me at ease straight away by telling me how much he loved reading *Films and Filming* over the years and that as a boy, living in a village with one cinema that only opened once a week, he lived for the movies, especially the glamorous Hollywood films of Rita Hayworth. Vladek was beaming at the sight of us getting on so well. We toasted the evening with champagne, and dinner was soon served. I wish I could remember everything that was said that night, yet it was one of those great evenings with no thoughts of tomorrow or taping interviews.

After Vladek's amazing dinner that was filled with gourmet delights, none of which was good for us, we continued our conversation over brandy in Vladek's living room, which was filled with his paintings and mementos from all over the world.

What happened next was the beginning of a classic French farce. There was a knock at the door, and when Vladek opened it, there stood a London bobby complete with the hat. Without any warning, he planted a kiss right on Vladek's mouth. "Sorry I didn't call first, love, but I am off as of ten minutes ago. Can I join the party?" It turned out that he was Vladek's latest conquest. The story of how they met is still vague, but believe me it was strange and very much in keeping with the master's offbeat lifestyle.

The best was yet to come. The four of us sat down, with Ismail very amused at that point by the current turn of events. We tried to pick up where we left off, but there was yet another knock at the door. This time it was not so amusing.

"Ismail, I know you are in there, so you might as well open the door!," we heard someone shout. "Ismail, what are you doing?"

Vladek looked at Ismail, who had turned very pale, and whispered, "Oh my God, it's James; he's found my appointment diary, and he gets like this when he has had too much to drink. James hates when this happens, that I go out on my own and keep him in the dark about it."

The knocking still continued, with more pleading from the other side of the door. "Let me in! I want to meet your lovers—all of them!"

Vladek was shocked at first, and then he began to laugh as only he could. "My God, what does he think we doing in here anyway? Ismail, go let James in and we will explain that young Mr. David is your new conquest."

"Very funny. Is there another way to get outside? I think it best that I take him home."

Vladek led Ismail out through the kitchen entrance so he could walk around to the front door without letting the overwrought James Ivory confront the three men inside, being much too tipsy to cope. To this day, I cannot see *Remains of the Day* or any Merchant/Ivory production without hearing the American half of that production company screaming, "Let me in! I want to meet *all* of your lovers!"

Vladek became a great friend of Bette Davis when he first came to Hollywood. She had just seen him in *From Russia With Love* and became a fan as well as a mentor. He took all of her advice to heart, including her now classic line, "Just be the bitch, darling, and you will always have work, if not a cult following." And of course it was true. Ms. Davis confided to him that she always narrowed her eyes, lowered her voice, and gave long pauses before saying her lines with a kind of whisper. If you watch some of Vladek's films you will see this method in action.

One of Vladek's favorite parts was that of "Mr. Boogaloo" in the mind-numbing future/rock/disco film, *The Apple* (1980). Today, that is a midnight cult film and, much like Ed Wood's *Plan Nine From Outer Space*, is regarded as one of those so-bad-it-is-good films. Vladek instinctively knew the film would be appreciated even though it took several years after his death for it to happen.

I remember Vladek showing me some audio tapes of all his songs he had kept from the film. The tapes were given to him by Menahem Golan, so he could learn all the lyrics at the time of filming in Germany back in 1979. Apparently, Menahem was just blown away by Vladek's ability to speak several languages. If you recall the scene where Mr. Boogaloo holds a press conference for a diverse group of international reporters and speaks to each one in his own language. One of his favorite stories about *The Apple* involved Grace Kennedy, the other lead singer who, after the film came out, married a millionaire who made it his business to try and find every print of his bride's infamous film and burn it on the spot. Luckily, the film has survived and is now on DVD for all to see.

In preparing this piece, I began to reread some of Vladek's letters written to me over the years, remembering what a loyal and generous spirit he was to me and anyone who came into his orbit and made him laugh. Vladek Sheybal passed away suddenly in his beloved flat off Farm House Road in London on October 16, 1992.

Vladek loved that line from *The Apple*: "Life is just a Casino Royale." He certainly knew how to be . . . a . . . *master*.

Chapter 35

A Cannon-Bury Tale

Jenny Craven

Once upon a time in Hollywood in the 1980s, a make-believe land that time forgot, there existed a film company that brazenly dreamt without guilt or shame of riches and fame as the seventh major studio in a self-conscious tinsel town that was only just aware of six. That ambitious company had already reinvented itself once without the butterfly effect.

The company's new moguls made it their top priority every year to make a pilgrimage amidst much media fanfare to the French Rivera, lusting openly for the highly sought-after prize—The Palm d'Or—awarded a at the legendary Cannes Film Festival. Think of that award as a modern equivalent of a literary pilgrimage to Canterbury. The Palm d'Or award is a far less lofty, yet seemingly enlightened ritual of show business—the naming of The Best in Cinema by your peers or the media.

Those men spared no expense in throwing the company's money around at the festival. They took out lavish ads for films being made or about to be made (even films that they were "thinking about" making in the near future were given ads and poster art). The parties at the Carleton Hotel for Stallone, Faye Dunaway, or Sharon Stone were legendary, even by Cannes standards of *dolce vita*. At the end of the day, it is still money that talks and the boys seemed to have plenty of that to go around. That force of nature, known throughout the then-current entertainment industry as The Cannon Film Group, was being obsessively ruled by a pair of cheerfully schizoid moguls—Menahem Golan and Yorum Globus—nicknamed the "the Go-Go boys." For the moment, the Go-Go boys were the golden boys, with the Mediterranean sun as their spotlight and a Hollywood complex for a stage.

Menahem and Yorum were cousins, who came into that wildly cinematic version of Chaucer from Israel with both their curly heads high in the clouds, dreaming of those $100 million three-picture-deals and, of course, *the movies*.

The Go-Go boys lived and breathed movies in much the same obsessive manner as the self-styled moguls of old Hollywood did, and that made them charming to the locals and, more importantly, to the press. I had already become very aware of The Cannon Group and their shenanigans, thanks to my friend, Martine Beswicke. Martine had been cast as the infamous "Happy Hooker," when Cannon picked up the franchise with their latest installment, *The Happy Hooker Goes Hollywood*. Martine signed on for an R-rated film and quickly found herself in what amounted to a soft-core sex film. As soon as she left the set, the producers brought in girls from the porn industry to do simulated sex scenes that would certainly give the film an X certificate and compromise Martine's reputation, which at the time was that of one of the James Bond girls, as well as her fame as a Hammer Horror Queen. She had to stand her ground with those sleaze merchants and make them honor their original agreement.

The film did little or nothing for Martine's career or the reputation of the Cannon Group, who already had most of the Hollywood insiders' tongues wagging about that renegade film company that had just made twenty-three films in one year, some of them not that bad considering the lack of taste or discrimination the company was becoming known for.

They produced critical favorites like *Runaway Train* and *Barfly*, as well as John Cassevetes' "art" film, *Love Streams*. That open-checkbook approach also attracted directors like Roman Polanski, John Huston, and even the iconic darling of the French new wave, Godard, to their banner, allowing a truly eclectic series of films to be made that would never have seen the light of day in today's film market.

Of course now, in the light of the new century, when the Cannon Film Group legacy is avidly discussed by film buffs that were not even born when the catalogue was new, thanks in part to their films being available on home video and DVD, it is usually the action flicks that are synonymous with the company's reputation. After all, they brought Charles Bronson's *Death Wish* franchise out of moth balls, and gave Sly Stallone the world's first arm wrestling, father-and-son bonding flick, *Over the Top*, the title of which sums up Sly's star performance in the production, as well. At the time, Stallone was paid an outrageous salary for that turkey, which also signaled to most Hollywood insiders the starting point of the long downward slide of the Cannon Group into bankruptcy by the end of the decade.

They created new action stars such as Michael Dudikoff, Chuck Norris, and the "muscles from Brussels," the decidedly short but altogether hunky Jean-Claude Van Damme (who, as the legend goes, was discovered by Menahem Golan one afternoon when the then out-of-work actor, who was moonlighting as a pizza delivery boy, brought a pizza up to the executive office. Jean-Claude waited for Golan to leave his office, and then he risked all to deliver more than a pizza—he placed a karate kick right over the mogul's head without touching so much as a hair. That bit of showmanship so impressed Golan that he placed Jean-Claude under contract, and the rest—as they say—is history.

The offices of the Cannon Film Group were never boring. You could always count on at least one screaming match between talent and their producers before lunch. All the staff basically hated the people they had to work for, making for a colorful environment to say the least. I will never forget walking off the elevator on the floor where the executive offices were located, only to see two Israeli guards, both armed with machine guns, standing on either side of the door leading into their offices. That was one reason I was glad not to have ever had to work within the building itself. The good news is that there were no incidents ever reported during the time the company was there.

My working connection to that infamous company arrived in the guise of British screenwriter Michael Armstrong, who lived with me during that time and introduced me to Jenny Craven, a producer he worked with at Cannon. Those two eccentric personalities both arrived in Hollywood from the UK. (My further recollections of Mike can be found in the "Marked by the Devil" chapter in this collection.) Every one of the personalities I met during that period came to remind me of the equally colorful characters one would encounter in the slightly more classical world of Chaucer's *Canterbury Tales*. Jenny would be the "Wife of Bath" who, instead of being an authority on marriage, would concentrate on her prowess of as a film producer.

Jenny can best be described as a comfortably neurotic woman with a terrific sense of survival that was constantly being undermined by being let down by those upon whom she had come to personally and professionally depend. I fell into both categories in about twelve months.

Both Jenny and Michael had enjoyed a working relationship with Cannon Films in the UK, Mike as a screenwriter on *House of the Long Shadows* (1981) and Jenny as one of the producers of Mike's film, as well as the 1985 Agatha Christie adaptation, *Ordeal By Innocence*. It is a known fact that once you begin to work behind the camera in the film industry, it is almost impossible to give up the notion that you belong there, and your mind cannot cope with anything less. Sadly, Jenny and especially Mike had to suffer their time in the thankless Purgatory of Development Hell until their friends and family finally broke through the induced coma of "I am just one deal away from major mega success" and brought them to the reality of just getting on with their lives and leaving Hollywood forever.

Menahem seemed to listen to Jenny's judgments from time to time and respond with fatherly remarks like, "Now Jenny, do you really think so?" Jenny felt that by being favored by Menahem, she was an officially anointed "Producer," and anyone not recognizing the fact would be sent packing from her circle.

Mike brought her around to my place for one of our many parties during his time with me. Jenny and Mike had their differences and fought most of the time over her involvement in *House of the Long Shadows*, which she apparently ruined by allowing director Pete Walker to remove footage that destroyed the pace of the film, yet she and I connected that year and became a team both out of respect as well as from a mutual need to be part of the industry.

Jenny had been staying off and on with a couple of English friends when she first arrived in Los Angeles. One of the most memorable as well as outrageous of her friends proved to be to be the incomparable April Ashley, who was living down the lane from Jenny off Havenhurst Drive in the West Hollywood area. We first met over cocktails at my friend Isobel Gray's cottage, which was down the lane from the one shared by April. I was captivated from day one, although both warned me that "April was in crisis mode, so be prepared for anything." Regardless, April is an original and well worth the effort, whatever that might be, and as I came to know her, there was no one more loyal and steadfast a friend.

April had been the toast of London café society, even becoming engaged to a peer of the realm, Lord Rowallan, when it was discovered that April was born a *man*. Since transsexuals were not that much in the news in 1961, April became the most notorious Englishman since Oscar Wilde. April lived life to the fullest and, when sober, looked and acted just like Vivian Leigh, with a voice to match. To her credit, she remained a lady of regal bearing regardless of circumstance. April had been one of London's top models when the scandal broke regarding her sex, the effects of which even removed her screen credit from *The Road to Hong Kong* with Bing Crosby and Bob Hope. April remained a pop culture personality to be reckoned with throughout the next three decades. She opened AD8, the infamous supper club in London, which had a spectacular opening with pop stars and royalty. She was exiled from society, and then returned to Hollywood. April was instantly welcomed into my life and we have remained friends to this day, although I have not seen her in at least five years. She now resides in San Diego, having just celebrated her seventieth birthday. Jenny had wanted to make a film of her life, and I wish he had pursued that with Menahem instead of going down that rabbit hole with her rock-and-roll Alice.

When Jenny Craven decided to give Hollywood a proper bash, she required a place of her own. The ideal flat would be quiet enough for writing and yet close enough to town to entertain without driving one's brains out. One of the most difficult as well as unpleasant tasks in Los Angeles has to be looking for a place to live. In Jenny's case, double that. We began a two week search that was turning up zero until one afternoon when we happened to be near Venice and felt the need of a cocktail followed by some lunch. Our regular place was the ever-popular Rose Cafe, a landmark in Venice and a great place to hang out anytime. On that particular occasion, I happened to be reading the local paper, a little two-page handout for the Venice beach area. There on the two-column rental section was an ad that read, "World's smallest house for rent. Only the special need apply." I immediately knew it should be Jenny's new abode.

That optimism led us straight over to what can only be described as "the smallest house at least in Venice, if not the state of California." The tiny cottage was sitting behind a large house on a quiet street. The cottage was charming and yes . . . very small. The bathroom had an antique tub with lion's head legs, and the kitchen had a built-in breakfast nook. Jenny loved the place on sight, and within minutes, we were in the lavish living room of the owners of the smallest house in the world, who also happened to live three houses down from the cottage. The owners were two very nice twenty-something gay guys who both had worked in films, so the vibes were on target for all concerned. Jenny had great rapport with most gay men, unless she felt they were not "getting" her, and then it could be dicey. If our whole house hunting episode did nothing else, it helped bond the two of us as close friends, and I am pleased to say we both needed that to happen at that point in time. Jenny became part of the passing parade, as Hollywood was about to find out for better or worse.

Jenny was hard at work in those days on a screenplay (who isn't in Hollywood?), which turned out to be a hard rock version of *Alice in Wonderland*. She decided early on that the best way to finance the film would be to secure the rights to several tunes that would constitute the soundtrack. Jenny was a marvel to behold when it came to tracking her prey for that project. She secured the services and council of Andy Summers, the great English guitarist and composer formally with The Police mega-band. Andy had just remarried his wife, Kate, that year, and was currently scoring *Down and Out in Beverly Hills* and the less than stellar *2010*.

Jenny felt a certain expertise with the music scene, primarily from her last experience as a film producer on *Ordeal By Innocence*. On that production, she managed to singled-handedly (in her opinion) secure the services The Dave Brubeck Quartet, the highly respected jazz musicians. The first choice for scoring the quaint English village mystery was the equally noted composer, Pino Donaggio. Jenny as producer rejected Pino in favor of a rather—to say the least—unorthodox jazz score. The film was not a major success upon release and many felt the score, however fine, was just not the right one for an Agatha Christie whodunit.

My time with Jenny then consisted of trekking down to the seedy clubs on the sunset strip, (especially the toilet that later became The Viper Room a decade later), to hear groups such as Chuck E. Weiss and The Godamn Liars that she was considering for the film's soundtrack. Sometimes with Andy in tow, and most of the time without, that is where I came into play as a supportive element to the project.

The most memorable encounter we had with a rock star had to be Billy Idol. Jenny had tracked the hard-rocking as well as hard-living musician until he agreed to read her screenplay. After about a week, Jenny kept calling Billy for some kind of commitment, since his name would certainly help in securing even higher-end talent, or so she hoped. After a few more calls, we were told that Billy was coming to her tiny place in Venice to drop off the script and give her some kind of answer. We were sitting by the front room window watching for his entourage to arrive, when all at once the unmistakable sound of motorcycles filled the air and a trio of bikers descended on her street. Billy Idol in full leather gear was the first to park his bike. As he was walking up stone steps to the front door, he suddenly turned away to walk over to where the clothes lines were still hanging somewhat full of wet clothes. Billy then made his way over by the back fence, where he unzipped his fly, taking a beer-sized piss, all the while talking to himself with lines like, "Oh, yeah man, that's it now, baby . . . ."

Unfortunately, it was just not the right day for a "white wedding." Billy, as it turned out, did not feel the project right for him. He was looking to star in a film rather than do a tune for one. So without too much fanfare, Billy departed the smallest house in the world quicker than it took him to take a leak. Jenny and I sat there afterwards and pondered an image from his last album. "Too much flesh and not enough fantasy," Jenny dubbed our albino rocker.

While Jenny focused more and more on getting her script made, my situation at home was getting rather desperate. Michael and I were both low on funds and he was in no position to help with the monthly bills, even though he was well into his fifth month as my most unlikely roommate. That is where Jenny proved to be aces once again. She advised us to get over to Cannon ASAP while she put in a call to Chris Pierce, who was then in charge of developing projects for the company, to give Mike and I scripts to read on a weekly basis at $35 a go. That proved to be a life-saver, so Michael Armstrong and I officially became script readers for The Cannon Group. Every week, we received at least twelve scripts to read, which worked out to six apiece. We were advised to make two sections: one for projects suitable for Charles Bronson, and the other for Chuck Norris. (Chris once repeated the slogan for a Norris picture at Cannon, "It has to be 100% Grade-A Chuck.) While a lot of what we received could have easily been done by either one of them, occasionally something really good came through (I remember one in particular by Rospo Pallenberg), but, of course, those films never got made. I remember how much Mike and I laughed over seeing what Cannon was up to. One day, we drove over to drop off our twelve scripts for the week, only to see a giant billboard on top of the roof at the Cannon offices below La Cineiga. "CHARLES BRONSON: Soon to be seen as *THE GOLEM*," the sign declared. That film, of course never happened.

If they had put old Charlie in monster make-up, it could not have been any worse than *The Apple* or *Masters of the Universe*. My favorite recollection of that film has to be running into that "actor's actor" of little people, the ubiquitous Billy Barty, in the front lobby at Cannon.

His career went all the way back to *The Wizard of Oz,* and he then had a substantial role in *Masters of the Universe.* Billy said to me, "Yeah, this is a blockbuster all right. We spent four hours yesterday waiting for He-Man to get out of make-up. He had this giant boil on his ass and the make-up guys had a time covering it up. You know his costume is such that his ass is hanging out of it 24/7, but the guy is built, no doubt about that. Did you see that broad he's livin' with . . . what's her name? Oh yeah, Grace Jones. Man, they ought to take the cameras over to their place and make a real movie." Billy was, if nothing else, candid in his observations.

Michael Armstrong had worked for a few weeks on the $30 million dollar *Lifeforce* for Cannon just before coming to the United States, and he told countless stories of just how out of control director Tobe Hooper was at that time. Tobe had made three pictures for Cannon, all of them bombs, and he was still reeling somewhat from all the rumors of just *who* had directed *Poltergeist,* which remains Tobe Hooper's only post-*Texas Chainsaw Massacre* hit.

Mike described miles of film being shot every day, so that no editor could make any sense out of what was being shot on any given day. By the time Mike left, the film was hopelessly over budget. Upon release, *Lifeforce* barely made back $10 million worldwide. That and his other films for Cannon, such as the tired remake of *Invaders From Mars* and the very unintentionally funny *The Texas Chainsaw Massacre* sequel with Dennis Hopper, certainly helped bring the company to its knees by the time the dust settled on both Hooper's career and Cannon's ability to survive.

The Go Go boys both openly admired Roger Corman, and yet

they learned nothing from him about following market trends, or about survival in the film business, even though one of them actually worked for Roger when he first arrived from Israel. Why they embarked on genre projects like *Pirates* that were out of favor with the public, or fads like the Lambada craze months after it was over and done with in America, remains a mystery. They made *Masters of the Universe* two whole years after the popularity of the comic was stone cold dead, yet they sunk millions into what Yoram was calling "The new *Star Wars*." That kind of thing did not endear them to the shareholders or the banks that lent them money.

There are literally hundreds of similar stories regarding Cannon Group, yet looking back with the vision and clarity of time, there is still much to recommend the efforts they made in allowing all types of films to come into being, some perhaps not so worthy, but in this brave new world of bad being so-bad-it-is-good, then Cannon Films is right up there with such now-revered companies as American International Pictures, Republic Pictures, as well as their British counterparts like Tigon Pictures and the Amicus Company. The Cannon legacy is a rich one, and it can be said with some authority that we will not see their like again.

As for Jenny Craven and Michael Armstrong, success eluded their efforts to remain players in the Hollywood of the 1980s. Jenny finally returned to England, whereupon her mother, Lady Craven, passed away in time, leaving her secure and well provided for, so perhaps one day Jenny will finally write her own memoir of those "Alice in Wonderland" experiences in show business. Michael Armstrong teaches theater and screen acting in London, where he still has a bit of a reputation as a survivor of "swinging London," and when asked, does an occasional lecture on his three genre films for students.

And what of the Go Go boys? Yoram and Menahem have reunited at least three times since my experience with the company. Menahem wrote and directed a film that almost no one has seen called *The Versace Murders* starring Franco Nero as the murdered fashion icon and, from all accounts, that one is a classic bad movie I for one have added to my must-see list of grade Z blockbusters. After 300 films and countless attempts to reorganize themselves as moguls, they are both, as of 2008, somewhat immortal, and as such, should be worshipped by film geeks of future generations for simply shepherding so many bad movies into existence. We just cannot begin to thank them enough for their vision and especially their tenacity.

Chapter 36

The Americanization of Christopher Lee

Christopher Lee

"You're writing an autobiography? Who is it about?"

That priceless remark was spoken to actor Christopher Lee by a P.R. woman from United Artists as he toured America promoting *The Man with the Golden Gun.* Christopher played the title character in that installment of the Roger Moore/James Bond films.

In May 1958, I was sitting in the balcony of one of those splendid old movie palaces from the "roaring twenties" that still existed in downtown Los Angeles at that time. I was the ripe old age of eleven, with my mother in tow (she was compelled to accompany me since the theater would not allow anyone under twelve inside), preparing to see what was to be a life-altering experience, as we watched for the first time *The Horror of Dracula* with Peter Cushing as Professor Van Helsing and Christopher Lee as Count Dracula, in blood-curdling Technicolor.

Up until that moment, my experience with horror films was viewing the black and white movies on television thanks to *Shock Theater* (the glorious exception being the 3-D shocker *House of Wax* in 1953). I was already hooked on Boris Karloff and especially Bela Lugosi. In fact, Lugosi had just died a couple of years before and left my child-hood a little darker because of it. I was so enamored of Lugosi's per-formance as the Count that his death was reported to me—then a rather intense seven year old—by my pal, the local theater manger (who had taken me under his wing) as I left a matinee performance of some current "giant bug flick" in 1956. He stopped me with the words, "Your friend, the horror actor, just died." That was the first time I think I realized it would not be possible to meet all the actors I admired on the silver screen, so on that very day, I vowed to never let any opportunity escape me to encounter my idols face-to-face and express what a difference their work made in allowing my imagina-tion to soar and marvel at the sorcery that was the movie-going expe-rience, especially in the young and obsessed.

Strange that I can still remember that afternoon in Los Angeles over forty years ago watching Christopher Lee in less than ten min-utes of actual screen time reinvent the role of Count Dracula for an entirely new generation of horror fans. At that age, I had a coward's habit of hiding behind the back of the theater seat in front of me just as something truly frightening was about to occur onscreen. When Dracula's bride bares her fangs to feast on the mild-mannered librar-ian's neck, the poor soul (John Van Eyssen) had just arrived at Castle Dracula to sort out the Count's books, when suddenly the library door bursts forth and in strides Christopher Lee, his face gorged on human blood, his eyes filled with red contact lenses. Hissing like an animal, Dracula leaps across the library table and hurls the female vampire to the floor like a rag doll. It was a defining moment that liberated the horror film as we knew it across the world.

I found myself both shocked and mesmerized by what I had just seen. I remained transfixed and somewhat frozen in my seat until the house lights finally went up and my mother took me, shaken and a bit stirred, from the theater, convinced her friends were right and horror films were indeed a bad influence on the minds of children. To her everlasting credit, she never prevented me from seeing one during my whole misspent childhood. In my case, it was far too late to save my soul from the damnation of Hammer films.

I kept faithful to that promise sworn in 1956. As the summer of 1971 unfolded, I found myself in London as Christopher Lee was about to give one of the then popular "John Player" lectures at the National Film Theater. At that time, Christopher was still making films for Hammer and wore those red contact lenses for at least another year before moving on to more mainstream fare in international films. The theater was filled to capacity that afternoon, so as soon as the film clips were at an end, Christopher Lee finished up his Q&A by informing his audience that "at the moment, I have fourteen films on offer." As he left the stage, I made a beeline for the lobby and, of course, I walked right into him, surrounded by the faithful, signing autographs, and I was soon engaging him in conversation. To my amazement, he seemed aware that was a preordained moment, so I was able to have my say, informing him once again what he must have heard dozens of times from fans my age: how his performance as Dracula was a defining moment in our childhoods, etc. Lee thoughtfully listened to what I had to say and was very kind and generous with his time. Somehow, I felt we would meet again.

Six years later, the fates decreed that I would actually be working in the business and living in Beverly Hills no less, enjoying the good life as a talent agent representing the Del Valle, Franklyn, and Levine Agency in Century City. One evening, I took some friends to see actress-turned-chanteuse Sally Kellerman trying out her "nightclub act" in West Hollywood at Studio One's infamous Backlot cabaret. We arrived late and found ourselves seated at a table with what turned out to be a most colorful, somewhat closeted character named Terry James. It seemed that the gentleman was at one time the "Lord Mayor of London," very well-connected to the British film colony in Hollywood and a real hoot in his own right. Terry acted the part and it was not unusual to see him dressed like a character right out of *A Passage to India*, complete with pith helmet, walking about West Hollywood "inspecting the colonies," as Terry was fond of saying, hoping to put us "Yanks" in our place.

During one of our many lunches around town, Terry was quick to discover that I was not only a devoted Anglophile, but that we shared a passion for film history, as well. One afternoon, he mentioned that he had dinner the night before with Christopher Lee, how difficult it was for him to adjust to life in Hollywood, and so on. I seized the moment at once, and I told Terry about my encounter with him at the National Theatre all those years ago. Once Terry realized how much Christopher Lee's films had meant to me growing up, he started to laugh, explaining how that information would amuse and inflate a certain British actor's already enormous ego. Terry then and there decided it was time that Christopher Lee and I were properly introduced. Terry did make it clear that if it was my intention to make the transition from fan to Hollywood professional, I should never bring up the "Count" or Hammer films unless the occasion warranted such a discussion.

Terry then issued a warning about Christopher's notorious way with money and that under no circumstances was I to pay for his meals beyond the ones I invited him to share with me. It seemed that over the course of their friendship in Hollywood, Christopher had begun a habit of letting Terry pick up the check, until one afternoon Terry let him have it by saying, "If you think it is some sort of honor to be seen dining in your company, then bloody well think again mate!" Frankly, it was kind of an urban legend around town regarding the British and how tight they all were with a dollar, so that did not deter me. If I had to be imposed upon, who better then "Count Dracula" himself to drain my pocketbook?

The Christopher Lees, (which consisted of his wife, Gitte, and their young daughter, Christina), had been living in Hollywood just about a year when I had my fateful meeting with "The Lord Mayor." They had taken up residence on the eighth floor of a Westwood high rise known as the "Wilshire Holmby." After a day or so, Terry telephoned with Lee's private number and a time I could call to properly introduce myself and perhaps join them for lunch.

My first phone conversation with Christopher Lee was a surprisingly long one filled with his serious questions about me being an artist's representative in Hollywood. He loved the fact I was a film buff working a management job in the business, since he felt most people in our business knew next to nothing of its history. "They have no idea who Garbo was!" he said. We spoke about the pitfalls of typecasting, our mutual friends in London, and a lengthy discussion on the real meaning behind the ending of Antonioni's *The Passenger*, which had just come out. Finally, we spoke about Studio One, where our mutual friend, Terry James, and I first met. When I explained that the disco was predominantly gay, he paused for a moment, and then he said in that deep baritone I knew so well from his films, "Well, if I do go there, perhaps I should come alone."

One of the things during that conversation that must have endeared me to him was when I quoted our mutual friend, the eminent fantasy writer, Ray Bradbury, who described Los Angeles as "Twenty-nine oranges in search of a navel." Christopher just roared at that. I felt he knew in his heart of hearts that Los Angeles was not his kind of town. We got along so well during our conversation that I asked him if he would care to have lunch with me later that week. To my surprise, he said yes, which left me with the responsibility of choosing the restaurant.

In those days, the only place to take a celebrity in Hollywood where they could be seen and you could bask in their reflected glory was Ma Maison, a seemingly modest French Bistro off Melrose that was run with perfection by Patrick Terrail, and later with his partner, Wolfgang Puck. The place was legendary in the film industry as the most difficult restaurant to get a table, not to mention its attitude— so haughty that it had an unlisted number. The enclosed-in-plastic garden room was the main dining area, with tables always very close together so you could overhear most of whatever conversation was going on at any given time. There was a dining area back near the kitchen by the bar, but that was always reserved for Orson Welles, who came in through the back of the restaurant with his little black poodle, "Kiki." Patrick allowed Orson the privilege of bringing in his pet like they tend to do for special customers in Europe.

I arrived at Ma Maison half an hour early to make sure we got our table because that was my first opportunity to impress my childhood hero in Tinsel Town. It was a good thing I did. The place was jammed for lunch, as usual, and I was told it might be ninety minutes before my table was ready. I decided to have a drink at the bar in hopes that Christopher might do the same if we were forced to wait that long even with my reservation.

I walked back to the bar and saw the great Orson already at his little table dining by himself. He noticed me looking at him and motioned for me to come over.

"If you are waiting for a table, you could be in this bar until dinnertime, the way things are looking."

I explained I was waiting for my luncheon guest, the newly arrived British actor, Christopher Lee.

Orson smiled at me for the longest time and said, "Aren't you that fellow Gary Graver was telling me about who is besotted about the horror film?"

I was so stunned that Gary had mentioned me. Gary worked as a cameraman, so I had asked him to have Orson sign a photograph from *Chimes at Midnight* for me since they were always hanging out together.

Orson then said to me in his best Mr. Arkadin voice, "Young sir, you march right over to that head waiter who handles the reservations and tell him you are waiting for *Christopher Lee,* and I guarantee you will be seated straight away, and when you are finished, please stop by my table," he concluded with a wink.

I was off to do as he suggested. Of course, it worked, and I was seated a good fifteen minutes before Christopher arrived.

I must say that when Christopher did make his entrance, it was worth the wait. He was a tall man at six-foot five, and he pretty much towered over most of the diners that day. He made his way over, and after the initial handshakes and so forth, we ordered drinks to start.

"I would adore a 'Kir' I think," said Christopher.

A 'Kir,' for the uninitiated, is a sublime concoction of white wine and crème de cassis on the rocks. That became my favorite drink with lunch for years after that. When I mentioned that Orson Welles was dining in the back, Christopher smiled and told me that he was once directed by the great Welles in a television production of *Moby Dick* in London, and was, of course, greatly impressed with Orson, remembering him saying after a take, "*Print* with *enthusiasm*!" When it came time to leave, Christopher was simply too shy to say hello to Welles. However, Orson had already left the building, so there was nothing to fear.

Our first lunch together was nothing if not a success. He was charming, funny, and filled with fascinating stories about filmmaking all over the world. Within an hour or so, we were finishing each others' sentences. I was careful about discussing the Hammer years with him during that first lunch, but the subject of his long association with Peter Cushing was discussed, especially Cushing's devotion to his late wife, Helen. Christopher was quite candid about how he felt regarding her. "She was a psychic vampire and that relationship was complex, to say the least. Helen's mental hold on her husband was absolute. Helen did not trust me for many years and actually said to me at one point, 'You think you are a bigger star than my husband, don't you?'"

At that point, Christopher smiled and then told me his reply to Helen. "Well, my dear, I am taller than Peter."

Christopher reflected for a moment after that and told me that a lot of Peter's mourning was a heavy combination of both remorse and guilt, for the temptations of working with some of the most beautiful women in the world sometimes proved too much for him, being a mortal man after all. However, after Helen's death, he became one of the living dead, unable to think or be with people. "Peter simply went into the grave with her at that point." He was inconsolable.

"You know, Peter and I went to great lengths in our separate careers not to be considered just a double-act in horror pictures, as typecasting is one of the worst pitfalls an actor can let happen in a career." However, it was the great man himself, Boris Karloff, who felt just the opposite and would be the first to tell you that if it had not been for his being cast as the Frankenstein monster in 1931, he might well be forgotten today and not revered as an icon, an honor Boris most richly deserves, by the way. My career was much like his, really, for I too became known after I played the creature for Hammer in *Curse of Frankenstein,* and then a year later—well, you know the rest don't you?"

I wound up doing at least three print interviews with him during his eight years in town. I don't think he ever adjusted to being so far from Europe. His only real outlet was golf, and sometimes he played five days a week between films. His wife Gitte, a stunning former model from Denmark, was always traveling abroad since Los Angeles was not her cup of tea either. Christopher was funny about that, too. "My wife stays with the richest families on the continent, and yet she calls me collect!" I could hear Terry James laughing at that remark.

Looking back simply does not get better than recalling that afternoon in 1979 lunching with Count Dracula, receiving advice on securing a table from "Citizen Kane," and even dining in that hopelessly pretentious Bistro known as "Ma Maison." The day remains cast in my memory with a golden hue of a paradise lost.

There was one lunch that I shall never forget, since it was a total comedy of errors filled with misinformation, not to mention an actor thinking out loud when silence would have saved the day. One of the downsides to being an agent is having scripts thrown at you on a daily basis. Everyone in Hollywood with the exception of yours truly has a script. There was this one instance where a script was brought to my attention by a kindly, caring woman named Flora Mock. Flora was a short stout woman of sixty with a benign round face topped with white hair. She also possessed a soft voice, which, combined with her gentle manner, made her an ideal person to have as a friend, not to mention that I was always meeting great-looking people at her parties. Flora was the proud mother of actress Laurie Mock, who appeared in the cult films *Hot Rods to Hell* and *Riot on the Sunset Strip*. Flora had spent several years writing a script entitled *Sub-Rosa*. It was an art film about youth and deception. There was one particular character in the script, an aristocrat of advancing years, "Count Andressi." As soon as I read the script I knew "the Count" was tailor-made for Christopher Lee.

Flora lived in one of those large, slightly rundown houses in Beverly Hills right across the street from a former residence of Greta Garbo. Sadly, her place was mortgaged to the hilt. Flora made ends meet by taking a loan on the house every year to pay for yet another season in Los Angeles. That script was her last chance to be a player in Hollywood. Her husband was in the business, as well. Long divorced from Flora, he married yet again to Claire Mock, a younger woman who became a casting director of some standing in Hollywood named. Flora had to make her film, and as time was starting to run out, she gave me the script with a director already in mind. She had her heart set on Joseph Losey, a world-class director, who was, at that time, quite unbankable thanks to Liz and Dick Burton and their over-the-top, addictive lifestyle (watch *Boom!* if you ever get the chance). I on the other hand wanted to see Christopher play in something worthwhile, so I called him and sent the script over for him to read. Over the phone, Christopher was very impressed with the script and wanted to be involved. I told him about Flora wanting Losey. "I know Joe Losey from London. Leave it to me." So with that, I suggested a lunch where Christopher could meet the writer and her producer, who was at that very moment setting up a trip to Cannes for them to try and market the whole thing as a package. I arranged the lunch at the Café Swiss in Beverly Hills, as we wanted a low-profile environment to discuss the project.

The day of the lunch, I arrived at Café Swiss early as usual, soon to be joined by Flora and her producer, another elegant-looking woman in her late forties. We then organized the table and the stage was set for them to meet Christopher Lee and set the project in motion for real. Christopher arrived and asked me to have a word with him before we went in and met the ladies. I learned that Christopher had spoken a bit hastily about having a current entree to Joseph Losey. They'd only met once, many years ago, at a film festival, so I had to go into that dining room with Christopher in tow, knowing between the two of us that we were no closer to securing a deal for those ladies than before I had placed myself in such a pointless predicament. Why film stars exaggerate their contacts is still a mystery to me, since nothing is really to be gained by it.

Lunch went without a hitch and the ladies were charmed by Christopher's knowledge and experience. Yet I learned a real lesson about trusting projects to hearsay and other people's contacts, not to mention its consequences when they are wrong. The film of *Sub-Rosa* never came to be made, and Flora returned from Europe a bitter woman out for revenge, since her producer cheated her out of money and then betrayed her. Flora spent the rest of her life trying to get even and confronted that woman in public at every opportunity. I never got involved with another script, and remained the better for it.

From that time on, I rang Christopher from my office, chatted if I had the time, or asked his advice regarding one of my clients. I was working with Barbara Steele at the time and I knew Christopher had made a film with her in London. At one time, they were quite friendly.

"Barbara is a damn fine actress," he would say when her name came up. He used her as an example of how limiting the casting process was in Hollywood, noting that a woman with Barbara's pedigree could not find work. "It is all based on youth and who is the next flavor of the month in this place."

I happened to mention that my friend, Martine Beswicke, was working in town, doing an episode of the popular television show, *The Fall Guy,* with Lee Majors.

Christopher knew her ex-lover, John Richardson, having starred opposite him in a remake of *She* for Hammer films back in the 1960s. "Are they still a couple? Did they ever tie the knot?"

I told him she was very much a free agent in that regard, and the next thing I knew, we were both invited up to his condo for drinks the next evening.

Martine Beswicke was a strikingly exotic and beautiful woman, who usually liked to spend the majority of her evenings out on the town with a distinctly younger crowd of men. However, an invitation like that was not to be missed. Martine seemed to recall meeting Christopher at Ascot in London back in her Hammer days in the early 1970s. Martine had played the title role in *Doctor Jekyll and Sister Hyde* for that studio, as well as *Prehistoric Women*. Both those films gave her a certain "camp" value with the current crop of producers like Allan Carr, who loved the fact that she was in those films in the first place, always promising to find "the perfect role" for his Amazon Queen, but alas it was not to be.

We arrived the next evening in her little black Volkswagen that Martine had affectionately named "Pearl" at the Wilshire Hombly on the designated hour. After a slight confusion at the front desk, we were finally given the okay to take the elevator up to the eighth floor. Christopher met us at the door dressed in blue jeans and a sports shirt to show off the belt buckle given him by the Stunt Men's Association in recognition for nearly drowning in *Airport 77*. "This buckle means more to me than an Oscar. Sorry you had a problem at the desk; all I can tell you both is Muhammad Ali had no trouble getting up here."

With that, we entered his condo, which was spacious, with bookcases dividing the rooms from one another. As we entered, I saw a large oriental figure at the door that was surrounded by screens of oriental design—items acquired from years of traveling to Hong Kong to film those "Fu Manchu" films, no doubt.

Watching those two survivors from the British film industry enjoy each other's company that evening was such a trip for me. Knowing her as well as I did, it was easy to see that she quite liked him. I thought to myself, *if people could only see this side of Christopher's personality that was so relaxed, displaying that wicked sense of humor of his, a lot of his detractors who found him to be aloof and humorless would undoubtedly change their opinions.* Christopher was such a cultivated and charming man in a mix like that evening, yet when he found himself in larger groups, his nerves brought out the pompous side of his nature and his persona became forever tied to it in the minds of Hollywood insiders.

When Christopher was filming the Chuck Norris action thriller, *An Eye For An Eye,* with Richard Roundtree, someone asked Richard what he thought of Christopher. Richard thought for a moment, and then said, "That cat is heavy . . . too heavy." Christopher was making one film after another in Hollywood, but the quality was not there. Even his film with Spielberg was not a success, and his patience was beginning to wear thin. He once told me his mantra for work: "*If* the money is there and the part is there...*I'm* there, and *I deliver!*"

After eight years, Christopher had achieved what he had set out to accomplish in America. "It was crucial for me to make myself available to the people in Hollywood to whom I had been just a name and a face on the screen, living thousands of miles away in Europe." Before he left altogether, I invited him over to my place for the last time to photograph him next to my billboard size poster for *Frankenstein* that I acquired from the late director Robert Florey. We had decided to send prints of the poster with and without Christopher to his neighbor in London, Mrs. Boris Karloff, as a surprise gift.

After the shoot, he walked around looking at all my memorabilia and, while standing by my fireplace, I asked him to pose with the Lugosi *Dracula* posters, something I don't think he had ever done before. "I wore a ring that Lugosi had worn in the last four of my Hammer Dracula films out of respect for this man who had worn his cape to the grave."

The very last time I saw Christopher after he finally moved out of his condo was in a rather modest motel on Wilshire Boulevard not far from their former abode. The Lees were staying there until the time for their flight back to the UK. I decided to interview him one last time to commemorate his eight years in the "Colonies," as the Lord Mayor would have said. We sat there talking with a tape recorder between us. His pet cat, "Renfield," slipped through the half open door and wandered out into the motel hall, so the last image I had at that moment in time of Christopher Lee, the definitive Dracula after Lugosi, was watching him chase after his cat, talking baby talk to it—"Where does daddy's little baby think its going?"—even through it was named after a certain fly-eating gentleman dreamed up by Bram Stoker.

Christopher Lee, after eight bizarre years living among the smog and palm trees below the Hollywood sign, returned to England where he underwent heart bypass surgery. He not only recovered beautifully, but went on to become one of show-business' hardest working character actors. Now well into his eighties, Christopher is still giving masterful performances in such blockbusters as *The Lord of the Rings* and *Star Wars*. He has become far more than the horror star of my youth. In point of fact, Christopher achieved a career that spanned over half a century. He deserves to be called "an icon of the British film industry." Knowing him, he is probably even prouder of being made a "Commander of the British Empire" (OBE). His late friend, Boris Karloff, would have been delighted had he lived to see his "successor" achieve so much and would have undoubtedly given his favorite compliment: *"Full marks!"*

Chapter 37

The Bitter Tears of Count Yorga

Robert Quarry

During the time I was involved in providing an audio commentary with actor David Hedison for the DVD project of *The Fly* {1958} over at 20th Century Fox the same producers were given the green light from MGM/UA to put together a seven-disc boxed-set of Vincent Price horror films, two of which—*Dr. Phibes Rises Again* and *Madhouse*—co-starred a relatively unknown character actor named Robert Quarry.

Quarry enjoyed a substantial career boost during the 1970s thanks to the unexpected success of a low-budget skin flick that changed its spots mid-production from a soft-core *The Loves of Count Yorga*. Legend has it that Quarry convinced producer, Michael Macready, to film it as a straight horror film and release it with a more mainstream title, *Count Yorga Vampire*. The marketing ploy was courtesy of American International Pictures, the studio that in time tried to groom Quarry into a horror star to take over from Vincent Price should he choose to leave the studio.

Count Yorga Vampire was a sleeper hit that summer, setting Quarry, a working actor for over twenty years, on a rollercoaster ride to near-stardom as the heir-apparent to Vincent Price. While I was still in town recording my remarks for a mini-documentary they were preparing to go out with the Vincent Price boxed-set, a call was made to secure Quarry for an interview and perhaps even an audio commentary regarding his work with Vincent. Apparently when Quarry answered his phone and listened to what the offer was, he turned it down flat by reminding the young man who called on behalf of the studio, "I am an old man now. Leave me alone."

When I asked the producer if Quarry was coming in to work, they told me what he had said, and then they asked if I knew him, but more to the point, did I know what the relationship was really like between Vincent and Quarry.

Did I know Robert Quarry? Yes. In fact, he was at one time in my life like a member of the family—the eccentric but lovable "Uncle Bob," but definitely not the kind of Uncle on whose knee you sat, either.

I have in past essays discussed a number of nightclubs and cabarets in Hollywood that figured rather prominently in my interaction with certain celebrities. I think this is the time to introduce an infamous fixture on the Sunset Strip that was known as Numbers, which used to be located at the entrance to Laurel Canyon from Sunset, directly across from what used to be the Virgin Mega Store.

That well-appointed restaurant/bar was often described by the locals as a nightclub, where mature gentlemen could find male companionship for the evening and beyond for a price. The young men employed there as bartenders or waiters all wore white muscle shirts that bore a number from one to fifteen. The "host" of the establishment was even given his own star billing on the sign, alerting patrons to park their cars in the back parking lot and descend the stairs to a chrome and leather hideaway complete with a full bar and restaurant. "Welcome to Numbers, with your host, Ernest." Ernest was a short, stocky slightly European fellow in his late forties, who looked a bit like the comic Bill Dana without the laugh track.

For an agent, Numbers was, on the right occasion, the perfect place to chat up working actors, the ones with high visibility in television, and in that way, hopefully acquire some clients that might actually make me some money for change. At that point, I represented way too many unknowns for my own good. Also, many producers and a variety of Hollywood types showed up at the watering hole like clockwork for years.

It was around 1980 that I first encountered the man behind "Count Yorga," as well as such familiar TV personalities as Richard Deacon, Charles Nelson Reilly, and, when he was in town, Paul Lynde. Numbers was a riot on weekends, especially during the summer when its eccentric show biz clientele attracted a zany cross section of people, both gay and straight. All were welcomed, and the better looking someone was, the wilder it got, since one could never forget that Numbers was all about taking care of business, as long as you ran it by "your host, Ernest."

The first occasion I really got to chat with Robert Quarry was at Richard Deacon's birthday, which was celebrated at Numbers on one long ago Friday night. Richard was a great guy and everyone that got to know him was the better for it. He was a generous, big-hearted man with a knockout sense of humor. He used to joke about how so few of his co-workers ever knew he was gay. "I always played such straight-laced men in suits." I, of course, remembered him from when I was a kid watching the old *Leave It To Beaver* show, on which Richard was Lumpy's dad. It was the night of Richard's party when I first noticed Count Yorga in the flesh, sitting at the far end of the bar nursing a martini. I first checked with Richard to see if that fellow was who I thought it was. Richard laughed and said, "Oh yeah, that's Bob alright, the ghoul from the graveyard. Go on over, and he'll get a real kick out of this."

My first conversation with Quarry was rather short. He was at first flattered that I knew so much about his films, but explained that he was really there to celebrate Richard's birthday, and he suggested that I call him and we would get together for a drink and a chat when not so much was going on. His parting line to me was a zinger: "Listen kid, I would buy you a drink, but at this point in the evening, it might dip into my 'trick' money, so let's have a rain check."

I made a point of keeping his number after such an arch introduction, so later in the week, I invited him over to my house to meet some of my friends. I decided to make it a real "horror film soiree," so I invited Curtis Harrington and Reggie Nalder to join us, and then invited Martine Beswicke, as well, since I knew she could hold her own against the bomber squad of arch fiends I had booked for the evening.

Robert enjoyed being social, so when he arrived at my front door, he was ready to party and dressed in Levi's and a work shirt, not exactly the attire I expected from Count Yorga Vampire, but definitely proper West Hollywood attire. He was a cool dude, to be sure. He seemed to have a really good time, however the next day, when we talked on the phone, he was rather acidic about the whole evening and singled out poor Reggie to rag on, saying to me, "I tried to have a conversation with this corpse, and by the time I left, I at least expected to see a pee stain materialize on his pants to show he was still alive." It seemed that Reggie was so put off by Quarry's humor that he just sat there in silence, pretending not to understand much of what was being said.

After a while, the thing I began to realize most about Quarry was his bitterness, justified or not, regarding his career in Hollywood. The whole "Count Yorga" thing had his back up as soon as the afterglow of publicity wore thin, not to mention his exclusive contract with Samuel Z. Arkoff, whom Quarry always referred to as "Mr. Heeb." He once sent a Christmas card to the Arkoff family, which depicted Count Yorga in full regalia sitting on a toilet. As Quarry later explained, "Arkoff, with little regard for building my chances of a real movie career, chose to put it firmly in the toilet with shitty films that exploited my name and little else, which is basically what he did to Vincent, as well."

Quarry had cultivated an intense hatred of the late Louis M. Heyward, who was head of European production when he was making *Dr. Phibes Rises Again* and *Madhouse* in London. According to Quarry, it was "Deke" Hayward who stabbed him in the back by going to some of Quarry's posh English friends during filming and "outing" him to them, as well as trying to take them away from him by slandering him in any way possible. When that gossip was related back to Quarry, he rightly or not never stopped feeling betrayed by all the bad blood. That probably led to his contract being terminated, but not, unfortunately, before an embarrassing swan song at AIP called *Sugar Hill*, a Black exploitation flick about zombies. In that film, Quarry plays a gangster, a part that was originally written for a Black actor. Lines like "Listen Fabulous, I may make an honest nigger out of you yet," really sounded ugly even in that era when political correctness had yet to appear.

I never got the impression from Vincent Price that he ever felt any real competition from Quarry as an actor or as a potential rival in the horror market. Vincent was always a *star*, whether in or out of horror films, not to mention a far better actor than he was given credit for in his lifetime. Quarry used to give interviews regarding Vincent and made observations about him relying too much on camp and never really creating characters beyond an extension of his personality.

That is a given with most movie stars. Think of John Wayne or Jack Nicholson. They always create their characters as extensions of their larger-than-life personas. I have seen most of Quarry's films, and there is not a one of them in which he is anything other than Robert Quarry reciting someone else's dialogue. I believe that Quarry had a deep respect for Vincent Price as an actor, yet circumstances combined with meddling producers to put a wedge between them. Who knows—in a perfect world they might even have forged a rapport reminiscent of what Vincent enjoyed with Peter Lorre, had chemistry instead of trumped-up rivalry been there. The funny stories Quarry used to tell regarding Vincent and wrap parties where Price got the nickname Vincent "Half-Price" due to his custom of taking back to his hotel room anything of value that was left on the craft-tables. He also told stories of when Quarry picked up the tab for the wrap party on the *Madhouse* set, when it became obvious that Vincent was not going to spring for it. All those anecdotes made for entertaining dinner conversation, but they certainly did not help create a bond between the actors.

Those were the kinds of memories crossing my mind, as I sat in that audio booth trying to conjure up bits and pieces of my friendship with Vincent and wondering if Quarry would turn up while I was still there. I had not seen him in a good many years. However, I had enough fond memories to remember his friendship and generosity with sincere affection. I couldn't help but recall wonderful gourmet dinners at his home, even those during really difficult times when his mother, Mimi, was ill and living with him during her last years, and I especially remembered our evenings out on the town.

Even though Quarry and I would never meet again, I was always in touch and aware of his comings and goings through mutual friends on the Internet, right up until his death in the first week of February 2009. His passing brought to the surface again just how much of a "lost horizon" his life was after all was said and done. It seemed to me that anyone who stayed afloat in Hollywood as long as Quarry did was not only a survivor, but a winner, as well. However, his dreams and ambitions were always just a little higher and harder to reach than the average working actor. He never fully recovered from Sam Arkoff and Louis "Deke" Heyward's treatment of his contract at American International Pictures, which placed him within reach of assuming Vincent Price's mantle as the top horror star in America during the late 1970s.

As Quarry explained the situation to me, Arkoff had offered him an exclusive contract to appear in horror films for the company beginning with *Dr. Phibes Rises Again* and followed with another starring role. The failure of the second *Dr. Phibes Rises Again* placed Quarry's career in a holding pattern that simply never took flight. Vincent Price was disgusted by then with his career and especially with what Arkoff had chosen for him after Jim Nicholson left to start his own company. Sadly, Jim died suddenly after making just one horror film, *The Legend of Hell House,* under his newly formed banner. Vincent Price ended his run with AIP in what could have been a *tour de force*, a horror version of *Sunset Boulevard* called *Madhouse.* That would have reunited both Quarry and Peter Cushing in the same film after both stars shared the screen in *Dr. Phibes Rises Again.*

Arkoff set the stage for disaster by promoting Quarry as Vincent's heir-apparent way before it should have happened, setting the two men in a negative relationship that they simply never attempted to rectify. Quarry invited Peter Cushing to homemade dinners, while Vincent entertained himself elsewhere. When the two turned up at the studio, the publicity department tried to organize interviews for them, but Vincent felt betrayed by AIP and simply ignored Quarry whenever possible. Quarry loved to talk about how cheap Vincent was and how jealous he was over all the attention Quarry received from AIP.

All of that changed during the filming, and according to Quarry, Deke Heyward went behind his back to his social circle in London telling all interested parties about his gay lifestyle, which he never really hid in the first place, openly living as he did with a Latin boy toy and having the time of his life.

When Quarry returned to Los Angeles, he sent the Sam Arkoffs a Christmas card that depicted himself in full Count Yoga costume sitting on a white porcelain toilet with his dress pants down and a vampire's shit-eating grin. Quarry was tired of pretending to play the game and had just received the final AIP project that ended his contract with the studio, *Sugar Hill,* in which Arkoff got his revenge by casting the *Count Yoga Vampire* star in what amounted to a minor heavy in the script. The catch was that his character was supposed to be played by a Black man, so lines involving Quarry using the N-word were peppered throughout the script, causing him to apologize before every take to his Black co-workers. He befriended the young actress playing Sugar Hill. One incident had nothing to do with Arkoff and everything to do with where they were filming. *Sugar Hill* placed Quarry in the role of a Civil Rights advocate, when he was told in a local dinner club that their policy was that they could not seat him with a Black woman. When they also reminded him he did not have a reservation, Quarry said that was not the case—he made a reservation in the name of Abraham Lincoln.

The second decline for Quarry happened a bit later in his career, when he was tapped to play the second lead in the remake of the old television series, *The Millionaire.* The premise was a forerunner of *Fantasy Island.* Each week, his character sought out worthy strangers on behalf of his master and gave them a check for $1 million, and then the rest of the hour was taken up with how they spent it. The production was first class all the way, and the producers assured Quarry at least a season of twelve episodes with the possibility of a second season, and from there the horizons looked blue indeed. On the strength of their enthusiasm, Quarry went right out and bought a brand new deluxe Cadillac and prepared to assume a lifestyle of the rich and famous . . . but then the pilot episode was aired, and bang! All was over.

No twelve episodes, and worse, no more paychecks.

Near-stardom in two different mediums was just too much for one man to bear, and yet Quarry kept the faith and continued to look for parts. More than once, he got them, so he remained afloat. The Robert Quarry I remember was a witty, acerbic gentleman with a potty mouth and a big heart. I will always miss him, and I feel lucky to have had him as a friend. I have a lasting example of the Quarry wit on a photograph he gave me from *Count Yorga Vampire*. It reads, "To David, a very special person—according to you!"

Chapter 38

The Gruesome Twosome

John Abbott and Martin Kosleck

I decided to revisit my experiences with two of Hollywood's most bizarre and talented character actors. The urbane and sophisticated John Abbott, whose unique voice and bulging eyes made him ideally type-cast as fussy professors or a timid murderer with a perverse kink in his psyche. Martin Kosleck, who was an equally colorful personality, was known internationally as one of Hollywood's master interpreters of Nazi villains, especially Joseph Goebbels, whom he played on film five times.

Those two men once appeared in a film together at Universal Studios in 1945 in one of the last of Basil Rathbone's Sherlock Holmes features, the lackluster *Pursuit To Algiers* . . . but more on that shortly.

I became acquainted with John first as a close friend and neighbor of my dear friend, Curtis Harrington. Curtis introduced us at one of the director's many parties at his Vine Way abode, and after a few encounters, we discovered a mutual interest in vintage films and British theater, so we became friends. John had retired from motion pictures when I knew him and had found a new and even more rewarding career as an acting teacher. He gave classes and workshops in his home until his health would no longer permit it.

Martin entered my life a bit later, oddly enough through one of John's students, a hunky lad we shall call "Tony," who befriended Martin and his longtime companion, Christopher Drake, visiting them regularly at their secluded Laurel Avenue home six blocks from Santa Monica Boulevard in West Hollywood. Tony also helped John run errands when needed and made a ritual of taking the fussy actor twice a week to Bob's Big Boy restaurant, where John indulged himself in several cups of what he always referred to as "the best dammed coffee in Los Angeles"

Both actors had appeared in so many classic films that it would be difficult to pick a favorite. However, since I was such a devotee of the horror genre, the films that made me remember them both with great pleasure were the few excursions they both made into that realm of the fantastic.

John was always a reliable supporting player, whether at Warner Bros. acting opposite such stars as Bette Davis and Claude Rains in *Deception,* or holding his own with scene-stealer Peter Lorre in the highly enjoyable mystery thriller, *The Mask of Dimitrios.* His greatest supporting role in films would have to be as the outrageously eccentric Frederick Farlie in the Wilkie Collins Gothic chestnut, *The Woman in White,* featuring a barnstorming performance by Sidney Greenstreet as the evil Count Fosco. John had a 16mm print of that film, and one night we screened it in the loft of my friend, photographer Dan Golden. The loft was on Boyd Street in downtown Los Angeles, where just the day before, he had Kenneth Anger show his new edit of *Lucifer Rising*. We wisely kept both events separate, although we had the same audience both nights.

There was only one occasion when John had his name above the title in a horror film and that was over at Republic Studios, a studio known for making primarily Westerns, in a little-known "B" picture, *The Vampire's Ghost*. That particular film, blessed with a literate script by Leigh Brackett, has acquired a substantial fan base over the years as a sleeper with a refreshingly unique take on the overdone vampire formula by creating a character who, while centuries old, is world-weary in a Byronic mode, rather than relying on the eternal character-ization of Stoker's oft-filmed *Dracula*.

The film is set in Africa and follows the trail of blood caused by the undead Webb Fallon, cursed during the reign of Queen Elizabeth I to wander the earth as a vampire. John's unusual features suit the character quite well, although it is startling to see him as the tough owner of a seedy tavern, the watering hole of drunken sailors and mis-fits. John plays this creature against type, as Webb Fallon could walk the earth in the daylight, and his blood-taking is all done off-camera. It was great to see John take on a lead role, allowing one to see what a great actor he could be when Hollywood allowed him to carry a film. My good friend at the time, author Richard Lamparski, quoted me regarding John Abbott in the 11th edition of his long running series of books on Hollywood celebrities, *Whatever Became Of… ?* I singled out *The Vampire Ghost*, John's star turn in a classic vampire film, which was a well-kept secret among horror fans.

When I was a monster kid growing up in the 1950s, Martin Kosleek caught my attention with multiple screenings on late night TV's *Shock Theater* package of horror films that included Universal's *The Mummy's Curse* and *House of Horrors*. The real star of that "horror noir" was the iconic Rondo Hatton, whose tragic real-life acromegaly made his participation in any movie scream of exploitation. Be that as it may, Rondo has a huge fan base among horror geeks. An award is even given online once a year in his name and image for those worthy of his blessing.

What makes that particular outing so unique is the odd chemistry on screen between Martin and non-actor Rondo Hatton. They are a bit like the double act of the Frankenstein monster and Ygor from *The Son of Frankenstein,* only without the pathos.

One might describe Martin as an actor much in the mode of Peter Lorre, with his accent and icy demeanor. The difference was, of course, that Peter was a great actor who lost interest in the Hollywood scene when it began to lose interest in him, and he began sending himself up for lack of any real passion for whatever projects the studios gave him by the end of the 1940s. Martin did not have a Fritz Lang in his life, nor did his performances rise to the level of art like Peter Lorre's did with UFA at the end of the 1920s. Having made that assessment, I would liken Martin's acting style more to Udo Keir and the kind of roles he has been doing in the last decade. If Martin was alive today and around Udo's current age, he would no doubt be working non-stop.

Martin enjoyed being a uniquely perverse individual in life, a lifelong homosexual, who made no real secret of his sexuality among his peers in show business. He was delightfully decadent in his style of acting, and his attitude sometimes infused his acting, particularly his performance in 1941's *The Mad Doctor,* which is discussed in more detail later on.

In *House of Horrors,* Martin is madly outré as poverty stricken artist Marcel DeLange. He lives alone except for his loyal cat in a cold studio with all his unsold sculptures. One night, disgusted with his lot in life, he decides to end it all by drowning himself. He drifts down in the midnight fog to the waterfront to throw himself in the Hudson River, when he sees another figure already floating in the water. This creature turns out to be a homicidal maniac known as "The Creeper," who has a nasty habit of breaking young women's spines for no particular reason. His character was a spin-off from Basil Rathbone's Sherlock Holmes series that was such a sensation at Universal during the war. The one with Rondo was called *Pearl of Death,* and this film was his reward. The mad artist fishes the hulking killer out of the icy river, somehow takes him back to his studio, undresses him, puts him in pajamas, and then tucks him in his bed. All of this is done off-camera, yet when I finally met Martin in 1985, we had a huge laugh over the overlooked homoerotic implications of this moment, where Marcel literally picks a strange (to say the least) man up and brings him into his studio, where they enter into an unholy partnership that could be considered quite domestic, as well. The film gets away with this subtext mainly because it is all done in a fifty-nine-minute horror film with a monster that seems asexual at best. It is because of the perverse intensity of Martin's acting, not to mention the fact he displays no interest whatsoever in women in this film, that this queer aspect begins to shade his character. There is also a queer attitude among some of the men in the film, particularly Howard Freeman (who plays one of the art critics fated to die at the hands of the Creeper). Howard plays his role as an old queen who likes to dress in loud silk robes while rolling his eyes at the slightest provocation.

Both John Abbott and Martin Kosleck were successful character actors in Hollywood, appearing once in awhile in those quickie horror films around the same time, and on occasion, might have run into each other on the back lots of Universal or Warner Bros. However, their personalities were different. John was far more closeted and conservative about his private life, and they never socialized at the time. I mention that to set up the situation that was about to present itself in the Hollywood of 1985.

John Abbott lived the life of a well-meaning snob in a (by Hollywood standards) modestly grand home high above the Hollywood freeway in mock-Tudor elegance. He enjoyed bringing his guests into his authentic recreation of an English pub, which he maintained off the dining area.

Although he taught both sexes, he had a definite preference for the attractive young men who came to Hollywood by the thousands hoping to be the next heart-throb in a weekly series, or maybe even a movie star. The only woman I ever heard John speak of with reverence or respect was Dame Flora Robson, who was his closest friend in show business next to actress Queenie Leonard, who was once married to George Sanders' brother, Tom Conway. One of the master bedrooms in John's home was always reserved for Dame Flora when she chose to come to the colonies. She was even filmed there once, in a documentary about Joseph Von Sternberg's ill-fated *I Claudius,*

The Epic that Never Was. John had made his film debut in Von Sternberg's *The Shanghai Gesture* years before, and that was how he arrived in Hollywood in the first place.

Unlike Martin, who was living openly with another man, John kept his feelings to himself until his retirement and his new career as an acting teacher. That new calling gave him a fresh circle of friends and students to keep him young at heart. It was just fate that I should know him as his relationship with a young film fan brought about a "Death in Venice" infatuation with a muscular redhead, John's erstwhile "Tadzio," if you will, from Canada, who was hopelessly obsessed with the Sherlock Holmes films of Basil Rathbone. Let's call that young man "Rick" for the moment, and yes, he wanted to be an actor as a result of his obsession with the great detective.

It was that young man's interest in all things Rathbone that brought about "the night of the long knives," when Martin and John spent an unforgettable evening together after years of avoiding each other in our Babylon called Hollywood.

John rang me one afternoon asking me if I was acquainted with any actors or actress who might have worked in the Rathbone/Holmes films. His friend was coming down from Canada and wanted to see and do everything that might bring him a little closer to the "divine Basil." The fact John had breathed the same air on a soundstage with Rathbone made him a total god in the eyes of young "Rick."

All of that drama got my curiosity going, so I reminded John that our mutual friend, Tony, knew Martin well, and since they both made a Holmes film together, nothing could be more perfect than a party for the *Pursuit to Algiers* surviving players.

When "Rick" finally arrived in Hollywood, John called again and suggested he bring him around to my apartment and let him watch a VHS tape I happened to have of one of Martin's films that "Rick" had longed to see, but which never played on Canadian TV. The film in question turned out to be my own personal favorite, *House of Horrors*! I could not help but notice how different John was behaving about "Rick" and what sacrifices he was willing to endure to please him. I never thought I would show such a film to John, who could have cared less about sitting down to watch a Universal horror film, especially when he was not even in it.

The next day, John arrived at my front door with "Rick," who was indeed very handsome, wholesome, and a decent guy. I had the film all set up so, after a few moments of chat, we sat down to watch the hulking Rondo Hatton take up his domestic relationship with the mad sculptor Martin played. "Rick" was a total fan watching the film, since he had seen stills from it all his life and then was actually getting to see it for real. John was tolerant throughout most of the film, but still could not resist ragging on Virginia Grey, who was playing the love interest. "That woman left her brains in the make-up chair."

It was so obvious that John had no patience for glamour girls of any kind at any time, even in a film. After the film, "Rick" asked if he could make a long distance call to let his girlfriend in Canada know that he had finally seen *House of Horrors* and was at the moment in a real cool apartment in Beverly Hills that had framed posters of Rathbone as Sherlock Holmes in the hall. On top of everything else, the guy was straight! However, that really was not the point at all, since John was not a predatory gay man. His feelings were not unlike that of Thomas Mann's character in *Death in Venice*: John was responding to the boy in the only way he could, as a mentor and guide through Hollywood and its golden past. That was about as classically Greek as it got in Lotus Land.

I had hoped seeing Martin in that film would jog some memories with John of their work on the Holmes film, which was shot in the same period of time. John remembered Martin of course, but as I already suspected did not socialize outside of shooting the film itself.

However, John did talk about working on a Nina Foch werewolf film over at Columbia called *Cry of the Werewolf*. "I am the first character you see in the film, and there was an actress in that film named Blanche Yurka, who played Nina's gypsy servant, and the studio felt we had real chemistry together! So believe it or not, Columbia wanted to pair us in a series of horror films calling us "The Gruesome Twosome." Blanche and I did some publicity for the werewolf film, and then all the interest seem to just fade away and no more "Gruesome Twosome." He laughed about the fact the studio had no budget for a werewolf, so they used German Shepherds. In the film's opening credits, the dogs had peanut butter placed on the roofs of their mouths so they would appear to howl on cue.

I tried to bring Martin up in the conversation again by mentioning that both actors had worked on the highly regarded TV series *Thriller*, with Boris Karloff as the host. John loved doing his "little bit" in one episode in which he kept the head of the Medusa on tap to "gorganize" evildoers. "That one was directed by a woman, Ida Lupino. She knew her business, and it was a pleasure to work with her." He was unaware that Martin had done one, as well. Martin's episode was one of the best, called *"Waxworks,"* from a short story by Robert Bloch. Both those men had such presence when they performed that it was a shame they never got to act in something together, or so I thought at the time.

As we began to plan that special evening for John's visitor from Canada, I decided to ask our mutual friend, Tony, to take me over to meet with Martin, something I had wanted to do in any case.

The next afternoon, Tony and I drove into West Hollywood to have drinks with talented Martin. The first thing I was told as we got closer to the house was that in the last few years Martin had suffered a stroke and his left arm was slightly paralyzed, so I was not to be surprised if his mood might change during the course of our visit. When we arrived, Martin was seated in his favorite chair in the living room of the little house he shared with his long time companion, Christopher Drake. Chris was an actor at one time, as well (they both appeared in the exploitation horror film, *The Flesh Eaters*, with Martin playing yet another Nazi). He was not the first actor Martin had chosen to share his home with. In fact, back in the 1940s he had lived with one of the young actors from *Pursuit to Algiers*, a not-so-talented blond named Leslie Vincent.

Martin was in a very receptive mood when we arrived, and he seemed to have polished off half a jumbo-size jug of vin rose wine with a label that read "Mother Ciber." I seem to remember seeing that vintage over at the local Trader Joe's, not the best by any means, but as Martin later testified, it got you there regardless of its quality. It was a bit alarming to watch him grab the glass handle of that huge jug with his one good hand and keep his glass filled. I suppose part of the logic in having the bottle by your side is not to ever feel the need to ask someone to fix your drink. Our Martin was nothing if not thoughtful.

Tony brought me over in front of Martin for a proper introduction, and he quickly took Tony's hand in his one good one, exclaiming, "Oh Tony, you look so tall and handsome today, doesn't he?" Of course I said yes, and then introduced myself. Martin then went into this somewhat prepared speech about movie interviewers especially for my benefit. "You see, David, I was taken advantage of by a deceitful young man, who called me up one day asking if he could interview me. So, I said fine, and before you knew it, he had come to my house with a tape recorder, did the interview, and then asked if he could borrow some of my posters and photographs from my horror films from the old days at Universal. Well, I never heard from him again and my posters were never returned. As you may realize, those pieces were worth quite a bit of money. I am only allowing this visit now because we love Tony, don't we, Chris?"

By then, Chris had tactfully disappeared into the back bedroom, so I seized the moment to assure Martin that I was only there to meet one of my favorite actors and had no evil plans up my sleeve to do him any mischief. Once we all had a drink in our hands, Tony and I took our seats in front of the great man and I began to try and break the ice. It did not take too long for Martin to warm up to me as I passed his tests of knowing something about actors and the business. I hesitated to tell him about my time as an agent for fear of another depressing anecdote.

I had brought a couple of stills from *House of Horrors* for him to sign, and once he realized that I probably had more movie memorabilia of my own then he ever did, Martin began to feel more relaxed, allowing the fascinating raconteur side of his personality to come forth, regaling us with tales about his life in the spotlight. Since he had lived a very full life by anyone's standards, I don't think he really cared much about how he appeared to other people, much less what they might have thought of him, thus making him all the more candid about his personal life.

Martin must have been one wildly charismatic charmer in his day, as his scrapbooks soon revealed. He was a much sought-after artist in New York, whose opening night exhibit program had a dedication by none other than the great Albert Einstein to attest to Martin's talent. He was also married around that time to a wealthy socialite named Eleanora Von Mendelssohn, but they apparently divorced in 1951. As fascinated as I was by all that, I did not ask too many questions on that first visit. There were examples of his artwork hanging on the walls of his bungalow, one of which he said was very much like the painting he gave Bette Davis, who he let me know was a close personal friend. He really did know all the important figures of his generation—and why not? He could charm the snakes from the pit if he set his mind to it. Martin had indeed led a charmed life, of that there was no doubt.

Martin did volunteer some information about his horror films at Universal by telling me just how much he loathed Lon Chaney Jr. "Chaney was a mean, roaring drunk, and we *hated* each other on sight. He would refer to me as 'that sawed off little Nazi cocksucker' to anyone who cared to listen. When we were filming *The Mummy's Curse,* he would start drinking as soon as the cameras stopped. At six in the morning, all made up in his mummy suit, he would then ask if anyone would like an eye-opener. It was absurd, as he only had one good eye to open in that make-up to begin with. The costume he wore for that was not made for a man to wear for very long at a time, as it could get very hot, and anyone in that costume was going to sweat like mad. Well, he made matters impossible by drinking in it, because it caused his whole body to smell like nothing you could imagine a human being smelling like, other than a mummy that had been dead for a few centuries. That I made more than one picture with that man is a miracle in itself.

"However, most of my time at Universal was fabulous. I was given a wonderful dressing room with my name on the door, and more to the point, I was treated with respect. My audition for *House of Horrors* was a simple scene with my cat. They found this sweet little stray cat that bonded with me instantly. I began this speech to the cat about not having any food to give it. I had the part by the time I finished. Universal had plans for me and I regret nothing I did there. I was very lucky."

I lived for moments like those, and so I sat spellbound listening to Martin paint a vivid picture with that unmistakable voice of his, describing what it must have been like to work in Hollywood during and after the Second World War.

When I asked about his friendship with Basil Rathbone, he seemed to glow with admiration and described the many kindnesses Rathbone had shown him during the films they made together.

"Basil always treated me as an equal in every way. When I was up for the film, *The Mad Doctor,* he would not allow the front office to audition me, telling them that my talent as an actor was there on the screen and my acting skills were beyond reproach! I mean such generosity as both an actor and a man. One thing that interfered with our friendship remaining as strong as it had become after that film was Basil's wife, Ouida. It seems that when the film was previewed, she got it in her mind that my personal feelings for her husband were, shall we say, unnatural. In other words, I made her feel jealous and she would not allow me to come to any of her parties after *The Mad Doctor* was released. Basil was a very cosmopolitan man of the world and he knew of my preferences by then. In fact, when we were making the Holmes film with your friend, John Abbott, I was involved with a young man who was not really a very talented actor, but through my influence, he was given a small role in the film. Basil took the time to advise me to leave this man, as he was not good enough for me. Imagine what Ouida Rathbone would have said to that! Basil Rathbone was one of Hollywood's greatest actors as well as one of my favorite people I have ever known in my life."

Martin paused from his recollection, and then he explained, "I don't work anymore because of my health, but even before my heart attack, I was done with what this town had turned into. Did you know that one of the last auditions I went on was for one page of lines in a cheap horror picture about a Black vampire in Hollywood?"

I was just sitting there with God knows what kind of expression on my face, when I blurted out, "You mean you had to audition for a scene in *Blacula*?"

"Yes my friend, that is exactly what I did and that was basically it for me in this town."

I told him that I think the part he was up for went to Elisha Cook Jr., and after a moment, he laughed at me, saying to Tony, "I can't believe this guy; he even knows who gets the parts when you lose out!"

The long afternoon had started to turn into evening, so we began to say our goodbyes. I will never forget his candor and humor during that visit. I am sure that with his illness and the depression his medication must have brought on, life was not so charming for a man who lived such a glamorous, exciting life. As his friend Bette Davis was fond of saying, "Growing old ain't for sissies." I wonder if Miss Davis realized the irony in that *bon mot*?

A few days later, John Abbott rang to let me know that he finally spoke with Martin and he had agreed to come over to John's house for a little party for "Rick" and the memory of *Pursuit to Algiers*. That was going to be a definite time capsule, so I went through my stills and found one from the film to copy so "Rick" would have something to take back to Canada to commemorate the evening. John had called a few times wanting to know if I could find some photos of Rathbone that John could purchase as gifts for "Rick" before he had to return home. I know John was enjoying having him as a houseguest and was well on his way to missing him already.

The day before the party, I got a rather odd call from our Martin, who wanted to know if John had a well-stocked bar and if I could somehow make sure there was enough Vodka for the evening—and it *had* to be Russian Vodka or he was not going to bother coming. We all know that when someone asks those kinds of questions, it means "by the book alcoholism," not that I hadn't noticed that Martin had become one during his bouts with illness and depression. For the first time, I began to worry, not for John, since I knew he could handle that sort of thing with ease, but our young Holmes fanatic did not need to deal with such situations during what was meant to be a holiday. So, attention must be paid . . . .

John had pulled out all the stops for "Rick's" tribute evening. He had gone all over Hollywood looking for little Sherlock mementos for him to take back to Canada. The house was simply glowing with candles and table settings laden with goodies of every kind. It all somehow reminded me of A Christmas Carol, with John as the reformed Scrooge. That meant that our young "Rick" was Tiny Tim, no doubt.

John was resplendent in his red smoking jacket and looked every inch the lord of the manor. "Rick" was on Cloud Nine the whole evening, which began as Martin arrived at the front door of Abbott Manor with a definite boozy glow on, but charming as only a professional actor on display can be. He played the part of the veteran actor to the hilt. Of course, John knew what was up from the start, and played the equally famous actor role to the max, as well. It was an even match, at least for the time being.

Martin was charmed by "Rick," as I knew he would be, and quickly found himself the center of attention. "Rick" proceeded to ask as much as he could about his beloved Rathbone. He was not to be disappointed. Martin was, as we knew, as fond of Basil as "Rick" was, so it was a super encounter for both of them. At one point in the festivities, I had John and Martin pose with a still from Pursuit to Algiers, which they both then signed for "Rick," who, by that time, was overwhelmed by all the attention. It did both actors a service to witness someone as young as him respond to classic films and actors with such reverence and respect.

I can't really remember the other guests, but there were only about a dozen. The evening was quite festive until about eleven o'clock. Martin was feeling his liquor by then and found his way into John's pub to be by himself, and pretty much stayed by his vodka, while "Rick" and the others chatted away. By then, Martin had shared what he could with "Rick" about the divine Basil, so the spotlight was off him and he more than took advantage of it by keeping out of everybody's way.

I kept going back to check on Martin and Chris, having been through that experience countless times, and I kept an eye on him, as well. To say there is a God can be an understatement, but it defiantly applied in that case since Martin was by midnight stoned out of his skull and could not even make conversation beyond a few mutterings, which only Chris could fully appreciate. Fortunately, "Rick" had retired to his room to look at all his mementos, and most of the other guests had said their goodbyes and departed without ever seeing the state that Martin had gotten himself in.

At that point, it was time to let John know that his guest of honor was out cold and resting soundly on the floor of his beloved English pub. I do wish camera phones had existed back then so I could have captured the remarkable expression of disgust that passed across John's face. He fully understood that his peer and colleague from days gone by had let himself go blissfully astray, which was just another night at Baskerville Hall for Martin. John followed me into the pub, muttering all the well-worn lines from films about drunks, complaining about how he dared to come into his house, and so on. When we reached our guest of honor, he looked quite dead to all concerned except for the rise and fall of his chest.

Without too much fanfare, Tony and Chris carried Martin out of Abbott Manor feet first, just like in the movies. As his body was going past the door, John stood in the alcove, saying with great aplomb, "There goes the saddest thing I think I have ever seen: a man who can't hold his liquor."

Chapter 39

Dreaming Dreams No Mortal Ever Dared to Dream Before

Curtis Harrington

The night before my dear friend, Curtis Harrington, passed away, I dreamt of him for the first time in ages. Curtis was hosting one of those intimate parties in that rambling pink house of his that towered above the Hollywood Freeway off Vine Way. I seemed to be helping him with small chores and going from room to room looking for objects, as he followed close behind advising me where things belonged. It was an odd dream. Curtis seemed tired and complained that his house would fill up with people he really didn't seem to know. "My library is full of strangers," he said at one point, and then I woke up.

The next morning, I received the news that Curtis Harrington had died during the night in his sleep within the very house I had helped put in order in my dream. During that terrible moment, reality as I knew it vanished long enough to release a flood of emotions, allowing forgotten memories to flow like Poe's "rapid river" through my mind. For nearly thirty years, Curtis had been a witness to my life. He attended every party I ever gave during that time and I was likewise a guest in his home over the years. Both of us shared the same passion for vintage films, making our friendship easy to maintain since we were always running into one another at screenings around town. In fact, one of the last events he attended before his death was my photo exhibition, "Nevermore," at the end of 2006 that honored the Poe films of Roger Corman. Curtis was a lifelong admirer of Edgar Allan Poe, and Roger was his mentor. Besides hiring Curtis to direct two features during his career, he lovingly paid for a day's location shooting for Curtis's final film, *Usher*.

It was his sincere passion for film that made Curtis so easy to like. Never once was I compelled to treat him like a celebrity, which he truly was in Hollywood society. The reason was that Curtis was a movie fan first, last, and always. Before he began directing films, he spent a lifetime watching them in his hometown of Beaumont, near Palm Springs. It was there as a child that he began a love affair with horror films and weird fiction thanks to the town library and a local drug store that was always well stocked with *Weird Tales* and *Black Cat Mysteries*.

In the summer of 1973, I was still a junior in college, living in the wilds of San Francisco. One particular evening, I happened to be on the look-out for a TV-movie-of-the-week entitled *The Cat Creature*, a valiant effort to capture the essence of a Val Lewton film, even to the point of casting veteran actor Kent Smith, who had been one of the leads in Lewton's classic *Cat People*. The director was Curtis Harrington, whose name was already well-known to me thanks to many late night viewings of *Night Tide,* which was his first and perhaps best foray into feature filmmaking, and also an homage to Val Lewton, with a mermaid filling in for the character of the cat woman.

At the time, I was preparing a trip to Los Angeles to interview Robert Bloch, always tops in his field, whose contributions to weird fiction and Alfred Hitchcock's legacy were already legendary. Robert had written the screenplay for Harrington's TV movie, thus setting the stage for my first real taste of "classic Hollywood" and a friendship that would last a lifetime. The Blochs lived in the Hollywood hills in one of those houses that you drove past that had no sidewalks, so it was easy to miss unless you knew where you were going.

Robert and his wife, "Ellie," were the nicest people you could hope to meet in a town not known for its hospitality. He had arranged for me to meet the director of his movie of the week the second day I was in town at a screening for the infamous "Count Dracula Society." The film we saw that day was Tod Browning's *Freaks*, which turned out to be not only one of Robert's favorite films, but Curtis's, as well. I was totally unprepared for meeting a film director that was such an ardent movie fan. Curtis was so unassuming and modest in his demeanor that he seemed like an old friend from the moment we met. The first thing I remember Curtis saying to me after the film was, "Can you imagine what it was like for stars like Harlow and Gable to see these strange, deformed people wandering around the soundstages of MGM in 1932?" That was followed by that great unmistakable laugh of his that I would hear off and on like the bells of Poe's famous poem for the next thirty years.

I did not spend time with Curtis again until late in 1977. By then, I was already living in Beverly Hills and about to start a new career as a theatrical agent. That situation made it possible for me to invite Curtis to parties and screenings for a change, to try and return the many kindnesses he showed me when I was still new to the Hollywood social scene.

One of my favorite hang-outs at that time was the Backlot Theater located behind the gay disco, Studio One, in West Hollywood. One of my best friends was a silver-haired young man named Steve Applegate, who managed the showroom, and it was through him I arranged for Curtis to see such veterans of the silver screen as Geraldine Fitzgerald, who was beautifully introduced on her opening night by her co-star, Bette Davis. Afterwards, we went backstage to see that amazing lady, who recalled her days at Warner Bros with Peter Lorre and Sidney Greenstreet during the filming of *Three Strangers*. She was very impressed with Lorre, who she said was a real intellectual, and with what a lady's man Sidney was in spite of his size. "Sidney was a favorite client at every whorehouse in Hollywood. Those ladies always called him a 'gent.'"

The actress who performed there next was none other than the Bride of Frankenstein, the sublime Elsa Lanchester. Curtis was thrilled to see that eccentric film icon camp her way through an evening of bawdy ballads she made famous in the English music halls of the 1920s. The highlight of the evening was a special selection of clips from *The Bride of Frankenstein*, followed by some very strange "home movies" of Elsa and her late husband, Charles Laughton, taken during their early days together in Hollywood. That was a magical night indeed, as we went backstage and Curtis shared with Elsa some of the times he had spent with the great director of *Frankenstein*, James

Whale. She seemed amazed that anyone would have known Whale after he quit making films in the late 1930s.

"Charles worked with him on *The Old Dark House* with Boris before we did *The Bride of Frankenstein*. I seem to recall having James to tea a few times after that, as well as attending some of his parties. Then, we just lost touch, as one tends to do in this business."

Elsa was a hard one to read, very eccentric, though for that evening she was on her best behavior and, being a trouper, she signed autographs and seemed more than pleased that her fame was assured thanks to a role of a lifetime, rather than just being the Bride of another monster—however sacred—the difficult and brilliant Charles Laughton.

The years from 1977 through 1983 were filled with what now seems like an endless wrap party for *The Day of the Locust*, and my friendship with Curtis was a major factor in all of it.

During that period, I got to know Shelley Winters, who acted for Curtis on two occasions. Curtis organized parties around her and we would all find ourselves sitting on the floor around an ornate loveseat in his living room. Shelley held court from her throne, and she loved to be the center of attention at all times. Why not? She was a big bad mama, after all. Curtis always got a laugh from the candid observation our mutual friend, Barbara Steele, made regarding Shelley, (whom she knew from her time in Hollywood as the second wife of screenwriter James Poe). "Shelley Winters is the kind of woman who would begin a conversation with you, then go to the bathroom and leave the door open."

Shelley bonded big time with Curtis on the set of *What's the Matter With Helen?* The project very much in the *Whatever Happened to*

Baby Jane? tradition, not a stretch considering the source material was from Henry Farrell who wrote the original. Hoping that lightening would strike twice, Shelley was paired with former musical-comedy star Debbie Reynolds, who gave the performance of her career in that film. While there was no duel of the divas like the fireworks caused by pairing Crawford and Davis in *Whatever Happened to Baby Jane?*, both ladies had high hopes for the film's success because *Whatever Happened to Baby Jane?* had brought both its stars Oscar nominations, not to mention a share of the profits.

Unfortunately, *What's the Matter With Helen?* was given no build-up whatsoever from Filmways, so the film opened and closed without any publicity for the two stars, who got some of the best critical notices at that point in their careers.

Curtis was also livid that some idiot in the publicity department created a poster that gave the whole ending away. The offending one-sheet had the temerity to show Debbie Reynolds as a corpse. Can you imagine *Psycho* advertised with Janet Leigh's dead body in the shower? It was that bad, and the whole experience would have buried a lesser director, yet Curtis continued to work even without that all important block buster that would admit him to the exalted realm of Hollywood players.

Shelley worked with Curtis once more, in England on a project she personally brought to American International Pictures entitled *The Gingerbread House*, a rather camp retelling of Hansel and Gretel with horror overtones. When it finally made the rounds stateside, it was known as *Who Slew Auntie Roo?*, to connect it once again to that sub-genre of once glamorous actresses of a certain age who wind up headlining in horror films. Curtis did it because Shelley asked for him personally. The perks were, of course, a trip to the UK and the joy of working with Sir Ralph Richardson, whom he adored. Curtis arranged for them to have lunch together every day during production.

Curtis absolutely hated Michael Gothard, whom AIP forced upon him after the actor's favorable reviews in Gordon Hessler's *Scream and Scream Again*. Gothard had also scored with a tour de force in Ken Russell's *The Devils*, yet Curtis found him unpleasant and difficult in the modest but key role of the sinister chauffeur. They squared off over Michael's long hair, which he refused to cut until Curtis threatened to fire him. I always wondered why Curtis was never offered any of those Poe films American International was making at the time in England. Perhaps the lack of success with the aforementioned films sealed his fate with that company.

In 1983, I became involved with the making of a documentary about the horror genre for PBS entitled *The Horror of it All*, working with a really wonderful producer, Gene Feldman, and his charming wife, Susie. They filmed most of the interviews in my apartment in Beverly Hills, and I made sure Curtis was one of the talking heads in the finished product. Curtis had known director James Whale towards the end of his life, which included a meeting in Paris, where Curtis was studying film. Whale made a point of spending time with Curtis while on vacation there, encouraging the young filmmaker by presenting him with a gift of $500 to stay on in France and finish his studies, (which included a monograph on Josef Von Sternberg that was much quoted at the time it was printed). Curtis never forgot Whale's generosity. Years later, he was instrumental in preserving one of Whale's early thrillers at Universal, T*he Old Dark House*, by scouting around the studio for the negative while shooting his only feature there, *Games*.

Actually, he was fortunate to have gotten *Games* off the ground at all, as then-studio-head Lew Wasserman was not especially "into" nostalgia, famously nixing Curtis's original casting choice of his idol, Von Sternberg's leading lady, Marlene Dietrich. As Wasserman explained to Curtis after he had already flown to Las Vegas to secure the services of his "dream actress," "Dietrich is all yesterdays, and you need something more 'today.'"

Ultimately, Curtis settled on the Oscar-winning actress of *Room at the Top*, Simone Signoret, who unfortunately for Curtis was, at the time of filming, losing her husband (Yves Montand) to another woman (Marilyn Monroe), so her heart was not in the project at all. Marlene Dietrich would have placed his film into the realm of the sublime. However, he did at least come away with something from the Vegas encounter. As he made his pitch to Dietrich in her dressing room, she realized that she was in the presence of a rabid fan, and asked him if he'd like one of her shoes. It was a memento he would always treasure.

The Horror of it All included appearances by such distinguished film personalities as John Carradine and the great director, Rouben Mamoulian. My contribution was locating author Robert Bloch, Hammer Horror Queen Martine Beswicke, Roger Corman, and of course, Curtis. Another one of the interviewees was 1950s producer/director Herman Cohen, who had caused a sensation by bringing teenage monsters to the screen with titles like *I Was a Teenage Frankenstein*.

We premiered the finished product on campus at USC to a packed house. Afterwards, a panel was set up on stage for a Q&A. While I was there waiting to be seated between Curtis and Martine, Herman Cohen came walking down the aisle in the company of a handsome blonde boy in his early twenties. Before they came within earshot, Curtis leaned over to me and whispered, "David, you do know about Herman and his 'boys' don't you?" Before I could say another word, Herman and the young man had made their way onto the stage and Herman introduced the lad by saying, "I want you both to meet the next Robert Redford." Curtis managed not to burst out laughing, but just barely. I lived for moments like that, and knowing Curtis, there were many more to come.

Curtis was among the second wave of American avant-garde filmmakers to show promise after the end of World War Two. He became fascinated with one of the true pioneers of experimental films, a legendary woman sometimes referred to as the High Priestess of experimental cinema, the great Maya Deren. Her first name can be interpreted as "illusion" in the Buddhist sense. Her film, *Meshes of the Afternoon,* was a major influence on both Curtis and Kenneth Anger in their own short films of the period. Maya died in 1961 after an intense study of Voodoo in Haiti, where her fascination turned to obsession. They say she even became a *Voudoun* priestess while filming hours of rituals and dance enchantments before her untimely death. Both Kenneth Anger and Curtis Harrington made their early experimental films under those influences, yet the two men were destined for very different paths in their personal lives, as well as their careers.

At the end of 2004, The Getty Museum sponsored an evening honoring the most influential surviving filmmakers of *avant garde* experimental cinema: they chose Stan Brakhage, who came down from San Francisco, followed by Curtis and the most notorious of the three, Kenneth Anger. That was bound to be an event. Many of us who knew those men well also knew that Kenneth and Curtis either were not speaking, feuding, or both for years.

If I may, at this point, I would like to offer the following observation based on my experiences with both of them. Curtis long ago gave up the *avant garde* to pursue a career in the very tough and real world of directing television for hire, and making the odd feature when the opportunity made itself known. End of story.

Kenneth, on the other hand, spent a lifetime living one moment in wealth and privilege with rock stars and the rest of the time in poverty and chaos—a life, I might add, of his own making. Kenneth was and is a destructive personality. However, with less than four hours of film to his name over the last five decades, he is nonetheless an acknowledged World Class filmmaker, whose body of work has influenced some of our premier directors around the world. He is somewhat of a genius, but that doesn't excuse the reckless and destructive behavior that is now his calling card.

On the night in question at the Getty, with fires raging all around Los Angeles, Kenneth Anger mounted that stage with his colleagues and both he and Curtis shined in a shared spotlight. Afterwards, there was a reception, and we all posed for pictures, and the two *vieux copains* were joyously macabre and seemingly on the best of terms. In a perfect world, that would have been the beginning of a dialogue between the two of them on the art of survival, having known each other since they were fourteen years old.

Kenneth had been very bitchy regarding Curtis's last project, which also proved to be his last film, *Usher*. After Curtis sent a copy to Kenneth, I got a call from Kenneth, who was having a fit about how Curtis could not return to the *avant garde* any old time he wanted to create art. "If Curtis thinks this little film will restore his reputation he can just think again." So you can imagine my relief when this night of nights arrived and the two of them chose very wisely to let bygones be just that. The Gods were kind to both of them that evening, a treasured moment in time for two very talented men.

There have been so many moments in the past thirty years involving my memories of Curtis that I cannot possibly remember them all in this essay, yet I always come back to a very special afternoon, when Curtis was invited to join me for an afternoon brunch in Chatsworth with composer Les Baxter. Les wanted Curtis there to try and convince him to use his music in his next film. Unfortunately, those two men had more in common than they realized, since neither one of them was in line for an assignment in films. In fact, Les had become so overwrought with anxiety that he went out and engaged the services of a male model to represent his new compositions. The model in question was telling the music executives that he was the composer ... very Phantom of the Opera.

What makes that day stick in my mind was the drive up to Les' compound, which was in a mountain area and very isolated. Right across the way from Les Baxter's house was a cemetery. As we were driving towards the Baxter home, Curtis suggested we pause for a moment and go into the graveyard, the reason being that both of Curtis Harrington's parents are buried there and he had yet to purchase gravestones for them. Before we arrived at the luncheon, where poor Les Baxter was hoping for a change in his luck, we were across the street picking out markers for the authors of Curtis's being.

Lunch was stellar, with both men seeming to enjoy each other's company. As we were readying ourselves to leave, Les handed Curtis a cassette of some of his music. We wound our way down the road and out to the freeway, and then Curtis let the tape fall out the window, saying to me, "Can you imagine the gall of that man, thinking I would even consider using any of his compositions when they are so déclassé?" Moments like that created an iron-clad rule: never talk about jobs socially. Nothing good can ever come of it.

One of the very last times I saw Curtis was at a memorial they gave at the American Cinematheque in Hollywood for Gary Graver, the writer/director/cameraman who worked on all of Orson Welles' films at the end of his career. Curtis was sitting by himself at one of those metal tables in front of the ice cream and candy shop in the courtyard of the Egyptian theater. Curtis was like a magnificent ruin, covered in liver spots and not wearing his partial for his lower teeth. I don't think he cared how he looked anymore and it gave him a sense of serenity that was almost otherworldly. We spoke for the better part of an hour. He told me that he was very happy with his lot in life. The traveling he had done in the last couple of years while screening *Usher* at festivals made him comfortable in his own skin. "I will be remembered for my work, this I know. My legacy is assured." It was great hearing him talk this way, and we parted with the understanding I would come to spend some time with him on my next visit into town.

At the memorial, many of Gravers' co-workers and friends spoke in-between film clips, but none were as eloquent as Curtis, who broke down during his speech as he described the way a native culture releases the spirit of their loved ones, and managed to break everyone's heart in the process. That they should pass away within months of each other is in itself a kind of tribute to their working collaboration, which was based on mutual respect and love.

Personally, I lost a great and loyal friend, and cinema also lost something: the kind of intellect and grace that came so easily to Curtis, the style and polish with which he framed a scene, and his wit and humor in the face of Hollywood indifference. Those qualities may not appear again in my lifetime, nor, I fear, in Hollywood at all.

I cherish the two video interviews we did together. One is still available from VCI Entertainment with the uncut version of *Ruby*, which was a film Curtis disowned for many years because of interference from producer Steve Krantz, the husband of soap queen author Judith Krantz. It still makes me laugh to remember getting a call from Curtis when he found out Steve had died. Curtis said, "I feel like getting some Jack Daniels and heading over to the cemetery to watch the gravediggers cover him up." The second interview was for my cable access show, *Sinister Image*, and that interview will soon be released in a boxed set with all my conversations done at that studio for a company in the UK in the next year. We had a wonderful time discussing his up and downs in nearly half a century in Hollywood.

Among the many films that Curtis and I enjoyed together over the years, one of our all-time favorites was a not-too-well regarded all-star black comedy on the funeral business in Los Angeles (based on a highly regarded novel by Evelyn Waugh). We are, of course, referring to Tony Richardson's film, *The Loved One.* That film has been much on my mind of late because of the macabre nature of what took place at Curtis Harrington's funeral in the Hollywood Forever Cemetery on Santa Monica Boulevard in Hollywood. Valentino is interred there, complete with yearly visits from the "Woman in Black," and films are run graveside on weekends. You can see the connection with Waugh's observations, which are truer now than when he penned the novel decades before. The day of Curtis's service, with his body on display prior to his cremation, Kenneth Anger arrived with a makeshift film crew and began filming away at Curtis's mortal remains, including two alternate takes of Kenneth kissing Curtis on the forehead. Not even the other Ken—Russell, that is—could top that sideshow behavior (not unlike Russell's film of *Valentino,* which incidentally, I saw with Curtis when it came out).

Jack Larson was the openly gay actor who played Jimmy Olson in the George Reeves *Superman* TV series, and at one point before could begin the eulogy, Kenneth sat front row center and did what amounted to an audio commentary of Curtis's funeral as it was in progress. In 2005, Kenneth interrupted a screening of *Usher* at the Arclight Theater by rising from the audience and doing a monologue on Curtis Harrington as a child, while Curtis sat quietly fuming since, as he said later, "Kenneth knows fucking all about my childhood, and he is just more bad news than it is worth to fuck with anymore."

Whether or not Curtis would have been amused at this, I think the answer would be a resounding "no," since just a few months ago, I was visiting Curtis at his home and we began a conversation about his lifelong relationship with Kenneth Anger. Curtis was very disappointed that after all that time, Kenneth could not in his final years appreciate his celebrity. Curtis said, "You know, they write about his work as if he is a genius like Jean Cocteau, and still he spends his life in torment over trifles, even to the point of putting my little short film down as if any of this shit really matters. As far as I'm concerned, life is too fucking short to spend it on Kenneth Fucking Anger." So I am sure that all this attention paid to Anger was not what Curtis had in mind for his final goodbye to his friends.

None of that really matters in the wake of losing such an irreplaceable personality like Curtis. I will always maintain a treasure trove of memories involving him, sharing films, and enjoying all the amazing people we met in the course of three decades.

I remember watching Curtis roll his eyes, as Hurd Hatfield, a survivor of the studio system and a real hoot to know, flew in from Ireland and tried to convince a hunky waiter to drop everything and go back to Ireland with him. I recall escorting Gale Sondergarrd to a Sherlock Holmes screening only to learn that they could not find a print of *Sherlock Holmes and the Spider Woman.* I look back on Curtis hosting an impromptu dinner party for my little Lovecraft group even though they were total strangers to him. I recollect him trying to get Samson DeBrier out of a party before the host punched him out for a slip of the tongue. Curtis enjoying my attempts to tell Yvonne Furneux what a goddess she was in the Hammer version of *The Mummy.* At first, she told Curtis she was throwing me in his swimming pool. However, we wound up at each other homes, and another friendship began at the House of Harrington. There is a line in John Ford's *The Last Hurrah* where Spencer Tracey is dying, so his old friends gather around for one last Hurrah, Tracey observes, "How can you thank a man for a lifetime of laughs?" Well, you can't! All you can do is keep the departed close to your heart and cherish those memories, and they will never be forgotten.

I believe Curtis would have appreciated lines by the Divine Edgar as a fitting farewell to a true gentleman: "And my soul from out that shadow that lies floating on the floor shall be lifted . . . nevermore."

Chapter 40

Home on the Strange: The Saga of Kelton the Cop

Paul Marco

The recent passing of Maila Nurmi has once again brought attention to the films of Ed Wood and that eccentric band of players who populated his films from the mid-to-late 1950s. Truth be told, the only reason we even remember his films at all is because three have the legendary Bela Lugosi in them and they would be the iconic actor's last hurrah. Maila appeared in just one Ed Wood film, but if she had to choose, then *Plan Nine from Outer Space* would be the one to place one's persona in view. However there was one other person besides Lugosi who appeared in a so-called trilogy of Ed Wood oddball masterpieces and that was a character simply known as "Kelton the Cop."

On May 14 2006, another of Ed Wood's stock company passed away in Hollywood at the ripe old age of eighty. His name was Paul Marco, and if that name does not sound familiar, don't worry, because it shouldn't. Nobody outside of diehard fans of *Plan Nine from Outer Space* or Ed Wood film buffs would recognize the name either.

Paul Marco is a classic textbook example of an impressionable young man spending his youth at the movies and dreaming of a day when it would be his turn to be up on the silver screen acting out all his fantasies, and for the world to finally acknowledge him as "*a star.*" When you think about it, why not? Paul was brought up practically under the Hollywood sign. He attended Hollywood High, worked as a child actor, and then graduated to bit parts, until that fateful day when his agent, Marge Usher, brought him to the attention of Ed Wood.

Since we are not talking John Ford here, I will not "print the legend," but I will tell you the facts as I came to understand them in the ten years I observed that man in a number of odd situations that would tax the patience of anyone unfamiliar with "the twilight people" of Ed Wood's Hollywood.

Ed Wood hired Paul mainly because Paul had some money saved up and chose to "invest" in Wood's latest film, then known as *Bride of the Atom*, starring the greatest of all film Draculas, Bela Lugosi. The making of that highly enjoyable turkey was documented beautifully, I thought, in Tim Burton's charming film about the hothouse director and his zany crew of misfits.

In real life, Paul Marco simply blossomed in the presence of Ed Wood, the low-budget movie maestro, and in no time at all, became his one-man-band for whatever the task at hand might be. His goal was always to make Ed's films happen. Paul appeared in the aforementioned three films, as well as helped with the casting, moving props, and perhaps greatest of all, served as Best Man at Lugosi's on August 25, 1955 wedding to Hope Lininger, his fifth and final wife. If nothing else ever happened to Paul in his lifelong quest for Hollywood fame, his friendships with Ed Wood and Lugosi would shine enough of a spotlight onto his own questionable resume to keep him in afterglow right up to the day of his death, where he was hours away from being filmed yet again as—what else?—"Kelton the Cop," for a direct-to-video project.

I came to know Paul "Kelton" Marco when, on one sunny afternoon in Silver Lake, I wandered into an old high school friend's apartment during a read-through of a script my friend had written based on *Plan Nine from Outer Space*, only that one was "Plan 13." He had apparently run into Marco at one of the memorabilia shops that used to populate Hollywood Boulevard in the 1980s. I seem to remember wondering why an "old-timer" like Paul would bother to come to something amateur like that, as nothing would ever really come of it. My friend, who shall be nameless, never really ever got any of his projects off the ground, a sad, more-than-common fate in Hollywood.

I soon realized that Paul was one truly fucked-up individual, who would do just about anything to keep one foot in the door of show business. The trouble with that concept was that Paul was doomed to encounter only deluded fans, who used him as a threadbare connection to get next to that "Lugosi/Wood" vibe by dealing with someone who was there in 1956 watching Lugosi and Wood play with a rubber octopus in Griffith Park.

As soon as Paul arrived, he treated the whole group of us as if we were sitting over at Paramount with the power to put the script and Kelton the Cop back on the screen as soon as the script could be fleshed out and a production deal hammered into a contract for Paul to sign. He did, however, advise all of us that day that the copyright involving Kelton for a proposed television series that was supposed to be around the corner was not negotiable, nor was his concept for Kelton to endorse Pepsi-Cola. Last but far from least, Paul simply would not ever consider doing sex or nude scenes, as "it would go against what my fans all over the world expect from Kelton the Cop."

I walked out of that apartment utterly shell-shocked that there really were demented guys like that hovering over Hollywood and I'd finally crossed the line into the "Outer Limits of Sunset Boulveard" by actually being a witness to what the late Criswell predicted (wrong as usual): "that Paul Marco would make it big in films." Paul kind of reminded me of the "Chauncey Gardener" character in *Being There*, because there was always some bullshit activity that seemed to crop up involving the Ed Wood films that kept the fantasy of his stardom alive, and no one was ever going to get in the way of that reality.

It took some time getting to know him, but Paul finally explained how he came upon the notion that he and his character of Kelton the Cop were so important in the world of cult celebrity. A few years ago, Paul was a prop master over at Paramount, with benefits and even a pension. He had even managed to save a buck or two in his bank account.

One fateful afternoon, all that went to Hell in a handbag during a wrap party on the Paramount lot. Paul had kept the flame going in his own way for Ed Wood, and his part in all the craziness surrounding the ever-growing myth about Lugosi and Wood and all the rest of the crypt-kickers. It took a misguided remark from fan-turned-director Joe Dante to forever change Paul's life.

Knowing that Joe openly admired grade-Z horror flicks (even writing about them for *Famous Monsters of Filmland* when he was just a lad in high school), Paul put together a decades-old headshot of himself in a frame, wrapped the whole thing up as a gift, and handed it personally to the energetic Joe Dante. When Joe unwrapped the package and got a load of what was inside, he exclaimed in what I am sure was genuine pleasure and surprise, "Oh wow, Paul, you are Kelton the Cop! I've seen all of Ed Wood's films. Paul Marco, you are a *cult star!*"

Those words hit Paul like the second coming. He went home that night high on believing that at last stardom was around the corner. The next day, he quit his job at Paramount and began his ascent to the Promised Land. He went to the bank, emptied out his savings account, and hit the photo labs with large orders for stills of himself from what would soon and forever be referred to as "The Kelton Trilogy," meaning those three epics: *Bride of the Monster,* followed by the most celebrated of the three, *Plan Nine from Outer Space,* and lastly the totally forgotten *Night of the Ghouls,* which was filmed in 1959 and collected dust for decades in a Hollywood lab because the tab was never paid. Once the VHS boom hit the industry, practically all the old grade-Z horror flicks hit the stores in special editions including, would you believe, "director cuts," so *Night of the Ghouls* created a respectable buzz when it was finally released in 1987, even though Ed Wood did not direct the film, nor did it have a Bela Lugosi or Vampira to recommend it. In Paul's mind, that was insignificant. After all, Kelton was there, so alert the media.

When the dust settled, Paul had spent well over half his savings on bumper stickers, balloons, and key chains, all extolling the image of the latest superstar on the horizon, Kelton the Cop. He began his own fan club that boasted himself as the president and, for the moment, the only card-carrying member.

At some point in the mid-to-late 1980s, way before the Tim Burton film would bring Ed Wood to the attention of, shall we say, a wider audience than the rabid fans of cult cinema, I found myself co-hosting a public access show called *Horror Talk*. The other host was a chap named Jay Jennings, who had been doing those kinds of tapings for a while from the audio/video department at Beverly Hills High School, which was, at that time, well-funded for projects like that one.

The experience was quite similar to the last time I saw Paul. As usual, he arrived with the idea that the show was live and going out to millions of people. The only other place you could possibly find a character like Paul Marco would have to be a sketch on *The Carol Burnett Show*.

I will always remember sitting across from Paul once the cameras were rolling, watching him transform into what in his mind's eye a cult star should be. He smiled at me, he smiled into the camera, then he explained, as if it were for the first, time how his fan club (which, as far I as know, was yet to have a meeting) operated.

"Well, David, we all get together in front of the television and watch my films [all three of them] and then we have ice cream and cake, and exchange stories about Kelton and all my forthcoming projects." Paul then unfolded three different styles of Kelton the Cop tee-shirts (they came in three colors—like the trilogy, get it?). On the back, a strip of film contained the titles of the Ed Wood films just so anyone walking behind you got a load of it, as well.

Paul did discuss his relationship with Lugosi, and his stories were touching, like the one about holding Lugosi's cue cards during *Bride of the Monster*. My personal favorite was having a black Christmas tree just for Lugosi to enjoy at his Yuletide party. Paul also claimed that he personally took the cape off Lugosi's corpse that Hope had substituted for the real *Dracula* cape, so that Lugosi would lie for all time in the proper cape, the one he wore in 1931, not the cheap imitation he wore in his Vegas nightclub act. He ended the interview by putting on his Kelton hat and then saying, as if rehearsed, "Goodnight everybody. Good luck and remember, this is Kelton saying, 'I'll be seeing you.'"

Horror Talk on VHS is still available on the internet, I am told, and Paul has a personal website befitting a dead cult star. However, the best encounter of the third kind I ever had with Paul had to be around 1983 when his long-suffering lady friend and agent, Marge Usher, passed away. Marge lived in a modest but nice one-story Spanish style home in the area directly behind Century City on Kelton Avenue. It seems Marge gave Paul his character's name based on her address. Paul was living in Hollywood in a small one-bedroom upstairs apartment that was under rent control. Paul was at Marge's side when she died, and virtually moved into her home immediately afterwards, claiming she had left the house to him in her will.

The very next thing Paul decided to do was to throw a Kelton house-warming party, somewhat in honor of his late benefactor, for all his friends and acquaintances. The guest list included Dr. Donald A Reed, the deranged president of the Count Dracula Society (not to mention an asshole of epic proportions), Peter Coe and his good looking son, and a number of other Hollywood Boulevard types I just can't seem to remember. The important thing to know is that Maila Nurmi was not in attendance, as she always had taste and style.

Peter Coe had been under contract to Universal during World

War Two, and as such, appeared in *House of Frankenstein* and the Maria Montez classic, *Gypsy Wildcat*. It was in Peter's apartment that Ed Wood and his wife, Kathy, took refuge when Ed was evicted with nowhere else to go. During the party, Peter told me with great emotion about the day his friend passed away, how Eddie begged for a Vodka and orange juice at eight o'clock in the morning, and literally crawled from the bedroom into the kitchen refrigerator to get one. During that ordeal, Ed caught sight of himself in the hall mirror, and the image of a man so in the grip of addiction shook him up enough to agree to check into the hospital. Peter then demanded he go to hospital immediately, but gave in to waiting one more day.

Ed Wood died later that afternoon by simply going into the bedroom and lying down on the bed, never to get up again. Peter said the look of horror on his face when they found him was so terrifying that it would haunt Coe for the rest of his life. He then told me that they put Ed Wood's body out in the hall to await the coroner's arrival, and how shocked they were to discover it missing when they finally turned up. So many tales have been circulated since then, who can be sure which one to believe? I wish now I had put Peter Coe's story on tape, as he was an eye-witness to Ed Wood's final day on earth.

Most of us present that night advised Paul to see a lawyer about his rights regarding Marge Usher's will and his right to live in that house so soon after her death. Paul could not be reasoned with, having already moved in and told everybody, "Possession is nine tenths of the law." I remember telling Paul that it really depends on who is being possessed, if you follow my drift, not that he ever did.

The oddest thing of all regarding that episode in the Paul Marco saga was the son from out of left field that just seemed to turn up one day, living with Paul (who was never married, as far as anyone could tell), and that was just one more "Kelton" myth to be taken on faith. Paul had lived way back in the 1950s with the openly gay actor, John (Bunny) Breckenridge, who had also appeared in *Plan Nine from Outer Space* as the alien leader. Breckenridge was from a wealthy family and lived life mostly on his own terms. In 1959, he was convicted on ten counts of sexual perversion and spent a year in jail. He survived all that and live to the age of ninety-four, dying peacefully in a nursing home on the California coast. Bill Murray played him in the Tim Burton film, *Ed Wood*.

All everyone can seem to remember is that the kid was living at Paul's apartment in Hollywood. One just accepted the fact and both men were cool with it—at least that is what it looked like to outsiders. The story turns very Joe Orton at that point since, a few weeks after Paul and his "son" moved into Marge Usher's house, the boy, who had been seen riding around the neighborhood on a motorcycle, peeled out of the driveway one morning and promptly fell off the bike, hitting his head on a rock and dying. Poor Paul not only had that freak accident to deal with, but Marge Usher's family stepped in and demanded he vacate the property as soon as possible. Paul was understandably upset, and finally packed up and moved back into Hollywood, that time alone. Late one night, not long after he was back in his old place, I got a weird call from Paul. I think he had been drinking, since he had at one time been a heavy drinker, as all the Ed Wood stock company had been. Paul was desperate for some male companionship and wanted to know if I could find him a hustler who would just be there for him to talk to if nothing else. When I began to prove less than helpful, he blurted out, "Listen, David, just get me a trick!" I was more than surprised to hear that from Paul, since he always struck me as being closeted about being gay, which was obvious to anyone who cared to think about it at all.

I did not like the way Paul sounded on the phone, so after he vented for another forty-five minutes, I promised to help him locate a shoulder to lean on or whatever, but I insisted on seeing him beforehand just to make sure he was really up to company, or more likely the hospital emergency room. The most interesting thing about that phone conversation was Paul freely admitting that the kid whom he called his "son" was really a boyfriend. He was just always too up-tight to acknowledge such a thing to himself, or more importantly, to his alter ego, Kelton the Cop.

If I had given it any thought at all, I would have remembered that Paul ceased to deal with Ed Wood the more the alcoholic director descended into soft-core porn. Paul had his standards and remained true to them for the rest of his life.

Not long after Paul's passing, his friends and fans gathered for a memorial party at the well-known Hollywood landmark bar and grill known as the Formosa Café, giving the bereaved opportunities to compare weird stories of what Paul had done to each and every one of us at one time or another. One rather touching moment occurred as we entered the banquet room: set aside for the occasion was an empty table, and placed on the table lay Paul Marco's policeman's hat and flashlight, a fitting tribute to a fallen "cop."

If fellow *Plan Nine from Outer Space* performer, Criswell, had lived to attend the tribute that day, he might have been inspired to draw material for his eulogy from one of Kelton's trilogy of films, the mind-boggling *Night of the Ghouls*: "This is a story of those in the twilight time, once human, now monsters in a void between the living and the dead. Monsters to be pitied, monsters to be despised."

When all was said and done, Paul Marco did it his way.

Chapter 41

La Perversa: the Phantom of the Ferris Wheel

Samson De Brier

Hollywood has been known for spawning many myths over the years regarding its inhabitants, both famous and infamous. During the twenty-five years that I called Beverly Hills home, I witnessed first-hand my share of those myths-in-progress.

I cannot remember when I first physically set eyes on that little diminutive, white-haired creature know far and wide as Samson De Brier, who in a certain light, looked to me exactly like an illustration of an English witch during the time of Matthew Hopkins (although Kenneth Anger always thought of him visually as the old sorcerer in *Fantasia* that has Mickey Mouse as an apprentice). The end result regarding Samson's appearance was always an occult reference, which makes sense when you understand the groove in which those people worked and played.

As I began to put this together, I realized that for the sake of accuracy I will reveal that I had first seen a photograph of Samson as a child in—of all things—a monster magazine! It was an early issue of Forrest J Ackerman's *Famous Monsters of Filmland* in the early

1960s, when I was about twelve years old. Ackerman used to run a mystery photo in every issue, so he ran this really creepy photo of a weird-looking, demonic creature with huge fingernails dressed in what looked like a spider web painted on a shroud. Ackerman identified the picture as a scene from *The Phantom of the Ferris Wheel* by Ray Bradbury, as if it was a lost film of the author's *Dark Carnival*. I never forgot that image, and it was years later that I discovered it was a frame enlargement from Kenneth Anger's *Inauguration of the Pleasure Dome*. I still remember the Proust-like moment when I finally saw the garment for real in a dusty frame in Samson's parlor decades later.

Before you read any further, I must advise that there are spoilers ahead for anyone who still remains starry-eyed regarding the mythology surrounding *avant-garde* filmmaker Kenneth Anger and his self-conscious social circle of friends in Hollywood. I will confess to being one of those who was once dazzled by the idea of actually meeting some of those characters, although at the time I did not fully grasp the phrase, "Be careful what you wish for." If you read enough of my observations from this period, you will soon discover that I became, shall we say, "disenchanted" with the reality vs. the myth of those dilettantish creatures with their cruel intentions and insincere friends.

On paper, the concept that one could actually have lunch and kind of hang out with characters out of *Inauguration of the Pleasure Dome* is a trippy one, to be sure. I was born too late to have ever met most of Kenneth Anger's inspirations, like the Great Beast Aleister Crowley (also known as "the wickedest man in the world), Sergi Eisenstein (a world-class director and cinema god) or Jean Cocteau, all geniuses in their field. I did, however, get around to meeting three of the characters out of *Inauguration of the Pleasure Dome*: director Kenneth Anger, who played Hecate in the film, Curtis Harrington, who played the role of "slave" in a Caligari make-up and the subject of this chapter, Samson De Brier, on whom Kenneth bestowed three roles as Lord Shiva, The Great Beast, and Osiris.

It was Samson's home and social contacts that made him of interest to Anger in the making of that film, rather than any artistic similarities, and I realized much later that it was the superficial and artifice of Samson and the famous people passing through his life that made him a celebrity rather than any real accomplishment in the arts.

It had to have been around the time I was getting to know both Curtis Harrington and Kenneth Anger, probably around 1976. Samson is, of course, a character, not a real person, rather the invention of an aging self-styled Hollywood courtesan, who knew only too well that time was always on his side, especially if he outlived all the witnesses to his life.

According to Sam (as I always called him), he started out as a young man arriving in Hollywood from the east coast (by way of Paris) under the name Arthur Jasmine, determined to write and learn about that wicked town in the manner of Elinor Glyn, if you were to really believe all the hyperbole of those early days of the roaring twenties. According to his nephew, Antonio R. Modica, "Arthur Jasmine" was the name under which Sam, as a young man, wished to be published. Apparently, Sam then met the legendary Alla Nazimova and was immediately cast in the small but showy role of Herodias in her notorious, all-gay version of Oscar Wilde's *Salome*, with great attention paid to Beardsley's brilliant illustrations when it came to creating the sets, which were spectacular.

I, for one, do not believe that Sam is really in the film at all. I find it fascinating that both Kenneth Anger and Sam have these juvenile appearances in films that nobody will ever be able to accurately document that either one positively was the actor they claimed to be. For the record, Kenneth Anger has always maintained that he was the Changeling Prince in Max Reinhardt's MGM all-star production of *A Midsummer Night's Dream* (1935). However, bear in mind that is the same man who has said in print interviews that he was sodomized by Puck (i.e. Mickey Rooney) in the same film (off-camera, of course). So who are you to believe when all is said and done?

According to his nephew, Sam made his living, first as a nurse in a home for the insane, and then as a landlord. The one true reality regarding Sam and his reputation as a celebrity is that for a period of time in the 1950s and 1960s, and perhaps even into the early 1970s, Sam used his Hollywood home as a salon for like-minded artistic types to meet and converse. He really did attract movie stars such as Marlon Brando, as well as the Los Angeles intelligentsia, including people like Anais Nin, into his home. Sam must have been quite a different person in those days, and I, for one, wish I had known that Sam rather than the rancid version I am recalling here for posterity. It was those glory days that allowed Sam to enjoy the benefits of having first-hand gossip to use as his passport for invitations to countless Hollywood dinner parties over the years.

By the time I got to know Sam, the salons were long a thing of the past and he was on the dinner circuit based primarily for having been part of Kenneth Anger's legendary *Inauguration of the Pleasure Dome* (1954), which was indeed shot in his ramshackle home off Vine and

El Centro Streets, to this day a dangerous, seedy part of Hollywood. The film flatters the location more than you know, because when you were actually in Sam's place, there was very little that would make you aware it was ever filmed there at all. Any documentation you can find regarding Samson or his place in Hollywood history will always be as a footnote in Kenneth Anger's filmography.

When I try and think back to just when Sam came to my house, I seem to remember a party around 1977, when I was beginning to see a lot of Curtis Harrington socially at his home and then at mine. Sam just turned up one evening at my apartment and seated himself in a corner of my living room, where I had placed an old Spanish chair that could be said to resemble a throne of sorts. It was there that "La Perversa," as Curtis liked to call him, held forth during that first evening. I remember he was wearing an antique necklace in the shape of a dragon, which suited him oddly enough. At first, I liked him. After all, he was a character, and in those days, still had a charm about him that came from years of telling people what they most want to hear. I suppose Sam wanted to find out why Curtis was accepting so many of my party invitations, and certainly he wanted to meet and connect with my circle of friends, who, for the most part, were all young and beautiful new faces, and who can really blame him for that?

Celebrity is like a drug in Hollywood; almost everyone I knew was taking it in one form or another. Kenneth Anger loved and despised Hollywood, while Curtis Harrington learned how to work within its system. Sam used his relationship with both men to travel in their circles when it suited him, and after so many years of networking, Sam had his own circle of old Hollywood friends, who found themselves fascinated with the seemingly wicked man, who really had no life of his own except as a reflection in other people. Sam desired to meet younger people and experience what was going on in the current Hollywood, which was moving well beyond his ability to keep up.

Looking back on the combined relationships of Sam, Curtis, and Kenneth, they all had one common denominator: they really disliked each other on a regular basis. Curtis had a long-standing feud with Kenneth, and vise-versa. I remember being told by each of them separately that I was not to discuss one with the other. Unfortunately, they forgot to tell Sam, who kept the flames burning throughout their lives, gossiping back and forth between the two directors, and then going to dinner parties and making fun of them both for their individual shortcomings. Sam really did not admire or respect anyone towards the end of his long and tedious life. What soured me on him for good was his disloyalty to the very people who made it possible for him to be accepted in Hollywood society in the first place.

I probably saw more of Sam than usual, when he allowed Kenneth Anger to rent his front house, saying at the time that he would "most likely live to regret it." The main house was large enough to accommodate Kenneth's ever-growing collection of movie memorabilia, not to mention books, tapes, antiques, and costumes for works-in-progress. Kenneth was flushed with money at the time, which was not a good sign since he always prided himself on being a spendthrift and he made good on that, believe you me. No sooner had he moved in than he began major redecorating. First, he repainted all the rooms in different colors, just like the rooms in Poe's *Masque of the Red Death*. The carpets were midnight blue, and he meticulously glued gold and silver stars and planets to the ceiling, completing the effect with expert lighting (as only a film director could). After dedicating a room to his first love, Rudolph Valentino, Ken was ready to rock. Kenneth had his pleasure dome installed, so all he needed was a Lucifer to share it. Within two months, Kenneth found a likely lad in a hunky twenty-two-year-old ex-Marine with a knack for dealing drugs, and he moved in for the duration. The happy couple then purchased an expensive dog, whose breed I just can't remember anymore. Needless to say, it was exotic.

Within weeks of all that domestic bliss, Kenneth had two major problems on his hands. His racism had gone unchecked in New York and was in full flood in Los Angeles. Soon, he found himself a prisoner in that house after dark, since he pissed-off a Latino gang that shot his dog and then trashed the front porch. That, of course, worried Sam to distraction, not that he felt any differently than Kenneth—he just never let his true feeling be known, especially in a neighborhood that was already by then (1988) over half-Latino. The next bit of bad news involved his companion: the ex-Marine was caught selling drugs across from Hollywood High School and arrested. Fortunately, I knew a gay attorney, Harry Weise, whom we all met on the set of *Sextette* with Mae West. Harry did his best, and finally the kid was let out of jail and promptly moved back to the Midwest. All that drama took its toll on Kenneth, and within six month, he, too, moved out of the house he had spent thousands of dollars redecorating, leaving Sam to moan about how "Absolutely no one will rent this place now." That incident put a strain on the long relationship between the two men that lasted almost until Sam's death.

It is amazing to me how so many intelligent people throughout my time in Hollywood could never see beyond the superficial when it came to people like Samson De Brier. For example, one of the most noteworthy things about Sam and his legacy were the celebrity salons that made his reputation. The house where so many glorious salons were held was now not unlike the banquet hall where Miss Havisham was to have her wedding dinner—a ruin.

I can still see his shack now. Since he never lived in the front house, which he rented out, the back house was like a shack in some backward part of the Ozarks, the porch filled with old newspapers and junk piled high with no sign of getting smaller anytime soon. The kitchen was the filthiest I think I have ever seen, with a sink so filled with mire that the idea that Sam actually still prepared meals there was simply inconceivable to me.

Supposedly, Sam and several friends formed an underground organization that found housing and work for individuals persecuted during the McCarthy era, when performers, writers, and directors were blackballed because they were suspected of being Communist sympathizers and being gay, and that is when his acquaintances with actors and actresses began his salons. I wish I had known that Sam, because the Sam I knew would never be a martyr to Gay Rights.

Sam was sometimes referred to in the Los Angeles press as "the American version of Quentin Crisp." Crisp was a brilliant personality, a gay icon the likes of which we will most likely never see again. Sam was, in comparison, not a man who ever allowed his sexuality to get in his way, nor did he really stand for anything other than self-indulgence. His one virtue was his imagination and his ability to see genius in other people.

I always loved the story my friend, Richard Lamparski, told me about a meeting he tried to work out for Sam to come face-to-face with his so-called counterpart, when Crisp was in Los Angeles doing his one-man show and was more than gracious in making time in his schedule to go out to Sam's house and have tea. When the day arrived and they made the pilgrimage to Sam's, he was nowhere to be found. Sam could not bring himself to meet the real deal when it appeared at his front door. He had lived a lifetime pretending to be famous and eccentric, yet he knew in his heart of hearts that he was no Quentin Crisp.

Sam kept a daily diary all recorded in that spidery script of his, and I am sure if one were to begin to read it in earnest, it would not be unlike reading Andy Warhol's diary, filled with nasty observations about people who thought they were his friends. When Sam was still living, he always bragged about its publication, but that was never to be, and perhaps it is for the best, although it might have shed some light, however fabricated, on just who he thought he was. Steven Arnold was another artist who fell under the spell of "La Perversa." I can recall vividly how Steven sat at Sam's feet in that crowded, dust-filled parlor with two lamps doing their best with 40-watt bulbs, as Sam read from his favorite passages of the diary. That would, of course, be the Parisian section from the early 1920s that was filled with references to a love affair between De Brier and Andre Gide, who died in 1951. I never saw proof such a relationship outside of that diary, so once again, time worked against the truth (for the record, his nephew claimed after Sam's death, he had a letter from Gide to Sam as proof of the affair, and that he entrusted the letter to one of Sam's friends, who was starting a library featuring primarily gay authors, and that the letter was later sold at auction at Christie's).

I do believe he knew the tragic Ramon Navarro since he was around Hollywood during the same time. Whether he also knew the two hustlers who killed Navarro, we will probably never really know. I always wondered why Kenneth never quoted Sam in any of his books on Hollywood, as he surely must have known some tidbits that would be of interest to the infamous author of two editions of *Hollywood Babylon.*

At the time of Sam's death in April 1995, he had lived at 6026 Barton Avenue for over fifty years and never cleaned it once after the salons ceased to exist in the early 1970s. There were mementos everywhere, some of value, others too absurd to contemplate. The costume he wore in *Pleasure Dome* was framed under glass, although it had been in that frame so long there was doubt it could be removed without damaging the piece altogether. There were antiques to be sure, but everything was covered in dust and grime, and things were piled on top of one another. Sam really did live like a bag lady, even clipping coupons and always dining out on everybody else. He slept in a small bedroom off from the parlor in a red and gold Chinese frame bed that looked like Anna May Wong might have owned it around 1915. He kept a loaded gun, also an antique, by his bed. It worked, he said, and he feared burglars all his time there. His house may have been nice when he bought it seventy years earlier, but the neighborhood declined to the point where gunshots could be heard on a nightly basis. Miraculously, he was never robbed or beaten up in the lifetime he lived there. One story had him walking out of the house, gun in hand, swinging it around in full view of the neighbors and yelling, "Has anyone seen them?" over and over, then turning and disappearing back into the house. He figured nobody would ever bother him once everyone knew he had a gun and might just be nuts enough to use it. In any case, it was a miracle the local thugs knew enough to leave him alone. It was even more of a miracle that he did not go up in flames like a witch in Salem because he chained-smoked cigarettes like Bette Davis on a slow day.

There was a time when I first got to know Sam that I used to take him to industry screenings at various locations around town, until one night in particular, when we went to see a John Waters film at the Gower Studios. I must tell you that Sam had no problem mouthing off to anybody who crossed his path the wrong way. In the past, he would tell somebody to be quiet and nothing ever came of it since people should be silent during a film. However, on that occasion, he found himself sitting behind Pat Ast, a very large, loud, and sometimes pissed-off actress on whose shit list I personally would not want to be. Pat was sitting with her group and her hair was teased very high on her head, so Sam tried to move to a different seat, which he did, in the same row, leaving me a seat or two away from him. During the movie, Pat kept talking to her friends at key points, yet it was not affecting the people around her except for Sam. As the film was into the last twenty minutes or so, Sam had reached his limit and told her to just shut her fucking mouth and watch the fucking film. Well, all 300 pounds of Pat Ast rose up and turned around to face her heckler and, seeing it was an old man, she still did not give a fuck, so she told him to shut his fucking mouth, and then she told him she was Miss Pat Ast. Sam (without missing a beat) replied, "Should that be Miss Fat Ass?" Well, by then, the film was no longer the center of attention. I managed to get Sam up and took him out the side exit to my car.

He kept asking me if I knew who the fat dyke was, and I told him not to give it a thought.

I believe that was the last screening I ever took La Perversa to see. I grew tired of the rudeness and bad manners that he felt were his right because of his age and that fact that nobody ever struck or hurt him physically in his entire life. Compare that with Quentin Crisp, who was beaten up so many times over his homosexuality that he simply refused to hide regardless of the risk. Maybe Sam's lifetime with a private income in Hollywood, where he never ventured out without companions, may have something to do with his amazing luck.

There are countless stories I could tell about Sam, yet they all end the same way. Yes, sometimes he was a trip to deal with and did possess on occasion a gallows humor in his observations about Hollywood. I think what disturbed me about my relationship with him was never knowing if he was a real friend or not. That became the ultimate turnoff in the end.

When he died, appropriately on April Fool's Day 1995, Curtis Harrington told me that Sam had something like $5 million in the bank (Sam's nephew disputes that claim and says his estate came to far less), and yet he lived his entire life a miser in a filthy old house by himself surrounded by objects that were too dusty to see or appreciate.

When all the considerable dust finally settled surrounding that man, I imagine his legacy will always be tied to Kenneth Anger, who had his faults to be sure, but remains a towering figure in the history of twentieth century cinema. Thus, Samson De Brier will finally have that footnote in history all to himself, as the man who lent his house to Kenneth Anger to make his film and played three roles in what is now a highly-regarded art film, *The Inauguration of the Pleasure Dome*. Let the marquee read "Samson De Brier as the Lord Shiva-Osiris and the Great Beast."

The other day, I noticed online that there was about to be an auction of the house Sam lived in throughout all the notoriety of his seven decades. The house is now valued at over $1 million despite the crappy neighborhood. The flyer for the house described it as follows: "Former home of the infamous celebrity warlock Samson De Brier. Check out this relic from Hollywood's pre-hippie LA freak show history."

I couldn't have said it better myself.

Chapter 42
Never Fall in Love with Your clients

Henry Willson

In past chapters of this book, I have mentioned my former career as a Hollywood talent agent, which eventually led me back to journalism after three years of toiling in and out of an industry I never much cared for, as it existed in 1979.

The current Guild laws regarding sexual harassment are clear and well-enforced today, but in 1979, it was very much like it was back in the heyday of agents like Henry Willson. My friend and colleague, Robert Hofler, published a book on Willson, coincidentally in time for another of Willson's clients, Tab Hunter, to put out his views on Hollywood and being gay in the 1950s.

Robert and I spent a great evening in the bar of the Peninsula hotel discussing Henry Willson for a then-to-be-published expose for *Vanity Fair*. The text he submitted to them was rejected, and rather than give up what amounted to several thousand words, Robert turned the essay into a book

My friendship with Henry began one evening at a West Hollywood cocktail lounge known with a nod and a wink to Tennessee Williams as The Garden District. That nightspot was the favorite watering hole for survivors of the Golden Age of Hollywood, as well as the Bronze Age! Hermoine Gingold could be seen in a booth with her fantasy sibling, photographer Roy Dean, well-established for his male nudes (free from hard-ons!) of which Roy was very proud. Not to mention older show biz types looking for younger show biz types, and so on.

On one of those Saturday night free-for-alls, Roy introduced me to the creator of the Adonis factory, Henry Willson. Henry was a regular on Saturday nights, positioning himself at the bar with a stool left open for the next Tab, Rock, or Guy to show up and get famous—or so they thought. Roy had mentioned the fact that Henry was a regular there, and that was my opportunity to get some essential pointers from the master agent himself. I had heard so much negative feedback about Henry from agents, who basically did the same thing to their clients, but without achieving results such as creating the next Rock Hudson.

Henry was a smooth talker, not to mention a namedropper, of epic proportions. His names, however, were worth dropping. Lana Turner, Joan Fontaine, and Natalie Wood were all former clients of his, so "bring it on" was my motto. We liked each other right away. He gave me some sound advice regarding the promotion of actors, as well as publicity, and how and when to use it. The one piece of advice that I never forgot, (and it even found its way into Robert's book), was "Never fall in love with your clients!"

When Henry passed that on to me, I replied, "Henry, with my client list, that isn't a problem!"

Henry had been not only a press agent for Selznick in the good old days, but for a time, he was the most powerful agent in Hollywood. His so-called "Adonis factory" had manufactured Guy Madison, Rory Calhoun, and Tab Hunter. It was through his creation of Rock Hudson from the meek lad once known to his mother as Roy Fitzgerald that both men ascended the heights of Hollywood immortality. Henry loved to dream up butch monikers for his golden boys, and Hollywood laughed behind his back as one after another of those homemade hunks would rise and fall in the Hollywood meltdown known as stardom. That was not the case with Rock Hudson; directors such as George Stevens and Douglas Sirk made sure that Hudson's star stayed bright and glowed on for decades after Henry Willson faded from view. The tragedy for Henry was that he broke his most cardinal rule and fell in love with his Eliza Doolittle.

I saw Henry at the Garden District every other weekend for around a year, and I sometimes took him to screenings if the film interested him at all. However, one Saturday came and went with no appearance from the star maker. That happened the following week, as well, and some of us grew concerned over Henry's well-being. A mutual friend and actor named John Wyche came in the club with the news that Henry was out at the Woodland Hills Motion Picture Home. His heavy drinking had led to health problems, and age and depression did the rest. I made it a point to see Henry out at the home at least twice a month, as did his other former clients, but never a word from the one that meant the most—the boy who came to him as Roy and walked away a Rock.

Chapter 43

Radio Daze: The Palm Springs Triangle

Frank Olsen

My curiosity was peaked the other day, when I happened upon an article in a November issue of *Vanity Fair* regarding the exploits of Lou Pearlman, who was known in the trade as "Big Poppa," a supposedly Svengali-like individual, who managed and controlled the most-hyped boy bands of the 1980s. Lou was the guiding force behind The Backstreet Boys, to name the most successful of the many groups he led to fame and riches.

The article went on to detail the man's reign of terror with allegations of sexual misconduct and fraud towards the boys in the band. The minute I finished the article, I felt a strange connection—an uncanny déjà vu—to the man and his exploits. You see, I, too, knew such a man as Lou Pearlman, and the similarities are simply too startling to ignore. The "Big Poppa" in my experience went by the name of Frank Olsen.

By the end of 1999, I chose to abandon Beverly Hills, not to mention the apartment I inhabited for over two decades, to embark on what I hoped was to be a new direction for me in the provocative world of talk radio. As the new Millennium filled the horizon with all manner of change, I was receiving encouraging phone calls from an old acquaintance of mine, former theatrical agent Maggie Abbott. She had recently relocated to Palm Springs and briefly had some dealings with an up-and-coming media group known as the Triangle Television/Radio Network.

Maggie is without doubt a textbook example of how to survive and stay above water in both Hollywood and the European film community's sometimes fickle concept of show business success. Maggie's reputation as a deal-maker had been very much like that of the infamous Sue Mengers here in Hollywood, a well-regarded agent both in Rome and London, with strong connections in film production, the kind you needed to "make it happen."

Maggie's dissatisfaction with the Hollywood system was especially profound considering that she was in a very select company of women excelling in a man's world. Maggie vividly recalled, "My London office was so vast that sometimes I could not even find the bloody telephone."

Maggie was a powerhouse in the days of "swinging London," where she knew Mick Jagger and David Bowie on a first-name-basis. She was Bowie's agent during the filming of *The Man Who Fell to Earth*.

By the time I came to know Maggie, all the rock-and-roll days of the late 1960s were well behind her and, after a less than satisfying attempt to manage the career of Maria Conchita Alonso, not to mention associate producing *Nightwing* (1979) and *American Pop* (1981), she was tired of being in "the war zone," as she referred to it. Hollywood was no longer fun anymore, and having been at the top of the heap, the only alternative to surviving the fallout was to exit stage left.

The exit presented itself shortly after a farewell engagement help-ing her old friend, Jackie Bisset, functioning as her confident/assis-tant. Maggie finally made up her mind and put Hollywood firmly behind her, moving lock, stock, and scrapbooks to "God's Waiting Room," which was otherwise known as Palm Springs.

Being Maggie, she quickly caught on to the subterranean ways of the desert community, and she began keeping a journal about the locals for future reference. Once you strip away the climate, the tour-ists, and the hype, what you have is a town where people come to reinvent themselves, or con others into believing they had become something else.

Maggie was enormously supportive regarding my relocating to the desert. She kept advising me, "David, you can really make a new life for yourself out here." After a couple of trial runs into Palm Springs night life, I was still having next to no luck in securing a place to live. Just as I was on my way out of town, I stopped by Maggie's condo to say goodbye and make her a present of a pocketbook version of the movie she co-produced, the infamous *Nightwing*, that I had just found in a thrift shop. However, she simply refused to give up on me, and rang up her friend, real estate broker Ruth Brewer. Soon after that, I found myself in front of a desert-style set of cottages owned by Ruth, signing a lease for my new place in the sun. I was officially a resident of Palm Springs.

The next order of business was finding a job, and she had already made overtures with her friend and ally, Vivienne Furlong, for me to au-dition at the Triangle Network as a potential host of my own program.

Here is where it all becomes a bit surreal. After all, when I arrived in Palm Springs at the end of August 1999, I had absolutely no experience in broadcast radio other than being a guest on various entertainment programs over the years in both Los Angeles and New York. Maggie and Vivienne explained that the CEO of that fledgling gay and lesbian media network was looking for "new talent," so all I had to do was win over a man named Frank Olsen.

The offices of the Triangle Radio Network were located at the corner of 1000 Tahquitz Canyon Way in what had once been the Sun System broadcasting company, a 1,200-square-foot, ground-floor set of studios and offices with broadcast capabilities.

After a couple of boozy "rock and roll" lunches (Maggie's term) at Ms. Abbott's condo, surrounded by her newly formed posse of desert divas with priceless names such as Vivienne Furlong and Ethel Hyde White (call me "Buzz.") A fun lady, she was the widow of character actor Wilfred Hyde White of *My Fair Lady* fame.

Each of the ladies present that day seemed to have their own take on just how to handle big Frank. Vivienne had come to Palm Springs from Las Vegas already a widow (not a good sign) and had already made a comfortable nest at the station not only with her #2 spot on Linda Christian's chat show, but as part of Franks inner circle (also not a good sign, as it would turn out). Ethel, on the other hand, was the real thing in a town filled with wannabes and phonies. She was exactly who she said she was, nothing more, and nothing less. Ethel was married to Wilfred Hyde White and was also the proud mother of actor Alex Hyde White. She loved films, having spent a lifetime in the highest circles of show business society on two continents. She pretended to know little of what Frank Olsen was up to, and really could not have cared less. However, she was savvy about what went on in Palm Springs, and it was Ethel who ultimately warned me off the place later on.

I was prepared to meet the Triangle mob head-on, so to speak. The first meeting turned out to be more of a Saturday morning breakfast at the station. The ladies advised me to ask no questions, just listen, and I would get the picture. They also made a point of telling me to not make too much of what Frank Olsen might do or say, since he was quite a "character"—an epic understatement of macabre proportions.

The breakfast was a buffet affair accommodating over fifty people. I met most of the regular studio crew that day, which appeared to consist entirely of well-built, good-looking Mexican boys in their late teens, as well as some of the radio talent. Television conductor Johnny Mann and his wife, Betty, were there, as well as a middle-aged couple that owned and operated a nude hotel right off Palm Canyon Drive. Vivienne brought actress Linda Christian (once married to Tyrone Power), who was signed to do a morning chat show for Triangle. Richard Weiner, the acting head of the station, was there to greet everyone. Richard was always charming, and his credentials included working for ABC Television for years, where, I believe, he won a Peabody Award for his efforts. Richard was also a practicing attorney for the company, as well.

I did not meet Frank Olsen that day, but his larger-than-life presence was felt nonetheless. From day one, it seemed everyone at the station was aware that Frank had a shady past. However, as long as Frank could create all that revenue, uncannily raising money from numerous backers, no one seemed to mind. His only visible connection to the gay community aside from being gay himself was the fact he had owned a string of gay bars in Seattle, as well as other business enterprises, including having bought and sold three other radio stations in the Pacific Northwest.

The game plan, as it was explained to me that morning, was for me to appear on at least three or four of the then-current radio programs at Triangle, to see if I could handle myself on the air. So the following Monday, I appeared on Linda Christian's program, with Vivienne acting as her co-host. It went quite well, and from there, I did two more, with the final test being Max Craig's talk show, *The Other Side*. Max was an acerbic gay man in his early forties, and also an attorney, who prided himself on being arch and funny. It was my appearance on his show that made it clear to the talent at Triangle that a new talk show host was born.

Max called me later that night and told me Frank Olsen wanted to meet with me in his office to discuss what kind of a show I might be right for at Triangle. The station was set up as you would imagine, an up-and-coming broadcast studio, not too grand but tasteful, with a lobby decorated in ultra modern style with overstuffed sofas in abundance. Completing the picture was a receptionist with her own desk facing a bird's eye view of the main recording chamber behind a soundproof glass wall.

My first impression of Frank was that he looked like a character out of *Star Wars*. He was very pale and quite overweight with a head of thin, white hair that fell about his face. He looked just like Jabba the Hutt. He spoke more like a bartender in a rough trade saloon. "Come on in here, Dave, I'm Frank Olsen. Why don't you just take a seat and let me map out what I have in mind for you here at Triangle." He then went on to say, "I can tell just by looking at you that you are thinking: 'Who is this fat old fart anyway?' Well, let me enlighten you on a few things. I have bought and sold more businesses in my lifetime than you ever will, I'll wager, not to mention I have a hell of a lot of money to back it up. And for your information, I also have the best-looking lover in this town, so never underestimate what I can do. So, if you will trust me, we will make some great fucking radio together, okay?"

I was, to put it mildly, a bit overwhelmed by his bulldozer personality, but I must admit he did know the radio business and seemed very sure of himself at all times. He quickly cut through the bullshit and came right to the point with, "Do you want to be a radio star? I can make you one if you really pay attention to my advice. I know what works on radio, and before I am through, so will you. Son, you are now enrolled in the School of Olsen." He asked me something else that day that was a bit shocking, but his candor could also win you over, as it did with me. Frank asked if I minded working for a boss who has been in jail. He explained that having been a gay man in Seattle back in the day had created a legal situation with an underage guy who was his first lover, and he had done time over it.

I reassured Frank that it was really none of my business to know such things. After all, 'love is blind, or in the eye of the beholder,' not to mention a four-letter word, so as long as everybody was on the same page about creating some kick-ass radio shows, then I was there 100% and ready to put out . . . so to speak.

From that day forward, I played out exactly the kind of tape Frank wanted to hear. After that interview, I went directly over to Richard Weiner's office, where he offered me a contract at $500 a week to broadcast my own hour-long program at the Triangle Television/radio Network.

The concept I had in mind all along was to do a live chat-type broadcast with phone–in guests that could help keep the topics and conversation lively. Since I had a reputation as a "film historian" with a special interest in fantasy and horror, it was decided that I should try doing the program like a horror host might do on television. I came up with a title that combined the horror genre with gay and lesbian overtones, and so *Tales from the Closet* came to life. I borrowed the title of the then-popular TV show based on the old DC comics, *Tales from the Crypt*, substituting the crypt with the dreaded image of the closet from which all gay men must emerge sooner or later.

My first broadcast was aired during the second week of September 1999 and went out live on the Internet as what must have been the first gay horror-themed chat show of its kind on radio. The great mystery to evolve from that week was why none of the programs could be heard in the greater Palm Springs area. The only actual radio stations that carried the Triangle Network live were along the Pacific Northwest from the Oregon coast all the way up to KBRO radio in Bremerton, Washington, and of course Seattle, which was Frank's hometown.

I was left pretty much to my own devices for the rest of the month, for which I was eternally grateful, since I was so green at all the technical aspects of doing live radio. My board operator was a seventeen-year-old-kid named Joey, who vaguely resembled C. Thomas Howell and never stopped chewing gum. As soon as he got my show up and running, he would split for thirty minutes at a time and I wisely never asked why.

The man who really ran the radio end of Triangle was a veteran of the network named Spike Chandler. Spike, who was then in his late thirties, had been a popular disc jockey in Southern California at one time and gave it all up to work in radio. Spike looked like a guy in training midway through army boot camp. He dressed in army fatigues 24/7, so after a while, he began to resemble an extra from the *M.A.S.H.* television show. I could not have survived the experience without his loyalty and kindness. Frank had promised Spike the moon to work the round-the-clock hours he did and I am sure he led Spike to believe he would one day be the director of the station, which, in a perfect world, should have been the case.

My best friend at Triangle was a beautiful lady with a kind heart, delicate features, long black hair, and a theatrical name to go along with her image: the great Daun De Vore. Her program, which aired just before mine, was called *Celebrities and More with Daun De Vore*. Daun was a tireless professional, who worked long hours, did her homework on her guests, and it all paid off because her show sparkled with charm and great conversation. She was also, like almost everyone at Triangle except for Spike and yours truly, a practicing attorney.

As we approached the new Millennium, the atmosphere at Triangle was super-charged. Frank began mapping out elaborate plans for one and all. He brought Daun and I into his office around Halloween and explained that Triangle was branching out to include television. He wanted me to create a character to host a weekly series introducing new and vintage horror films. Frank had signed a deal to broadcast *Auction Television* on weekends, which went out live throughout the Palm Springs area, as well as on the Internet. He created a huge line of credit with wholesale outlets such as Sam's Town purchasing thousands of dollars worth of home appliances to auction off on television. On weekends, those of us that wanted to make $75 to $100 a night could answer the phones at the station during *Auction TV's* bingo/lottery, which Frank supervised personally. At the end of that meeting, he grinned at me and promised, "I told you from day one I had big plans, and right now I have guys over in the prop department building you a coffin for your TV show." Looking back, he might as well have made a few more for the rest of us.

Frank arranged a day-long photo session for Daun and me for a proposed talk show for the two of us. We went ahead and posed for dozens of stills, where we pretended we were Sonny and Cher. Frank was always showing potential backers that material, raising more and more money for programs yet to be produced. At Triangle, everything was always just about to happen. Frank kept dangling carrots in front of everyone who worked for him, and it worked almost without fail.

Triangle brought in the year 2000 full of great expectations, and yet every day, there was one dramatic incident after another that made you wonder what was really going on. I was moved around in different time shots, first in a one-hour time frame, and then Frank decided on giving me a full three hours on the air in the evening from 8:00 until 10:00, six days a week.

Frank would come into the station at all hours of the day and night, bringing no less than a dozen people at a time and walking them through the complex, waving at those of us working in the sound booths with our shows. We were always on display for the backers, and yet after four months, none of our shows were being heard in

Palm Springs. Whenever one of us would bring that up at staff meetings, Frank hedged the issue or gave a date in the next few weeks for our local broadcast. Palm Spring was enjoying some attention with their film festival, and I tried to explain to Frank how difficult it was to attract guests with only Internet coverage and broadcasts in Seattle and the Pacific Northwest as the audience.

Frank was not an easy man to pin down, and as the weeks went by, he showed up less and less during business hours, deliberately missing appointments. During that period, I lost my phone–in callers, and he became more and more irritable regarding the shows and their content.

One evening, he came into the station right in the middle of my show and screamed at me to get the fuck in his office. "Listen, this is a gay radio station, understand!? Why are you not talking more about gay sex and less about these fucking old movies and gossiping about these dead movie stars!?" From that moment on, he demanded that I keep talking the entire three hours and start getting more guests to come down and talk in person.

Under that new policy, I at least got my call-in guests back, and I decided I better start giving Frank a sexually gay show or start looking for another job. I had recently had my old friend, author Richard Lamparski, on the show, and when I explained to him what was going on with Frank, he gave me the phone number of playwright Robert Patrick, author of the award winning *Kennedy's Children*, not to mention an encyclopedia of knowledge on every aspect of gay porn.

Frank was tuned in full-tilt the night I had Robert on the air, and after a brief discussion of Patrick's involvement with the legendary

Caffe Cino in Greenwich Village back in the turbulent 1960s, he got right down to business. Robert took full advantage of Triangle's sexual freedom policy to ask me on the air if he could discuss his favorite sexual pastime. I still was unsure where that was going, but wherever we went, it was all for Frank, so I gave Robert the floor.

At first, Robert was a bit reluctant to come right out with it, but he finally asked me if it would be alright to say on the air the Greek term for what he liked to do in bed.

Still in the dark, I said, "Fine, go on with your train of thought."

"Well David, you see, I am a firm supporter of Analingus. I will not apologize for enjoying it in the privacy of my bedroom, and, by the way, I have started a group to give some respect to the men who perform it, as well of those of us that like having it done to us."

The highlight of the broadcast, from my perspective, was Robert, a witty and erudite man, who tackled the program with great humor. He gave his contact information freely on the air, proving to be a man of his convictions and a true pioneer in the field of gay literature from the days of Stonewall into the twenty-first century.

Life at the Triangle Network was strained and getting more so with each week that followed. Deadlines where not met, we never got broadcast outside of the Portland/Seattle area, and more and more people were being paraded through the station at night to see Frank's work-in-progress. The station was filled to the rafters with appliances of every sort, including tractors, all to be auctioned off on television. Just before I arrived in the desert, Frank talked names like Ted Dawson and Lana Wood (Natalie's sister) to host *Auction Television*. During that period, I made friends with a charming lady named Elaine

Church, who came in to make some extra money. She had been in films at one time, appearing in two of my favorite British films, *Justine* and *The Killing of Sister George*.

Elaine was nobody's fool, and she quickly picked up on the bad vibes the station was generating in Palm Spring because more and more people became suspicious of Frank Olsen and all that money being raised for a radio station that never aired in town, as well as a television n Network with prizes that were won and often never collected by anyone. Elaine invited me to her home for a dinner party of around a dozen of her close friends. Afterwards, the whole evening was devoted to warning me to be careful about allowing my name to be used to sell stock or find backers for Frank's make-shift network. Elaine's friends kept reminding me that it was shows like mine that gave the impression to backers that Triangle was legit.

One incident in particular that really put the Frank Olsen situation in perspective came very soon after Elaine's dinner party. As luck would have it, Daun Devore had an uncanny talent for finding guests for her daily chat show and remained constantly on the lookout for celebrities. Daun had recently been in contact with former President Gerald Ford's public relations staff in Rancho Mirage. Ford remained, next to Bob Hope and Walter Annenberg, the most sought-after guest in town, and our own Daun Devore had the former President all but locked in for an appearance at Triangle. That would really put the station on the map, not to mention provide some much needed prestige, as well.

A few days before the Presidential visit was to take place, a black sedan arrived at the station filled with Secret Service men, who then proceeded to take down all the license numbers from the cars in the

Triangle packing lot reserved for the staff and crew. Within forty-eight hours after the visit from the Secret Service, the President's appearance was abruptly cancelled and never spoken of again. At the time, it remained a bit of a mystery, however hindsight is 20/20, and with the disclosures that have followed regarding Frank Olsen and several of his cohorts at Triangle, that turn of events was not at all surprising.

The drama continued through most of 2000, until Frank's boyfriend started driving the boss's Rolls Royce around the complex late at night trying to get women to have sex with him. He cornered Daun De Vore in her office late one night and pulled his cock out for her to see, explaining that his "awesome tool" was really made for women like her. Frank could only rent it from time to time. "I'm gay for pay, baby girl . . . Frank has promised me a million dollars to stay his lover."

By then, we all knew that Frank was the Titanic in search of an iceberg. One by one, people were getting pink slipped or their paychecks bounced. My hours were up to three a night, and Frank had hired a non-professional to read soft-core gay porn on the air. The provocative title of his show: *Gay Radio Reader with Samuel*. When I dared question Frank about that stellar addition to our radio family, he looked at me and said, "Well now, Dave, don't get all jealous on me. Samuel has an awesome voice. I just love listening to him talk about hard-ons."

Looking back after all that time, I am able to say that within the year I endured the broadcasters' "School of Olsen," I had some wonderful, articulate guests on my program, like the great Tab Hunter and British director Val Guest and his wife, Yo (both of whom lived in Palm Springs full-time), not to mention screenwriter (as well as the editor of *Films In Review*) Roy Frumkes, who kindly spent an hour with me when I really needed him, the lovely Anne Francis, who gave very generously of her time during Christmas, cult filmmaker Kenneth Anger, who revealed Hollywood secrets, Ron Chaney, grandson to acting legend Lon Chaney, who spent the entire program discussing a century of Chaneys, actor Richard Harrison (who was running for Mayor of Palm Springs at the time), Richard Lamparski, who discussed his next book all about his time in New York with his own radio program, and the late Roy Dean, who was already well-known as a photographer of male nudes, but, having been once many years before a very successful actor in the UK, chose to recite Shakespeare, even allowing us to play a scene together. He then read an original short ghost story about a lost gay love in Hawaii that was quite moving and a real highlight among my shows there at Triangle, especially now that he is gone.

They all did three-hour programs with me during 2000, and, of course, Robert Patrick (not the *X-Files* guy—can you imagine confusing those two?). When I was left to my own devices, it could be a lot of fun. I did, however, feel sorry for the dozens of people Frank swindled out of money, as the Triangle project spun out of control and finally just ended with an early morning phone call asking the talent not to come in since the shows were all cancelled, never to be revived

While I was putting this essay together, I discovered yet another article (this one online in *Frontiers*) that literally jumped out at me: "The Gay Enron-Q Television Terminates Its Signal." It seemed that after Frank Olsen defrauded countless investors over Triangle Television and Radio (from 1999 until it finally closed down in 2000, and later the whole complex was removed for good), he went on his obese little way right into another scam. That time, he reinvented the Triangle media name into Q Television, attracting even bigger names than when I worked for him. That time, he played the gay card for all it was worth, remaining always in the shadows on memos or faxes, just his name being enough to keep them guessing, 'Does this guy have the money and the balls to pull off an all-gay anything?' The players that time around included Steve Kmetko, Sandra Bernhard, and Reichen Lehmkuhl, who had their own shows on the network, and that time the show actually aired on cable, but not for long.

The article explains how Frank Olsen, "a former Seattle bar owner with a shady past," raised $15.5 million from investors for the premier gay television network "Q." Back to his old habits from Palm Springs, hiring muscle boys to act as floor managers, while picking up guys at the local Blockbuster to produce shows, Frank soon had the whole network running scared, as paychecks bounced and deadlines went unheeded. The whole ship began once more to sink.

Why is it no one ever does a background check on men like Frank? He has a felony-theft conviction on the books in Washington State from 1986, and a whole fallen empire in Palm Springs, where people are still owed money. There are folks out there who have lost their homes over the man's greed and dishonesty. Let's also take into account what his behavior did for the gay community—absolutely nothing, except creating mistrust and bad blood for anyone who fell in his path.

As the dust began to settle over this essay, I remembered Frank's birthday party in 2000 at some desert hotel out by Sunny Dunes. Everybody showed up to drink Frank's booze, eat his buffet, and pretend for one night that he was everybody's gay big daddy. All the muscle boys from the station were already in party mode, openly smoking bags of pot by the valet parking entrance. It was just so totally "Frank Olsen" already. I arrived with Maggie Abbott in tow. After exchanging a few puffs with the boys in the sand, we made our way inside. Never one to waste good money for a bad cause, Maggie remained reluctant to order a drink from the so-called open bar until she was absolutely positive it was *an open bar*, and then she quickly ordered a double-vodka.

Making a true movie star entrance from the back of the hall was Linda Christian, draped in floor length furs, with some boy candy on her arm, making her way into the center of the party, ready for a photo-op. Though long departed from the station, and far removed from Frank Olsen, the food and drink was on the Triangle tab, and let's face it, her beloved Ty Power was long dead, and so was her radio program.

Palm Springs remains the one town this side of Hollywood that loves to milk a celebrity corpse to death, not to mention claim them as resident desert flowers cut down too soon . . . cue Elvis and Liberace.

All of the Triangle "family" showed up for Frank's birthday, and the testimonials were ripe with praise for a man who had promised nearly everyone in that room a piece of the radio/television pie. After I had my share of cocktails, I decided to find a table, sit down, and finally take it all in. Who of all people should waddle over and take the chair closest to me but "Big Daddy Frank" himself. He puts his plate down and gave me the grinning "full Monty" version of Frank Olsen's media mogul leer. "Well Dave, I bet you never thought you would be sitting here in Palm Springs ready to rule?"

"No Frank, I certainly did not," was my reply.

"That's not just the half of it. As we speak, I've got those prop boys over at the station putting the finishing touches on that coffin of yours."

Really Frank? I was just about to say the same thing to you.

Chapter 44

Viva Hugs a Tree

Viva

My favorite anecdote about Viva, the former Warhol superstar and successful painter of landscapes, has to be the story her longtime friend, Barbara Steele, told me. She and Viva were enjoying a hike in the woods, when all at once—confronted by a tree of great beauty—Viva went into a self-induced state of rapture, ran towards her object of desire, and wrapped herself with abandon around the mighty oak, discarding her wardrobe as she went. However, her bliss was short-lived. She discovered the tree was covered with small insects and debris that attached to her nude body.

Viva soon let out a shriek as only she was capable of, and Barbara, not quite sure what was wrong, went over to see what she could do to help her distraught companion. Viva was screaming that she was being bitten and itched like mad, so Barbara knelt down in front of her and began to pick away as many insects and offending objects as she could. While that was taking place, a group of boy scouts chose that particular moment to come walking by, just in time to observe what appeared from a distance to be two middle-aged lesbians engaged in some depraved sexual act.

I was introduced to Viva by Barbara early in 1978 as a potential client for my talent agency. I already represented Barbara, and Viva was looking for an agent since she was in need of money, a situation that presented itself often in her life.

The first thing that people noticed about Viva was her enormous green eyes. In films, she had the ability to transform into a goddess, with a face both aquiline and aristocratic with hyper-hollow cheeks offset by hair most usually done in a frizzed-out, unkempt style. The look was, however, disrupted whenever Viva spoke because her voice did not match her looks. Viva had a whiny, tedious voice that could really make you want to hang up on her if she was on a rampage complaining about the world in which she was forced to live.

So much time has passed since Viva and I knew each other that it is important to realize how much the image and legacy of Andy Warhol continues to play in her life. I used to wonder what connection placed Barbara Steele and Viva—two very different personalities—as friends. It is not so difficult to understand when you compare their film personas. Both owed their careers to one man. For Viva, it will always be Warhol, and for Barbara, it will always be Fellini. In Barbara's case, one might want to add to that the Italian Horror master, Mario Bava, since Barbara's film career really began with *Black Sunday*, but Bava did not impact her as a person like Fellini did. His influence resonated throughout her life and work in films.

Viva was crowned a superstar by Warhol in 1967, and for three years, she appeared in films like *Bike Boy* (1967), *Nude Restaurant* (1967), *The Loves of Ondine* (1968), *Blue Movie* (1969), and *Lonesome Cowboys* (1968). Every one of those films share one thing in common: Viva speaks a kind of intellectual babble while undressing, and in the case of *Blue Movie*, doing the sex act for real on-camera with Louis Waldon.

Nothing Viva did after that had the same impact since her connection to Andy Warhol's Factory, and, like Barbara, she played off her Warhol persona in other director's films such as Agnes Vada's *Lions Love* in which Viva plays herself, a film goddess on the lam, visually Garbo acting like Zasu Pitts on drugs. After that, except for vanity projects in the form of video diaries made by her then-husband Michel Auber, Viva existed in effective cameos in such films as *Midnight Cowboy* and *Cisco Pike*. Woody Allen liked her energy and outré style enough to use her in *Play it Again Sam*.

I can't say enough about *Cisco Pike*. As one of the most underrated films of the 1970s, it was a failure when it was released in 1972, which was a shame because all of the performances were exceptional. The depiction of Los Angeles was totally on-target for the times, yet it is let down by the even-then dated references to the hippie movement, not to mention treating grass like it was a hard drug. I was one of the few people who actually saw *Cisco Pike* in a theater, and Viva is what I remembered best. The female lead is supposed to be Karen Black, yet when Viva is on camera, she is the one you notice because of her off-kilter line readings. In 1972 she was a fresh face in Hollywood, not to mention that she was several months pregnant during the filming of her scenes. When Barbara asked me to see Viva, it was *Cisco Pike* that convinced me she should be working in Hollywood. Viva was and is a unique personality, and unlike some cult figures of the underground, she was capable of so much more as an artist.

For me as their agent, another similarity between Viva and Barbara was trying to explain to Hollywood producers exactly who they were and why all their films were hard to see, and in some cases, hard to watch. It did not help that Viva appeared in the Warhol films speaking her own dialogue in situations that were largely improvised. In other words, the question remained whether she could really act. For Barbara, it was slightly different, yet most of her Italian films were dubbed, so her performances were visual, and those directors tended to use her like architecture, which added to her mystique.

By the time Viva came to me, her husband, Michel Aubar, was not in her life, at least at that time. She was raising her daughter, Alexandra, by herself. They were the two musketeers and they were soul mates, as well.

I remember so well the first time they came to Century Park East, where the Del Valle, Franklin, and Levine Agency did its business on the 13th floor. Viva and Alexandra arrived with shopping bags full of magazines—mostly old copies of *Interview* and *Rolling Stone*, collector's items even then, with Viva on the covers of some and articles in all of them about her adventures at the Factory with Warhol. The one thing she did not bring were her photographs. I had specifically explained to her on the phone, "I need head shots for both the *Academy Players Directory* and one great shot for me to send around town," to get the word out that Viva Superstar was in Hollywood and ready for her close-up. If only we were in the Hollywood of the 1920s, where a personality such as Viva would have been entirely at home, and no matter how many films she made, Mr. and Mrs. First-Nighter would have never heard that voice of hers.

Viva brought me an autographed photo of herself from her latest film, *Forbidden Zone*, which would be released a year later (1980), achieving immediate cult status since it featured the Oingo-Boingo band with the then-unknown Danny Elfman. Viva was dressed for the film like a Christmas tree ornament on LSD and it suited her somehow. She had no headshots with her, but since she had been in the New York scene with the likes of Warhol, she should have had boxes of 8x 10s by that stage of the game. What I did not take fully into account was she constantly moved from one location to another, with perhaps only the infamous Chelsea Hotel as a constant, and so she found it difficult to hold on to memorabilia.

I was surprised a few years later, when we did our interview for *Films and Filming*. I discovered that Joe Dallesandro had two boxes of photos. He would have had more, but Paul Morrissey borrowed all his stills from *Dracula* and *Frankenstein* that he did in Italy and never gave them back . . . poor Little Joe.

My plan for Viva was to let Hollywood know that she was a legend in underground cinema and was ready to become a Hollywood legend. I knew that was what she really wanted in an odd way, and for all her protests about the mediocrity of the bourgeoisie, Viva wanted mom and dad to see their little girl finally make it big in films other than those that resided in the abyss of underground cinema screening from the grind houses on 42nd Street.

After our initial meeting at the office, I set about sending off some publicity stills taken from *Lions Love* over to Mike McLean, a great guy, who happened to be casting a comedy about Dracula. *Love at First Bite* brought George Hamilton back into the public eye in what was to become a major hit upon release. However, Bob Kaufman's original script had a much funnier reason for Dracula's departure from Transylvania than they would end up with in the final film. It seemed that the Count had a Countess, who nagged and nagged until even the grave was no escape, so he packs up his coffin and takes his slave, Reinfeld, to the Big Apple. I think Mike had seen the Warhol horror films, and with that in mind, the fact that I had a client who was forever linked to Andy's Factory stars made him more than interested in seeing what Viva Superstar had to offer.

That moment in my working relationship with Viva was the best because all the planets were in alignment. I phoned her with the news, and, of course, the first thing out of her mouth was to ask how fast she could get a paycheck from those bastards at the front office. I was so hyped about finding a part for her that I just said whatever she wanted to hear because she was at last in line to do some really good work in a film that would be seen by the entire world. With any luck, that would launch her on a career as a comedic talent that I was convinced was her destiny.

I know all good things must come to an end, but not before they even have a chance to get started! It was but three days later that I received the news that the studio was canceling negotiations with my client because she was "blacklisted" from working in Hollywood over a dispute with the makers of *Cisco Pike*. It turned out that Viva was to do some publicity for the film in New York and was sent there by the producers for that purpose. After they gave her the expense money and airline tickets, she went to New York alright, but then she just kept going until she arrived in Paris, never to return or do anything she was contracted to do regarding *Cisco Pike*. That little tidbit was never brought to my attention during all my conversations with Viva over the previous three months after Barbara put us together hoping I could find her some work.

I will always regret that Viva did not play Countess Dracula in the George Hamilton film because when Viva is right for something, there is just no one else to play it but Viva. It is no accident that she never really took off after her glory days with the Factory. Warhol liked to play God with his superstars, and they all suffered for it in one way or another. The Factory was known for its in-house paranoia and dishonesty among the "golden lads and lassies," and Viva was quick to lash out at her mentor and lost favor with him after some ugly business in Paris where she tried to force Warhol to send her money by threatening to write about what she saw at the Factory and naming names.

Our relationship did not end with the demise of the Hamilton project, and for a few more weeks, I kept trying new things even though the blacklist was an obstacle almost impossible to overcome. It did not help either that Viva would phone me at the agency at least three times a day to inquire as to how and when something was going to pop up and pay her bills. I knew that routine by heart, since Kenneth Anger had the same problem in life: fame with no possibility of an income because of it. Artists such as Viva and Kenneth needed patrons to survive. Both of them could write, and in Viva's case, her true calling was to paint, but it would be decades before she realized what she always knew since childhood: that she had a gift for art and that one day it would take her back to where she always needed to be—in front of a canvas.

During that period, she lived in West Hollywood off Robertson. There was a landmark on the corner of her street, just inside the courtyard of The Sundance Cafe —a plaster statue of John Huston on a horse as the fictional character, "Buck Loner," from *Myra Breckenridge.* The Sundance Cafe was a Tex-Mex joint with a patio, and there were tables inside near walls that were covered with autographs of the famous that have eaten there. Barbara and I had many a taco in that place over the years, and when they closed it, she tried to buy the colorful wooden chairs they used inside.

Viva had rented a small house, which was barely furnished with books, magazines, and the odd table and chairs. One night, I got a call from her. She was freaking out because she had apparently just figured out that West Hollywood was primarily gay and her neighborhood was no exception. At night after the bars closed, the gay men that lived all around her stood naked in their front doors in the dark, as cars slowly drove by looking for some late night action.

"David, you have got to get over here and check this out—oh, my God, there goes the same guy back around again!"

Viva was concerned how that might affect her daughter, although as young as Alexandra was at the time, she had lived in the land of Bohemia more than most children her age. I was convinced she would survive—at least more than her mother seemed to be at the moment.

I lived so close to Viva that I decided to walk over and calm her down. The summer night was hot, and I was sure that would be a hoot on many levels. What happened next was beyond the valley of the dolls.

Viva was suitably distraught when I arrived at her front door, quickly ushered me inside, and turned off all the lights so we could watch unobserved, as the sexual conga line of cars made their way around the block, over and over. Viva had rolled a joint for us, and I brought some wine, so we sat there on her floor with the door open listening to the mating dance of West Hollywood. I seem to remember one song that kept being played on her radio that night: it was "Lola" by The Kinks, and I can never hear it to this day without remembering the "electric candlelight" that glowed that night so many summers ago because it indirectly resulted in my one and only one-night-stand with Viva Superstar. The combination of grass, booze, and some kind of sexual voodoo happened every once in a blue moon, and that created a window for the impossible to happen. She and I had never felt any chemistry during our relationship as agent/client. One must just take a line from the era and just blame it on the boogie.

A few days later, Viva stormed into my office and demanded that I end my representation of her. She was leaving Del Valle, Franklin, and Levine for lack of progress in getting her a job. Before I could say, "fine, have a nice day," Viva went over to where I had placed several frames of clients we represented and removed her autographed still from *Forbidden Zone* and then asked me for any of her copies of *Interview* that I had on hand plus her headshots. As she departed, her final put down to me was, "The only job you ever gave me was a blow job!" and with that, Viva Superstar headed for the elevator screaming, "You belong on the 13th floor!"

I, of course, told that whole story to Barbara Steele, who was most amused and thought it a shame that Viva was so impossible to help. They remained friends forever it seemed, and later on, she and I added Mary Wornov to the mix.

Several years later, I was helping Barbara with her Thanksgiving dinner because she was entertaining around twenty of her friends. As I was arriving with wine and a second turkey to help with the overflow, Barbara took me aside and said, "Guess who is here?" I dared not even guess, when she whispered, "Viva, and she wants to make up."

So, in the holiday spirit of the evening, I walked over to Viva, still recognizable after all that time, and when she saw me, she looked and said, "Oh yeah, I remember you now. Barbara said we got it on once. Is that so?" As she said that, Genevieve Waite came over to us and I immediately changed the subject by telling her I still had my cast album of *Man in the Moon*, her Broadway show with music by her then-husband, John Phillips. The show lasted one performance on Broadway and featured another one of my clients, Monique Van Vooren.

The last time I saw Viva was in 2005 at the Getty in Los Angeles. She was there with Alexandra and we had a wonderful time chatting away. Alexandra is a beautiful and intelligent woman, and Viva remains her best friend. Time has mellowed Viva, and she is painting full-time now. I am told she is a success living in my old stomping grounds of Palm Springs. It will always amaze me just how much genius can alter the lives of those it touches.

For Barbara, the experience of making *8 ½* has stayed with her a lifetime, and I was there when she gave Fellini a final embrace when he came to Los Angeles for the last time before he passed away.

As for Viva, her time with Warhol lasted less than five years, yet his legacy will always be a profound one, and she has had more than had the fifteen minutes of fame Andy predicted we all would have in this life. For a woman named after a paper towel, Janet Susan Hoffman, also known as "Viva," outlived her critics and mentor to reside where Hollywood chose to recreate their *Lost Horizon* in the 1930s. Viva had a lost horizon when acting was her goal, but all that is behind her, and her horizon looks very bright indeed.

Chapter 45

Welcome to the Breakfast Show

Kenneth Anger

Dreams have always been a mystery to me. Sometimes, I felt like they were private screenings that no one would ever watch, outside of me while deep in sleep. During most of 1983, I helped to research the sequel to Kenneth Anger's infamous *Hollywood Babylon*, to be titled (what else?) *Hollywood Babylon II*. That endeavor created many dreams, some of which I will never recall, and others I will never forget.

Kenneth was still living in New York, at that time, and he had already started sending me want lists of photographs he was planning to include with the text, as well as early drafts of certain chapters he knew would be of particular interest to me. As an aficionado of the horror genre, Kenneth knew I would want to see what he had uncovered on Lionel Atwill, so that was one of the first he sent to me typed on E.P. Dutton letterhead. In his familiar red penmanship, he wrote at the top of the chapter page, "For your eyes only; do not show to my enemies like Curtis [Harrington]." Kenneth was in the midst of yet another feud with his longtime colleague, and I was in the middle, since I was friends with both of them.

Kenneth had planned for years to do a follow-up to his legendary *Hollywood Babylon,* the international success of which made him even more infamous than his films ever did. The great obstacle was always trying to top the first one in revelations of the private lives of the stars, and as time marched on, America became less likely to accommodate the author with shock and awe, when pop culture wallowing in scandal and gossip without any help from the Magus of Tinseltown. That situation has only worsened with time, and reality shows and the Internet have made Kenneth's books with scandalous tales of stars of a bygone era (however classic) somewhat redundant.

As Kenneth entered his dotage with the media forever focused on his conduct, however unbecoming, it is important to emphasize what a monumental influence he had on twentieth century pop culture. His experimental films are landmarks of *avant-garde* and homoerotic cinema. Kenneth is also the father of the music video, creating the format years before anyone really knew what to do with it. Even the *Hollywood Babylon* books are now important references for anyone studying film history or simply curious about pop culture.

Kenneth loved the cinema from childhood, especially since it was in the golden days of the studio system, when MGM had more stars than the heavens and its stars misbehaved not unlike the gods of Mount Olympus at their zenith.

The *Hollywood Babylon* books were meant to draw attention to the futility of Hollywood trying to set a standard for moral authority where none existed. What could be more apropos than to compare Hollywood with ancient Babylon? In the 1920s, even that Babylon had a hard time catching up with characters like Barbara La Marr or Alla

Nazimova. The original French edition of *Hollywood Babylon* was more of a coffee-table book, oversized with beautiful reproductions of stills Kenneth spent a lifetime collecting. Anyone who was fortunate enough to own a copy would be disappointed in the American editions, which had none of the glamour of that first notorious 1959 edition.

One of the tragic aspects of the Babylon saga as it unfolded before me that year was the lack of preparation allowed Kenneth for a proper follow-up to the first edition. E.P. Dutton had advanced Kenneth a sizable sum that evaporated before he ever got to Hollywood to spend it. A self-confessed spendthrift, advances seldom encouraged results.

Kenneth arrived at my apartment at 9136 Beverly Boulevard with the following items in tow: a white violin trimmed in blue neon, a prop from one of the fabled "Gold Digger" films of the 1930s (and it still lit up on its own white pedestal); a six-sheet (81x81) poster from Eddie Cantor's *Whoopie!* (1930). The poster was a hoot, since it had multiple images of Cantor's huge eyes, resulting in a psychedelic montage in dazzling colors on linen. Last, but far from least, he brought a large framed autographed portrait of Rudolph Valentino. Kenneth also brought a suitcase and briefcase, but no typewriter.

At that stage of the book's development, I had seen the text of the Lionel Atwill chapter, which was culled from old movie magazines of the 1940s that chronicled Atwill's fall from grace during a sensational trial regarding a Christmas party at his Pacific Palisades abode, where two underage girls set the old boy up by telling all to the press. The end result was disgrace and financial ruin for Atwill and a field day for the Hollywood press, who by then had a lot of experience with those Hollywood hound dogs in Hamlet attire.

Kenneth hired me to provide photos and background information from the usual sources such as the library at The Academy of
Motion Picture Arts and Sciences, and the American Film Institute.
He quickly settled on a portrait I had of Atwill in profile from *Murders in the Zoo*, a pre-Code film with lots of sadism and cruelty. That
particular still had Atwill in the shadow of a mamba, which made the
leering actor all the more sinister. Atwill, for those of you that may
not know the name, has been forever immortalized by Mel Brooks (of
all people) in his film and later musical versions of *Young Frankenstein*.
In the film, actor Kenneth Mars plays an inspector with a wooden
arm, a character based entirely on Atwill's unforgettable performance
in *Son of Frankenstein,* Universal's last classic Frankenstein with Boris
Karloff as the monster.

In today's world view, what Atwill did in the privacy of his home
on that Christmas Eve over half a century ago would not even merit
a nod on *Entertainment Tonight,* and I mentioned that to Kenneth at
the time that those tales of long ago need to be off the charts to make
it shocking even in the 1980s. However, lodged in Kenneth's imagination was that image of Atwill as the kink of all kinks in the Hollywood
he so admired that he was to have a place in it no matter what anyone
might say to the contrary.

As the days went by, it became clear to me that Kenneth had lost
his mojo when it came to putting that book to rest. He enjoyed the
research and loved looking though stacks of photographs, but when
it came time to create a narrative for it, lawyers at E. P. Dutton quickly
took the wind right out of his sails. He had to depend on the old ad-
age, "A picture is worth a thousand words." For example, he could not

come out and say Cary Grant was having a sexual relationship with Randolph Scott, but he could imply it by showing a series of suggestive photos of the two men living together in Hollywood bliss with the boys at breakfast and at play in their very own playhouse.

The "coroner to the stars," Thomas Noguchi, who was in charge of all the famous autopsies of the famous for fifteen years became a favored source for many of the more unsavory stills in both editions. Kenneth had made a contact in Noguchi's office and scored many death shots, some of which remain unpublished. Noguchi loved the limelight and was very aware of Kenneth Anger and his books. Whether or not the two ever met is still a mystery. Noguchi was tossed out of office for revealing too much regarding the deaths of both William Holden and John Belushi, which in its own perverse way was very Kenneth Anger, but hey—this is Hollywood, after all.

Kenneth became so distraught over the book that he even at one point cooked up a plan to inform his editors in New York that the book would have to be put on hold because he was ill with HIV (which of course he wasn't). It took all my powers of persuasion to talk him out of that one, and he had gone so far as to ask around town for a doctor willing to go along with his plan.

I feel the need to explain just how generous a friend Kenneth was then. We had been good friends for at least five years, and he was never anything but a loyal and caring person at all times, in spite of what has been written about him in print. The Kenneth Anger of the 1980s was stubborn and insensitive to minorities always, and yet he loaned money to any colleague he felt needed assistance. The fact that he was famous never really meant much to him since this was not something he could take to the bank when the rent was due. I can't tell you how many times at universities (of all places) he would be approached by a student congratulating him on writing *Look Back in Anger*. If he felt like it, he corrected them with, "Sorry, that was John Osborne." More often than not, he would just sigh at the prospect that colleges ceased to teach anything anymore.

It was not easy adjusting to "life with Anger" and I felt uneasy when I was home because Kenneth went for hours without saying a word. He found a corner of the bedroom and just sat in the dark with his thoughts. I remember one particular morning during his stay when my phone rang way too early in the morning for my taste. When I finally answered, it was Helen Bilke, my neighbor across the courtyard, who rang me up at seven in the morning to find out who that wonderful man was who was staying with me. When I first asked why she needed to know—especially at seven in the morning—she replied, "Well, honey, he is on his knees in the courtyard cleaning the wedges between the tiles in the walkway with a toothbrush! I mean, your friend has been at it since daybreak and it looks wonderful."

That was my introduction to Kenneth's drug habits, and had they all been so constructive, they might never have been written about at all. When he was on speed or uppers, he was like a demonic Joan Crawford, and dirt look out! My mother came to visit during Kenneth's stay with me, and when she saw my living room after two weeks with Kenneth as a house guest, the first words out of her mouth were, "Marry him. He is a keeper!" My living room glowed from Pine Sol and window cleaner, every picture frame was so clear they looked transparent, the floors were mirror-like; the whole apartment was a showplace, especially with that neon violin glowing in one corner and the *Whoopee!* Poster lit up in another. Now that was Kenneth Anger management at its best!

One weekend afternoon, I took him to the autograph collectors show over at Beverly Garland's hotel, and I watched as he worked the room. At one point, we ran into an acquaintance of mine, Joe Dante, who directed films, was a fan at heart, and collected like one. I introduced him to Kenneth and Joe, who was visibly impressed. I told him who he was, and Kenneth smiled and said, "Oh, Joe Dante. Yes, I think I've seen your magic act in New York." Joe's smile quickly went upside down, and he coldly replied, "I am a film director, not a magician," to which Kenneth shot back, "Well maybe you should try magic. People might then know your work," and then walked away leaving Joe very pissed off.

Among the things Kenneth could not tolerate with admirers and fans was the mispronunciation of the name of his idol, Aleister Crowley. So many people say the last name as if it sounded like "cowly" instead of Crow, like the bird. To do that was grounds for banishment. He also could not stand smoking of any kind and really never had more than a glass of wine. His bête-noir would always be drugs just like his idol, the great beast, Crowley. In the glory days, when Kenneth was house Magus for the Rolling Stones and quite the rage, he ran into a man who introduced himself as "Chemist to Her Majesty, the Queen." He confided to Kenneth that the royal family got their prescriptions in giant crystal apothecary jars and the one that contained cocaine had the instructions on it, "Take as needed." Ken loved to tell that story to anyone who cared to hear it.

As the weeks worn on, I began to feel some concern regarding the book, as well as Kenneth's ability to get the thing done. He really wanted the book to be successful, and to accomplish that, it had to be as daring and scandalous as the first had been in 1959. E.P. Dutton wanted the book to succeed as well, but they simply did not understand what Kenneth was trying to create with his off-kilter vision of Hollywood, at least the Hollywood in his imagination. They wanted tell-alls without the backlash, and that was not a task even Kenneth could accomplish without bringing the lawyers down on him (and ultimately, the publishing house). Looking back, it was providential that the photographs could say what he could not. The final result was a beautiful failure, since the life was taken out early on and even Dr. Frankenstein would have a hard time resurrecting that Babylon.

One night not long after we did our last round of libraries and bookshops, he wanted to see Martin Scorsese's new film. Martin was a longtime admirer of Kenneth's films. On occasion, he lent Kenneth his editing rooms in New York to work on his projects. Martin's new film was *King of Comedy,* and so off we went to Westwood with my then-girlfriend, Susan, in tow. The film was not one of Ken's favorites, but he did respond to the obsession-with-celebrity aspect of the piece. We were all surprised at how well Jerry Lewis responded to Martin's direction.

The film did place Kenneth in an odd frame of mind, and afterwards, he treated us to a ride in one of those horse-drawn carriages that used to be available for hire in Westwood to take in the sights around the square. When we arrived back at the apartment, I served some wine, and Susan and I got a little high. The emotions I had suppressed came out of all at once, and I begged him to try and finish the book since it was so important to his career. As soon as I started talking, I knew that was not what he wanted to hear, least of all from me, so after a rather awkward silence, he went off to bed and so did we.

The next morning, we woke up to find that Kenneth had quietly packed all his things and left before daybreak for New York. He left me a note that read:

> "David,
>
> I tried to sleep after your comments last night and I decided that the only way to finish this thing is to go home now and just focus on the work at hand. I am very moved that you care so much about what happens to me. There are not too many people in my life that do. Thank you for all your support and especially for the use of your wonderful photos. I have left you and Susan two signed posters that my friend Page Wood made for *Lucifer Rising* . . . Oh, by the way, I can't get that funny story out of my head about your favorite actor Zucco . . . may have to do something about it.
>
> Love,
>
> Ken"

The letter and Ken's abrupt departure left me feeling a bit guilty, but if it got him to the place he needed to be to finally get *Hollywood Babylon II* off and running, then so be it. His reference to Zucco—meaning the late character actor George Zucco—was not so surprising since we had a very amusing evening during his stay talking about how roles sometimes stay with an actor and what might happen if an actor should become like Ronald Coleman in *A Double Life* and just wig out and become their character.

I had showed Kenneth a VHS copy of an old Monogram quickie starring Bela Lugosi called *Voodoo Man,* which features my old pal, George Zucco, as a high priest dressed in a black magician's robe, while wearing the most unfortunate headdress of feathers. Well, it was a sight. The whole film was like an Ed Wood fever-dream with Zucco calling out to the god Ramboona for guidance—whoever Ramboona might have been...

When the film was over, Kenneth and I had a great time second-guessing what happened to both Lugosi and Zucco after letting themselves go in such an undignified way. I speculated that Zucco probably went a bit off and ran out of Gower Gulch, where Monogram made their little seven-day-wonders, and went screaming down Hollywood Boulevard about the god, Ramboona. Lugosi, on the other hand, probably just went to his cigar shop on the boulevard, bought his usual drugs, went home, got happy, and then just crashed.

I now realize only too well to be very careful what you put in other peoples' psyches, because Kenneth was just desperate enough for copy that he took my little fantasy and went all the way with it, creating out of nowhere a whole scenario where Zucco goes off the deep end and takes his wife and daughter with him to the funny farm. Now, that was bad enough, but not too long after his book came out, I discovered that Stella Zucco was not only very much alive but beside herself over what Kenneth put out there about her loved ones. When

I heard about all of that, I managed to get a letter to her explaining that I adored her husband's work and that all was a terrible misunderstanding. I, of course, never got a reply.

The other tale from the book that was way, way off was the one about James Dean. All those tales of passing out in leather bars and having cigarettes put out on him were true—the problem was they happened to Montgomery Clift, not James Dean! My favorite contribution to the book was the photo of Vincent Price sporting fangs for a film not many people ever saw (and that includes his horror following), a British portmanteau known as *The Monster Club*. The image of Vincent smiling through his fangs seemed to be in on Kenneth's cosmic joke that Hollywood is, after all, fabrication on a grand scale. It was Vincent Price who told me one afternoon, "Hollywood is one of the most evil cities on the planet," and he had personally witnessed enough in his lifetime there not to kid around when it came to the Babylon known as Hollywood.

Not too long after all that went down, I had one of my Technicolor dreams and, as luck would have it, I remembered it and always will. In my dream, George Zucco was not only alive and kicking, he was also singing and dancing . . . at the Backlot at Studio One. In my dream, George had a cabaret act and I was there front row center as he came out in a tux, just like he looked in *The Adventures of Sherlock Holmes*, where he shined as Professor Moriarty, giving perhaps a definitive take on the role. There was George Zucco with a mike in one hand coming from behind the curtain as the band opened with "That Old Black Magic," which George handled a bit like Rex Harrison in *My Fair Lady* and with a touch of Fred Astaire. After his opening number, he said to the audience, "Welcome to the breakfast show!" After a couple of jokes like, "I just finished a picture over at PRC. The salary is such a comfort as it pays all my postage," he got a laugh from the industry crowd who knew all too well that PRC paid zip to their talent. That went on in my mind for a while, and it was *so real* you just would not believe it. Then, the actor known to his fans as "the man with the neon eyes" pulled up a stool and was then hit with a yellowish spotlight. With his eyes in full flood, he began to sing in that cat-like purr of his the tune written by Barry Manilow, "Mandy." I can never forget hearing my favorite character actor from the 1940s singing lyrics such as "Oh, Mandy you came and you gave without taking . . . ."

Welcome to the breakfast show!

Chapter 46
Everything the Traffic Will Allow

David Del Valle

While still at college, I was given a reading of Tarot cards by a silver-haired medium known in the occult circles of North Beach as Tarquin, a veteran actor. He lived and worked near the Geary Theater in San Francisco. He also specialized in playing wizards and kings on the stage, as well as at renaissance fairs.

After examining the cards I had been dealt, Tarquin said, "Your life is like a riverboat, and as long as you remain on board, you will prosper and survive; however, you will be tempted to step off that boat and walk the land. There are many dark corners and hidden dangers at every port, so remember to always come back to the safety of that riverboat, which will continue on down the river until the end of your days."

I have always remembered the old wizard's advice to stay on course, yet being human, I still manage to rock that riverboat from time to time as the traffic will allow.

I have mentioned at various times during the writing of these recollections that I was at one time a theatrical agent in Hollywood during the late 1970s. While this was true enough, I feel the time has come to embellish that period and explain just how a movie fan becomes a movie agent and lives to tell the tale.

From my perspective, the rise and fall of the talent agency known as Del Valle, Franklin, and Levine will always represent the culmination of the Hollywood dream. All my life, I wanted to be a part of the motion picture industry. As a child of the 1950s, maturing beneath the glow of a television screen, I watched old movies in reruns, like most baby boomers, but I always assumed I would be an actor. It did not take even a year living in Los Angeles for me to realize that everybody wanted what I wanted, and unless fate somehow gave me a break, an actor's life was not for me. I loved the movie business and the people who toiled in it to make it shine. I also knew that I could never just be content to throw parties and attend premiers as guests of those celebrities I would chat up at parties I shamelessly crashed in those youthful days of living it up in the shadow of the Hollywood sign.

The desire to be a star must be imbedded in the DNA of certain people, whether it is conscious or not. One has but to spend a weekend in Hollywood to witness the lengths human beings will go to achieve that goal. I remember so well driving by the Hollywood post office every Saturday to pick up a copy of a gossip rag in the form of a newspaper called *The Hollywood Star*, which was edited by a demented movie fan who chose to be called "Bill Dakota." The headlines alone stopped traffic, and yet there was a lurid charm about the way he described the antics of starlets and young men who came to Hollywood by the busload, followed their dreams, and then ended working as waiters and busboys. *The Hollywood Star* reported them through sexy and steamy stories, which made it all the more exciting for those of us still waiting to be seduced, or so one might imagine.

My first exposure to such things began at Tiberio's on Canon Drive in the heart of Beverly Hills, which—like Hollywood—is a city with no heart. Tiberio's was an Art Deco institution located back to back with The Bistro bar and restaurant. It was made famous by loads of celebrities, including Warren Beatty, who shot some key scenes for *Shampoo* within its hallowed walls.

Paul Tiberio looked like Peter Lawford, very tanned with silver hair and matching sideburns. However, the similarity ended right there. Paul was a real movie queen, who loved to wear enough gold bracelets and chains to give Mr. T a run for his money, if Mr. T went that way. Paul loved MGM musicals, and Barbra Streisand was his diva of choice in more ways than one. I started to work at Tiberio's in the summer of 1976 and soon found myself managing the store and meeting more stars than there were in the heavens, as the newsreels used to say about MGM.

I soon discovered that being right next door to The Bistro was like being a magnet for movie stars and their agents. As the rich and famous waited for their cars in the alley that separated our buildings, Paul often persuaded me to go out and try to reel them into the store to buy some of his wonderful but overpriced *objects d'art*. That practice, embarrassing as it was, could be a hoot if the circumstances were right and the subjects willing. If you need any resurgence that I am talking about the late 1970s, Paul created a business card for Tiberio's that was black with silver lettering on one side, as well as a mirrored Mylar side on the back. As Mr. Tiberio loved to explain, "I personally designed those cards that way so you can do your coke on the backside."

Those were the golden days of Beverly Hills. Looking back, I would not have missed any of it for the world. Joan Collins came in and shopped with us from time to time, as did Rod Stewart with his then-wife, Britt.

Barry Krost dropped in very late in the evening for a drink or to do a line before going on to cruise the rest of Beverly Hills and West Hollywood for Latin boys. Barry produced the very successful horror film, *When a Stranger Calls*, with Carol Kane playing a babysitter terrorized by a psycho. The film almost became a franchise, when a sequel was done years later called *When a Stranger Calls Back*.

Richard Donner came in one day with Stanley Mann, and we closed the shop just for them. Donner described for me the four films he was planning to make from *The Omen*, which had just opened to great success. His ideas were fantastic, and if the studio had been willing, those would have been horror classics.

Barbra Streisand brought Paul to his knees on every occasion she appeared in the shop. She could never agree on a price for anything, so he wound up just making a present of whatever it was she wanted. No wonder those people get so spoiled.

I had my own epiphany with the arrival one afternoon of a very chic, elegant woman who browsed with the eye of a true connoisseur. I soon discovered I was in the presence of Audrey Wilder, the talented wife of the great director, Billy Wilder. I must have made some kind of impression as I began to explain how I was a movie buff and had started to organize a section of memorabilia to sell in the shop, which, at that time, was unusual. Posters and photographs were still a few years away from being considered works of art. Mrs. Wilder asked me if I had any memorabilia from her husband's films, and thank God I had a *Sunset Boulevard* poster and two window cards from *Some Like it Hot* on tap. She asked if I had a favorite, to which I demurred: when you are a master like Billy Wilder, they are *all* favorites, like Hitchcock. She laughed when I told her that, and then she surprised me by promising to tell her husband about the shop and wished me luck.

Paul was furious when he came back from his two-hour lunch next door, where he had been drinking Bloody Marys with the then-always-in-the-bag Donald O'Connor, who was in pretty bad shape and grossly overweight from all the booze. "You mean she was in the shop and you didn't come in The Bistro and get me?" Are you kidding? I knew even then when to keep things running smoothly, and I also knew how to handle Paul, as well.

The next day, a messenger brought two packages into the shop for the two of us! I was given a personally autographed photo of Mr. Wilder standing by a lamppost and street sign that read "Sunset Boulevard." Paul was given a beautifully framed reproduction of the poster for *Double Indemnity*, also signed by Wilder.

From that day forward, Billy Wilder came into the shop at least twice a month, sometimes on his way to The Bistro and sometimes just to stop by and chat for a moment, as life seemed to be always on his terms. It was during those visits that Wilder asked what exactly did I hope to accomplish working in an Art Deco shop in Beverly Hills. It was then that the whole concept of working for actors rather than trying to be one of them began to take shape. Mr. Wilder gave me an introduction to his good friend, Walter Kohner, who with his brother Paul was one of the premier talent agents in Hollywood, if not the world.

The following Friday, I told Paul I had to see a dentist, but instead went promptly over to Scandia's on Sunset to my very first "power lunch," as the boys over at William Morris called them. Mr. Wilder had generously opened the first door for me, and it was all up to me. I was having lunch with Walter Kohner and a wonderful writer named Gavin Lambert, who had written the screenplay for Natalie Wood's *Inside Daisy Clover*, a personal favorite of mine. That lunch changed my life, and for the first time, I just sat and took in all the wisdom that was being tossed in my direction.

It was an unforgettable experience listening to Walter, who looked a bit like George Burns in the *Oh, God!* films. He talked like an old-time agent would talk. For example, I asked him what it was like representing the great Erich Von Stroheim, to which he replied, "Von Stroheim was not really a "Von" at all, and while we are on the subject, not much of a grosser at the box-office. Now, Bergman (referring to Ingmar, also a client), he delivers, and under budget." Having said that he gave me a big smile and sipped on his cocktail.

To this day, whenever I think of the legendary director, I always remember that he works cheap and brings home the bacon. Mr. Kohner felt I had potential as an agent and Gavin thought my love of movies was a plus, as so many in that field had no working knowledge of film history or the importance of the background of the talent they represented. By the time lunch was over, I had an appointment to apply to start work in the mailroom at William Morris, which was how that process began.

The problem with such an opportunity was twofold. First, I had to decide if I was prepared to make such a commitment to a profession that never crossed my mind before that magic luncheon. Second, I had to decide how to leave Paul without a replacement. Since I had already decided to "seize the moment" and try my hand at being a talent agent, I then set about finding someone to take my place at Tiberio's.

The answer to that was easily solved. My good friend from San Francisco, Chris Dietrich, was staying with me at the time, and he was in need a job and a more permanent place to stay. Paul was very pleased to meet Chris, and that arrangement turned into a life-altering moment for Chris, as well. It was not long after their first meeting that Chris was invited to move in with Paul. They began a relationship that lasted nearly two years. Paul was one of the best things that ever happened to Chris because, through working with Paul, Chris got to travel the world for the first time with someone who needed companionship and had the money to indulge the two of them in the best things in life, at least for awhile.

As for the mailroom at William Morris, that was an endurance test from day one, since all the guys that were currently employed in the mailroom all wanted to be actors and were just waiting for that golden opportunity when they could leave. The mantra we all were taught there was, "Never say no to the talent." That meant, of course, that at any given moment of the day or night, one of us might be asked to drive anywhere in the city and beyond in service of William Morris clients, and that, of course, included the agents. That also meant long hours, and weekends were never our own, so we couldn't even think about that.

The two biggest stars in the agency at that time were John Travolta and Richard Gere. John's mother died during pre-production work on *American Gigolo,* so it was no accident that Richard filled-in to star in the film in John's absence. I remember the stills they shot of John in character for the poster art in the same pose that Richard struck a few months later. We will never know if the film would have been a bigger box office hit if John had stayed with it instead of Richard.

I lasted about a month at the mailroom in William Morris before I simply failed to meet a request for an appointment or something. I did not return to the office the next day, and that was the end of my time with the agency. However, I could not let the likes of Billy Wilder down for long, and so I started asking around for any agency that might be looking for a sub-agent because I had a list of talent that might go with me if I could just secure an office.

I secured an office alright . . . at 1800 North Highland Avenue, with the unlikely help of a demented actress named Jane Ross. Jane was one of those people God puts in front of you just to see how far you will go before questioning your own sanity. Jane came to Hollywood from New York in the late 1950s fresh from a failed marriage to an older man. He had left her with a condo on the corner of Doheny and Sunset and a fever-dream of Hollywood stardom that could not be brought down no matter how many obstacles were placed in her way. Her major obstacle was that she could not under any circumstances *act*. She could, however, sell pot to her actor friends, and that is what Jane did most of the time in between circling ads in *Dramalogue* or *The Hollywood Reporter*. Jane had found representation, but only if she could bring a sub-agent in to handle her as well as the agency's overload of clients. .

The TRT Agency was the brainchild of one J. Toby Tolber, a large, affable Black man, who looked very much like Don King. He had a great laugh and a sunny disposition to match. As Toby explained his vision to me, all kinds of bells went off in my head saying, "David, this is not such a good idea," yet I decided to hear the man out since nobody else seemed to be on the horizon at this stage of the game. Toby explained that TRT meant "Today's Rising Talent" because, as he sagely pointed out, "No matter what your talent is, it is always rising." Toby had been in his tiny office on the main floor of the 1800 building for about a year. He was just barely getting by and keeping the creditors at bay when I came along. I was well aware that the situation was miles from where I had been even in the mailroom of a respectable agency like William Morris, yet the outrageousness of the situation took hold and I said yes, if nothing else than to give poor Jane Ross the chance to say she finally had an agent.

In theory, Toby was an experienced teacher about how the business worked, and he personally drove me all over town to meet with the casting agents that he knew, or at least knew of, yet never had the right people skills to connect with on his own. Within a month, I had met with Reuben Cannon, Jennifer Shull, Mike Fenton, and Jane Feinberg, who together maintained Fenton/Feinberg Casting. I added Marion Dougherty, Ross Brown, and Hank McCann to the mix, and with those talent seekers willing to look at our client list, J. Toby Tolber and I had credibility to send clients to the top casting agents in Hollywood, provided they had what it took to make us look good.

The six months or so I worked with Toby were, at least in my view at the time, as good an education in the methods and skills required to work as a buffer between casting directors and talent as I would have gotten at William Morris, or so I thought. During all that time, there was a bit of a mystery with good old Toby since he never trusted me with a key to the office and particularly his desk, which was always locked.

One afternoon on a Saturday, I was in Hollywood to see a film, and I discovered I had the starting times all muddled, so I decided to walk over to the office and see if Toby was working, since he had left a couple of messages on my service about getting together to go over breakdowns that evening. That was to be an afternoon I would never forget, and oddly enough would also act as a catalyst for my immediate future as a talent agent. I went to the office and noticed Toby's car was parked in the usual place, so he was there after all. When I tried to open our office door, it was locked, yet I could hear disco music from Toby's boom box, which he kept on the file cabinet to listen to audition tapes and such. I knocked and called his name, and after a bit of fumbling, out popped Toby in a t-shirt, looking rather the worse for wear. Just behind him was a Chinese girl of no more than eighteen years of age and about five-foot four in her stocking feet. She was dressed up like an exotic dancer with her midriff on display.

Toby introduced the girl by her "stage" name of "December-Lee." He explained that we "represented" her and that she was working down the street at the Ivar Theater. I had been working as close with Toby as one could without actually living with him, and that was news to me. Even I knew that the Ivar was a strip club that catered to the raincoat brigade, as well as service personnel on leave with time to kill on Hollywood Boulevard. "December-Lee" was pretty, buxom, and seemed to know the score, but she realized that I was not supposed to know about that side of the agency—at least not yet, anyway.

Toby spent the rest of the evening explaining that we did indeed "handle" strippers and that was what was paying my salary and the agency expenses at least until we had a few breaks without client list. I just listened and tried to think what if anything I should do next. He excused himself and said he would drop "December-Lee" back at the Ivar and then we would talk. While he was gone, I noticed that he left the desk drawer unlocked, so I took the opportunity to see what was in Bluebeard's closet, as it were.

Nothing could have prepared me for the contents of Toby Tolber's desk. Inside were literally dozens of Polaroids of young girls, mostly Asian, all under twenty (some I dared not think just how young they were), all in various states of undress. The thing that really sent a chill down my spine was the fact that almost all of them were photographed in our office, which was only big enough to accommodate three people at any given time. I should have left right then and there, but my curiosity was up and I felt like I had to sort this out since my name was now connected to TRT, a set of initials that began to take on a decidedly sinister connection by the minute.

The next day was a Sunday, and Toby had tried his best to explain it all away as a means to an end, saying that there was nothing wrong with booking talent at the Ivar and even suggesting that I check out the show gratis since my name was now at the door (lucky me). So, over I went to the Ivar Theater just in time to catch "December-Lee's" set. The Ivar was a trip because it was a burlesque house and at one time had been a movie house, as well. It also contained the stickiest floor I have ever tried to walk on in my life.

"December-Lee" did not disappoint with her many talents, and what an act that girl had! There was a runway leading out into the audience, which on that particular day consisted of a few very old men. There was one in particular that was in a wheelchair and wore glasses. I mention this because our Miss Lee bumped her way over to this gentleman and, without using her hands, removed his glasses (which were by that time all steamed up anyway). She also could pick up change with her vagina, or so she said, but there was only so much of her talent that I could handle at one time.

After the performance, I was invited upstairs to the dressing room to meet the other stars of the runway, and what a bomber crew the Ivar had at that time. Oddly enough, all of the young ladies were diminutive, all were no more than five-foot six in height, and I liked every one of them almost instantly. There was vulnerability in the face of each and every one of those girls that made you care about them. Their stories all varied, but one thing was true in each and every case, and that was that they came to Hollywood looking to fulfill a dream. Stripping was not what they would have wished for in any case. I wanted to know more, and the girls were all starving for junk food, so I loaded up my car with Ivar strippers. Off we went to the Sunset Arby's for Jamoca shakes and roast beef sandwiches. "December Lee" sat next to me and reminded the other girls that I was *her* agent and they should take notice not to take advantage, whatever that could have meant.

I spent more time with the girls, and within a week, I must have seen every variation on a theme in the art of striptease at the Ivar. I realized that, one by one, those girls were all making plans to go to Canada to appear at some tacky theater way across the border with a contract for at least a year. I soon discovered that my partner in crime, J. Toby Tolber, was responsible for their bookings, so the plot thickened.

I knew the situation was intolerable and had to end immediately, so I began to plan just how I could leave Toby without making any accusations, except perhaps to warn him that white slavery is a very serious offence. If that was what he was really all about, and if the agency was the only way he could make money, then he really was not an agent in the first place—at least not an agent in show business.

My next move would be decided for me by yet another Black man with the unlikely name of Jimmy Bond. Jimmy was a very successful attorney in Century City that was good friends with a fellow memorabilia collector I knew named Bob Scherl. Bob was informed of my plight with Toby from the start and was my guest for a night or two at the Ivar, so he knew what was at stake. Lucky for me that Jimmy had been "blown away" by my poster collection the first time he ever came to my place for a drink and was already in my corner career-wise.

Jimmy came over to my apartment on Beverly one night, as I was struggling with just what to do to remove myself from Today's Rising Talent. Jimmy wanted me to meet an attorney friend of his named Allan Levin, who kept offices in Century City. Jimmy set up a meeting that very night for the following day. I went for the last time to see Toby, and ironically, it was Toby who drove me over to Century City for my first meeting with Allan Levine.

Allan Levine wanted to invest in something and a talent agency seemed like a good idea since he was dating perennial starlet Edy Williams (the former Mrs. Russ Meyer) at the time. He wasted no time in bringing in another investor in to make our agency a threesome. Carol Franklin was a petite lady with beautiful Elizabeth Taylor eyes and a good heart. She was in the middle of a relationship with a sound editor named Marvin Kosberg, who was unwilling to commit to marriage, so in lieu of that she, decided to get involved with the agency to get back into business. Carol had owned the pharmacy that dominated the Century City area for years. She had a lot of show business clients and especially remembered helping the late Susan Hayward during her final bout with cancer.

What is truly extraordinary about this progression of events is how little experience I really had in the talent agency business to garner all that attention. It was less than a year in the making from the day I had lunch with Walter Kohner until the business meeting with Allan and Carol. I had a lot of confidence in those days and it would take every bit of it to convince those people to sign up for a $50,000 loan at the bank to start what would soon become Del Valle, Franklin, and Levine Talent Agency, with the swank address of 2049 Century Park East.

We opened our office on the 13th floor of the Century City East building. The atmosphere was charged with optimism, as we began to interview actors for a solid month before presenting our client list to the casting agencies. It was a SAG rule that every agency had to audition actors at least one day out of each and every month, whether we were looking for actors or not.

The moments I cherish the most about this process were, of course, meeting and watching—sometimes in total disbelief—what material would be chosen to impress us, but most of all, just who would show up. The second week, we were holding readings with a small nondescript lady in her late fifties. She arrived and introduced herself as Madelyn Cates. The name did not immediately ring any bells until she looked at me and said, "They told me you were a film buff and you don't know me? 'I'm the concierge. My husband was the concierge but he's dead. Now I'm the concierge.'"

"*The Producers!*" I declared at once, and Carol looked dumbfounded at me.

"What are you talking about David?"

I then explained to my partner that we were looking at one of the funniest bits in Mel Brooks' greatest film—the actress who played the concierge in Mel's comic masterpiece was right in front of us. Just for me, Madelyn did the whole sketch from memory and of course we signed her on the spot. Before the end, I was able to place her in the film, *The Devil and Max Devlin,* as the character Mrs. Trent. My other client, Reggie Nalder, played the Devil in that one and just hated Bill Cosby.

The other character I shall never forget was the completely mad Fox Harris, who is forever immortalized as the driver of the toxic car in *Repo Man.* He came in for a reading and brought a fifth of tequila, which he drank in two gulps and then delivered the most insane, demented monologue ever heard (by me at least). Fox had a wonderful voice, very Barrymore and yet very hip at the same time. Carol was so frightened by him that we took a pass on representing him, something I will always regret.

The arrangement we worked out among the three of us was to use Allan for contracts, and his participation would not go too far beyond that since he was very busy with his law practice. Carol and I would both cover the studios on a daily basis. In 1978, we could have a moment with just about every major casting director in town by five o'clock in the evening. One casting director in particular, Bobby Hoffman, (who became a good friend to us), worked over at Paramount casting *Mork & Mindy,* as well as *Happy Days* for Gary Marshall Productions. Bobby always took the time to have lunch with us, usually at Nicodell's, which was a favorite with executives around the Paramount lot, as was Lucy's El Adobe, which was right across the street. In those days, it was not be unusual to see Governor Jerry Brown dining there with Linda Ronstadt.

Within three months, Carol and I had relaxed into a good working relationship, but we were not prepared like a proper agency needed to be to survive. I should have insisted on hiring at least two other sub-agents to keep the clients at interviews during the week. The two of us just could not cover the city the way the major agencies did in those days before cell phones and laptops kept everyone close for auditions. It was really up to us to keep up the pace, but my lack of experience was starting to show, when clients became restless in a way I had not anticipated at all.

The worst thing about representing any actor was that the insecurities they possessed naturally intensified once they found representation. We both had actors calling the office all day every day wanting to know why they were not out doing auditions. Carol had a great response at first, saying to whomever, "If we are here answering your calls, then you must know we are not doing our job, which is being out there at the studios representing you." That was true, of course, but the reality of the situation was not always so cut-and-dry. Having young up-and-coming actors was indeed the lifeblood of an agency, yet it meant nothing if we didn't have some established stars to open the doors for the rest, especially in television.

Looking back, that project could easily have gone one way or the other considering that I did have a lot of casting agents willing to see our clients. The basic problem was trying to sell the ones I brought with me, which were recognized names, at least to me. I had Viva from the Warhol films and Barbara Steele from the horror films, but those two ladies were not in-demand, as I would soon find out. The Breakdown Service, at that time, was essential in sending out clients for work. Since we opened in 1978, the Breakdown Service was relatively new. That service was started by two young out-of-work actors, who struck gold with the concept of getting all the studios to give them breakdowns of what they were casting for on any given day, in both features and television. That service came in the form of mimeographed sheets of paper that arrived at my office by eight o'clock every morning. I quickly learned that my competitors were getting the service delivered to their homes at six o'clock, and quickly followed suit.

I became determined to sign some well-known names for the agency. I had my hands full attempting to keep Hermione Baddeley in line or following the further adventures of Calvin Lockhart. Calvin turned on the charm for Carol more than once, and had we been able to keep afloat for a longer period of time, I think we could have gotten him a series since he was a talented man, who sadly is no longer with us.

When I think of Carol Franklin, I can't help but remember one smoggy afternoon driving along Sunset Boulevard with her, when she suddenly put her hand on mine and said, "You know, David, with my son Jeff starting to take off in television with his writing and you making this agency shine, I am so happy to have both my favorite young men in my life right now." I only wish that I could have made good on that thought, but the cards were stacked the other way regarding Del Valle, Franklin, and Levine.

During the beginning of the summer of 1979, Carol and Allan got wind of a deal that seemed just too ideal to pass up. The Dorothy Day

Otis Agency was up for sale and Allan believed we could solve a lot of our current problems by merging with a more established agency. That agency had some established clients, none of whom I can remember, yet I do remember that a lot of them were children and all of them were working in television.

Carol and I went to the Dorothy Day offices for a formal meeting and also to inspect their client list. Just try to imagine walking into yet another phase of this well-established business by simply taking over. It was a done deal after about forty-five minutes of conversation. It seemed that Dorothy's husband was ill and she had to sell the agency in order to spend more time taking care of him. We certainly appeared to be working agents, at least in her mind. The deciding factor was that both my partners had impressive credentials at the bank. That was yet another fantasy in the making: to become the owners of a respected agency that was making money with their people. That made Del Valle, Franklin, and Levine seem like it truly had the Midas touch.

All this was just too good to be true, and so it would prove to be. No sooner had we signed the contracts and begun to make announcements of relocating our present agency to a new location than the industry was hit with a full blown commercial strike. The irony of this was that if we had just stayed put as we were, that would not have had an immediate effect on us since we had no commercial ties to the industry yet.

The last vestige of hope arrived soon after in the personage of the legendary Joyce Selznick, was discovered Tony Curtis and many other stars during her time in the business. I met Joyce at a dinner party and we hit it off straight away. She loved old movies and film history as much as I did, and before long, we had exchanged cards. She kept in touch with me through to the end of the agency and was just about to make some introductions for me to become an assistant casting director. That gave me the hope of being able to hire all the people I tried in vain to help as an agent. I would have followed any advice Joyce cared to give, but it was not to be because Joyce was dying. Within six months of our last phone conversation, she was gone, and with her went my last hope of staying in the business.

"Be careful what you wish for" certainly came to mind, when Carol and Allan tried to get us out of the contract because there was no telling how long the strike would last and we were in no position to buy another agency with no working clients to help pay the difference. Our own agency was still so new that we were not breaking even yet, even with Calvin doing *Starsky and Hutch* episodes or Hermione doing another *Love Boat.*

By the end of 1979, the grand old firm of Del Valle, Franklin, and Levine was about to close after less than two years of business. For me, that whole experience was a ride and a half into a world that offered the Faustian ideal, yet I always knew it was just too much fun to last forever. However, at thirty year of age, I still had the mountains of the blue moon to climb, so I rolled with the program.

The hardest thing to deal with then was informing my own clients that what started as the greatest bit of luck for all concerned was about to end. Actors do not handle that kind of stress well, and in my situation, most of my clients were also friends, so I had to break the information to them gracefully or not at all. The solution that seemed best for all concerned was that I remained a personal manger and continued to work for them sending them out and maintaining the breakdown service until I could find them another agency to go to.

That was a decision that led to my involvement with Timmy

Stone and United Kingdom Management as a transition from Del Valle, Franklin, and Levine. Tim Stone was the son of Richard Stone, who was a very well-connected agent in London. Tim had heard of my plight and very kindly offered to give me office space at his agency and bring my working clients with me. Tim represented his father's clients from the UK and acted as their guide whenever any of them found themselves in Hollywood.

I remember Tim wanted me to try and work with David Essex, the pop star, who made a bit of a splash stateside with his hit single, "Rock On." David had also made an interesting film about the pitfalls of fame called *Stardust*. Unfortunately, none of that meant much in Hollywood then, and so I could not rise to the occasion and secure our Mr. Essex a job. I maintained a desk with Tim for awhile, but we both soon realized that without money coming in from somewhere I needed to move on and make a living for myself, even if it meant leaving the glittering world of representing actors to find it.

The reality of my agency experience was without a doubt my own Lost Horizon, and the memory of it will always to be bittersweet. However, I had a fabulous time, met fabulous people, and for a moment, felt the kind of success you almost believe you deserve.

The one sobering image I have is the day the office supply people came to take away our desks and bookcases. My father called, and I picked up the phone just as the workmen took my chair away.

He said, "Hey, son—I am going to be in L.A. next weekend. Think you can ask that actress you handle from *Flying High* if she would like to party? Oh, how is everything going out there?"

"Everything is just *beaucoup* fantastic, Dad."